MANAGERIAL ETHICS

DILEMMAS AND DECISION MAKING

MANAGERIAL ETHICS

DILEMMAS AND DECISION MAKING

Poonam Sharma
Kanika T. Bhal

SAGE Publications
New Delhi ■ Thousand Oaks ■ London

First published in 2004 by

Sage Publications India Pvt Ltd
B-42, Panchsheel Enclave
New Delhi 110 017

Sage Publications Inc   **Sage Publications Ltd**
2455 Teller Road   1 Oliver's Yard, 55 City
Thousand Oaks, California 91320   London EC1Y 1SP

Published by Tejeshwar Singh for Sage Publications India Pvt Ltd, typeset in 10/12 Calisto MT by Prism Graphix, and printed at Chaman Enterprises, New Delhi.

Library of Congress Cataloging-in-Publication data

Sharma, Poonam, 1968–
    Managerial ethics: dilemmas and decision making/Poonam Sharma,
Kanika T. Bhal.
        p. cm.
    Includes bibliographical references and index.
    1. Management. 2. Decision making—Moral and ethical aspects.
    3. Management—Moral and ethical aspects. 4. Business ethics. I. Bhal,
Kanika T., 1964– II. Title.
HD30.23.S4956   174′.4—dc22   2004   2004018826

ISBN: 0–7619–3249–6 (Hb)   81–7829–384–6 (India Hb)

Sage Production Team: Leela Gupta, Mathew P.J. and Santosh Rawat

To Our Families...

CONTENTS

LIST OF TABLES

ANNEX TABLES

LIST OF FIGURES

LIST OF ABBREVIATIONS

ANOVA	Analysis of Variance
CSIR	Council of Industrial and Scientific Research
D Prag	Difference in the Organizational and Individual Pragmatic Ethical Framework
D Rel	Difference in the Organizational and Individual Religious Ethical Framework
EJOB	Extrinsic Job Satisfaction
FLED	Authoritarian Leadership
HRM	Human Resource Management
IJOB	Intrinsic Job Satisfaction
I Prag	Individual Pragmatic Framework
I Rel	Individual Religious Framework
ISO	International Organization of Standards
LOC	Locus of Control
LOCT	Mean Scores on Locus of Control
LS	Leadership Style
M	Mean
Mac	Machiavellianism
MACT	Mean Scores on Machiavellianism Construct
MRGUNA	Mean Scores on *Rajas Guna*
MSGUNA	Mean Scores on *Sattwa Guna*
MTGUNA	Mean Scores on *Tamas Guna*
N	Number of Cases
NRI	Non Resident Indians
NTLED	Nurturent Task Leadership Style
O Rel	Organizational Religious Ethical Framework
O Prag	Organizational Pragmatic Ethical Framework
P	Probability Level
PLE	Participative Leadership Style
PSU	Public Sector Undertakings

Pub. Org   Public Sector Organization
Pvt. Org   Private Sector Organization
r   Correlation
R   Multiple Regression
R & D   Research and Development
SD   Standard Deviation

PREFACE

Issues of ethics in business and the ethical conduct of managers occupy not only the pages of contemporary writings, but also the mind space of practitioners and researchers alike. Ethics and morality are very old concepts that have been studied by experts in various fields and have taken the shape and size of the discipline they come from. Most business ethicists have focused on identifying ethically appropriate standards of performance and making a judgment on the appropriateness of the act. These ethical philosophers are keen to provide prescriptive or normative definitions of ethics. We offer this definition to the reader only by way of contrast, because what we look at in this book is a social science view of ethics, instead of the philosophical one. Hence, we focus on what is, instead of what should be, and follow the empirical school of thought on addressing the issues of ethics in practice. Viewed in this light, the focus is on the cognitive processes, justifications of, and feelings towards, ethical issues and ethical decision making of managers. Though purists are likely to see these two approaches as independent of each other, there is a cyclical dependence between the two. The principles around which ethics in practice is assessed are often taken from the prescriptive school of thought and the perception and logic of people often provide the framework for identifying normative behaviour. Thus, though our methodology and focus is on ethics in practice, we have used the normative models as standards, and hope that the insights generated in this book would help in refining the prescriptive theories in their subsequent conceptualization.

We begin by indicating our perspective and its role in the study of business ethics. Since the focus is on managers' perceptions, we have used the phrase 'managerial ethics'. The book then addresses the methodological issues in detail, as the assertions and findings are derived heavily from the research which follows a positivist model. Beginning with the cognitive framework and perceived ethicality of various commonplace business issues, we have explored the role of individual personality factors, situations, culture and their interrelationships. In identifying the mental models of managers, we have used both western as well as Indian concepts, instead of treating them as an either or category—they are thus viewed in tandem with one another. The concepts of *Guna*s and other personality constructs, like Machiavellianism and the locus of control, are juxtaposed for a wholistic understanding of the ethical orientation of managers.

This book, like most other books of this kind, owes a lot to many people. The idea of working on ethics in practice had originated many years ago during informal discussions with philosopher friends. The lack of comfort in our discussions regarding how ethics needed to be dealt with and taught, were the first seeds of this present work. We would like to thank our friends who despite their ill ease and discomfort in discussing the subject, helped to bring out this book.

In addition, many people and their inspirations have helped to shape this book. To begin with, we would like to sincerely thank Professor R.S. Sirohi, Director, Indian Institute of Technology (IIT), Delhi, for providing the environment and support to undertake the research activity. The lessons of Professor Ansari in positivist methodology have now been passed on to the next generation. We thank him for all the support, help and guidance that he has consistently given. The support of the colleagues in the Department of Management Studies is also sincerely acknowledged. We gratefully acknowledge the support of Professor Vinayshil Gautam, Professor P.K. Jain, Professor D.K. Banwet, Professor Sushil, Professor Rajat K. Baisya, Professor S.S. Yadav, and Dr S.K. Jain, who have helped us with research at various points of time in more ways than one. Mr Harish Chaudhry's critical assessment towards our research has been invaluable. The support of the office staff, Mr Narang, Mr Bose, Mr Jacob, Mr Prem Singh and Mr Dalchand is also appreciated and acknowledged. A book like this is very dependent on the managers who participate in these studies. We would like to thank all those who made this work possible, by giving not only their time, but also their honest and sincere worldviews.

Finally, our heartfelt thanks to our families who have been a constant source of inspiration and emotional support for us.

New Delhi   **Poonam Sharma**
March 2004   **Kanika T. Bhal**

1

THE STARTING POINT

The present revolutionary phase called globalization has fewer trade restrictions and easier flow of wealth on the one hand, and tough competition and need for greater vigilance on the other. National boundaries are thus diminishing and the world is moving towards a global economy—which has a lot of potential, but at the same time, *portends more disruption*. By definition, a global economy is as big as it can get. This means that the scale of both the opportunity and the consequences are at its peak (Costa, 1998). The phenomenon of globalization has permeated our lives, influencing the personal values of individuals. World events influence personal values, and individual choices affect a global reality. However, this interdependence between the individual and the economy, although intellectually understandable, remains remote from our experience and news headlines frequently become the topic of discussion at the breakfast table (see Box 1.1).

Box 1.1
Some News Headlines

Patna, 18 June 2002:The CBI has intensified its investigation into the alleged role of the officials of the Medical Store Depot (MSD), Kolkata, in the medicines scam (*The Times of India*)

New Delhi, 30 July 2003: The reported incidence of product piracy and counterfeiting in the country is far higher than the levels reported in the Asia-Pacific region in the last two years, according to the findings of Pricewaterhouse Coopers' global economic crime survey 2003 (*Financial Daily*).

Friday, 6 June 2003: Coal India chief suspended—Under cloud on charges of corruption (*Financial Daily*).

Wednesday, 5 February 2003: Case against Air India officials, for their alleged role in a controversial aircraft leasing deal—Ministry to vet options (*Financial Daily*).

The Central Bureau of Investigation on Wednesday (30 April 2003) arrested former Delhi High Court judge in New Delhi in the Delhi Development Authority land scam case (*The Hindu*).

These incidents appear to be a mix of hope, despair, generosity and greed. Flashes of opportunity and breakthroughs are likely to be tainted by exploitation and personal advantage. As technology and science have greatly expanded the reach of the human mind, they have also greatly increased the stakes of wrongdoing. Therefore, in this post-Enron era, there is an intense need to adopt a proactive approach to develop a more ethical business environment. To some extent, many employers have reacted positively to the call for greater social awareness, adopting ethical and environmental criteria to govern the way in which they do business. However, the ideal remains a remote dream.

McCoy (1985) provided a contemporary and pragmatic view of the need to study business ethics. According to him, concern with moral issues in the business community stems in part from well-publicized stories of bribery, fraud and questionable practices by corporations and corporate executives. Management and directors, especially those who are ethically committed, fear that accounts of malpractice in the media, whether or not accurate, will undermine public confidence. Thus, interest in ethics arises from a perceived need among executives to maintain a good public image of business. Second, concern with ethics among bussiness leaders derives in part from the heightened standards of performance applied to most societal institutions, corporations, etc. Third, the rising interest in ethics derives not only from external pressures, but also in part from the genuine concern of many executives for the well-being of the society. Finally, corporate executives want to be good at their jobs. Increasingly, it is becoming clear that excellence in managing and performance demands attention to corporate culture and values, and that policy making requires ethical insight and moral courage, as well as technical know-how and organizational skills.

Gupta (2001) reported that DePaul University, Chicago, had arrived at conclusive evidence to show that the companies that make a public commitment to ethics achieve higher performance standards than those that do not. In other words, by making an ethical pledge to relevant stakeholders, a company significantly boosts its bottom line. This is also confirmed by the Stern Stewart analysis of Market Value Added, the *Fortune* magazine analysis of the most admired companies, and by the ranking released by *Business Week* in the US.

The socio-economic and competitive character of a corporate entails that it has to make a careful choice of its competitive strategy within the ambit of legal, social and ethical boundaries.

In this context, business organizations have enormous responsibility to follow and support the practices of business ethic that avoids short cuts and unethical practices, build a management style to reflect this practice, and quickly promote an active public strategy that is in tune with the environment in which it operates. In the long run, this approach makes business sense as customers are likely to be much more discriminating in a world of information and transparency, and are likely to gravitate to those institutions that have impeccable standing, enlightened leadership and a strong element of social responsiveness. In other words, the basic ingredients of good governance are— clarity of responsibility, transparency, checks and balances and thus, greater accountability.

Hence, studying the ethical issues in business is the need of the hour. The word ethics is a new entrant into business lexicon and the term has been used in as many ways as the number of people who use it. It may be relevant at this point to study how the term has been understood.

THE NATURE OF ETHICS

According to Taylor (1975), ethics would necessarily mean an inquiry into the nature and background of morality. In this definition, the term 'morality' is taken to mean moral judgments, standards, and rules of conduct. Ethics involves fundamental human relationships, and deals with 'what should be done' questions with reference to the behaviour that might harm or benefit human beings. Ethics deals with the internal evaluation of action by persons and communities who are themselves involved in social interaction. In other words, it is an activity that examines the moral standards of the individual himself or that of the society. This evaluation may be an appraisal of their own action, or actions of other persons and communities. It is, however, evaluation performed according to criteria and standards developed by those doing the evaluation, not by an outside enforcer.

Every society has its own customs, approved conduct, and conception of good character, that is, its morality, wherein certain actions and goals are valued, but others are not. A society thus, has comprehensive beliefs and cultural values that provide legitimization for particular purposes and ways of living. There are also sanctions to reinforce these social judgments and discourage goals and lifestyles regarded as less desirable. Ethics is the continuing reflection on the moral significance of action by means of which communities and individuals relate customs and conduct to values and beliefs (McCoy, 1985).

According to Henderson (1982: 38), 'Ethics is commonly defined as a set of principles prescribing a behaviour that can explain what is good and right or bad and wrong; it may even outline moral duty and obligations'. Given the dynamic environment in which business must operate today, this conventional definition is far too static to be useful. It presumes a consensus about ethical principles that does not exist in this pluralistic age. The absence of such a consensus may be due to numerous changes that have occurred over time in the business environment, including the growth of conflicting interest groups, shifts in basic cultural values, and the increasing use of legal criteria in ethical decision making.

A simple but dynamic working definition of ethics could be that it is concerned with clarifying what constitutes human welfare and the kind of conduct necessary to promote it. Ethical issues emerge when our perception of what constitutes human welfare receives or requires clarifications to a moral dilemma.

According to Rest (1986), a moral judgment is a considered opinion of what should be done (i.e., a decision about the morally right thing to do) when confronted with an ethical dilemma. He considered moral judgment to be one of the psychological processes involved in producing moral behaviour, but others (Ferrell, et al., 1989; Hunt and Vitell, 1986; Jones, 1991; Trevino, 1986) have conceptualized moral judgment as a component of ethical decision making.

Ethics is a system of standards for moral judgment. Group, organizational, and cultural ethics all exist. Each of these attempts to define acceptable behaviour. Together, they influence the personal set of values that defines an individual's own code of ethics, which can exert a major influence on his/her behaviour in an organization (Dunham, 1984).

According to Velasquez (1998), an individual's moral standards are initially absorbed as a child from family, friends, and various societal influences such as, the church, school, television, magazines, music and associations. Later, experience, learning, and intellectual development may lead the mature individual to revise these standards. Some will be discarded and the new ones will be adopted to replace them.

Hopefully, through this maturing process, the individual will develop the standards that are more intellectually adequate to enable him/her to deal with the moral dilemmas of adult life.

ETHICS AND BUSINESS ACTIVITIES

In the present context, our scope of query is studying the ethical behaviour of the individual managers in their workplace. Business ethics are rules, standards, or principles that provide guidelines for morally appropriate behaviour for businesses (Galbraith and Stephenson, 1993). Business is concerned with economics and profit, and in common parlance there is little or no connection between economics and ethics.

In English, the word 'economy' has three meanings: avoidance of waste of money; control and management of money, and other resources of a community, society, or household; and system of political economy (*The Advanced Learner's Dictionary*). So understood, economy has nothing to do with ethics. However, the Chinese word for economy—*Jing Ji* (or *Ching Chi*, in the old alphabetic system of writing)—is related to ethical value. It means: 'to govern the world in harmony and to bring about the well-being of the people'. The noted Japanese scholar, Dr Iwao Taka, comments on this connection in his paper, 'Business ethics in Japan': 'In Japanese, the word economy is read as Kei Zai. Kei Zai is a compound word consisting of Kei and Zai, originally stemming from the Chinese word, Ching-Chi. While Kei means governing the world in harmony, Zai means bring about the well-being of the people. Therefore, in this sense, the word economy does essentially include morality or ethics in its wide and fundamental meaning and scope' (Taka, 1996). Economic value can be either with or without ethical value. Therefore, to speak of economic value with ethical value does not deny economic value. Rather, it stresses and affirms their interdependence. More core business ethics concepts can be found and created if we keep our eye on this all-important point.

It becomes apparent that business and ethics are far from being mutually exclusive in the long term. Although there is scanty evidence to support this notion at present, we have very good reasons to expect highly ethical businesses to also be highly successful long-term survivors, like the Tatas, to prove this point.

After establishing the interdependence of business and ethics, we can define business ethics as the framework of values under which a business functions. Business ethics is, according to Donaldson (1994), a systematic study of moral questions related to business life, industry or other institutions.

Business ethics is a specialized study of moral right or wrong. It concentrates on moral standards as they apply particularly to business policies, institutions, and behaviour. The issues that business ethics covers encompass a wide variety of topics. Often, we come across the question regarding the importance of ethics in business. Although the answer to this question might be rather obvious, it can be explicitly asked why we should even concern ourselves with ethics in business. This question can be answered by each individual.

First, it is fair to say that most people want a just (or a good) society. A fundamental characteristic of a good society is that justice and charity prevails therein. Second, a practical concern of life is business ethics. People always live in some kind of economic system. This system can endure only if it operates so that justice prevails. If the system lacks legitimacy, it is likely to fail (Takala and Uusitalo, 1995).

Further, ethical considerations are important for the operation of an economy in many different ways. What happens in an economy depends on what people in that economy choose to do, and this is naturally influenced by their respective ethics.

Ethical considerations are of profound relevance to the nature and functioning of any economy. Since individual behaviour is central to the working of an economy, ethics has crucial influence on individual behaviour. This is treated in literature as managerial ethics, though it impinges directly on business ethics.

Managing business ethics is no doubt a critical social problem for business organizations. It is also a very complex problem which requires an in-depth understanding of the many factors which contribute to the employees' decision to behave ethically or otherwise (Stead et al., 1990).

Donaldson (1994) enumerates the key features of business ethics and considers the most important ones to be business activities. Most of the working population depends on business for its livelihood. The rest are dependent on it as consumers. As a force in society, it can certainly stand comparison with religion, politics, or anything else. The other reason of inquiry into the business activity is the self-interest of the businesses themselves to inquire into the ethics of business activity. There are three ways in which ethical inquiry can serve that interest: first, in terms of relations with consumers and the public at large; second, in terms of relationships with the employees; and finally, in terms of relationships among businesses.

Unethical conduct is not simply an individual decision, but is also a reflection of institutional culture with the result that such conduct may be related more to attributes of the business itself, than to the attributes of the individual employee (McCuddy et al., 1983). However, at heart is the issue of individual ethical behaviour, i.e., managerial ethics, which is the unit of ethical inquiry.

It may be worthwhile to explore the nature of ethical theories as studied by philosophers and psychologists in the past.

ETHICAL THEORIES

Ethical theories mainly concern themselves with identifying the basis for judging the ethical content of an act. The earliest understanding of ethical theories is divided into two fundamental types: teleological and deontological (Murphy and Lascznaiak, 1981). The two types entail different conclusions about what ought to be done.

Teleological theories emphasize the importance of the consequences of actions or practices. According to the teleologists, the consequences of an action or practice determine its moral worth. The most widely studied teleological theory is Utilitarianism, especially in the context of business and public policy. According to utilitarianism, an action or practice is right if it leads to the greatest possible balance of good consequences, or to the least possible balance of bad consequences for all the people involved. In other words, an action is right from an ethical point of view, if and only if the sum total of utilities produced by that act is greater than the sum total of the utilities produced by any other act the agent could have performed in its place.

When the utilitarian principle says that the right action for a particular occasion is the one that produces greater utility than any other possible action, it does not mean that the right action is that which produces the most utility for the person performing the action. Rather, an action is right if it produces the most utility for all persons affected by the action, including the person performing the action (Mill, 1991).

Both the immediate and all future costs (that can be foreseen) and benefits that each alternative will provide for each individual must be taken into account, as well as any significant indirect effects.

Deontologism (derived from the Greek word for 'duty') emphasizes that the concept of duty is independent of the concept of good, and that the actions are not justified by their consequences. Besides good outcome, there are other factors as well which determine the rightness of the action—for example, the fairness of distribution, a personal promise, a debt to another person, or contractual relationships like parent-child, business affiliations and contracts, and friendships which are non consequential but also enrich an individual's moral life. Deontological 'duties' are from this perspective, an important feature of ethics in general, and business ethics in particular. One of the most popular deontological theories is 'Categorical Imperative', propounded by Immanuel Kant, an eighteenth century philosopher. He emphasized on performing one's duty for the sake of duty, and not for any other reason. He also insisted that all persons act not only in accordance with duty but also for the sake of duty.

In fact, Kant attempts to show that there are certain moral rights and duties that all human beings possess, regardless of any utilitarian benefits that the exercise of those rights and duties may provide for others. He provides at least two ways of formulating this basic moral principle; each formulation serves as an explanation of the meaning of this basic moral right and correlative duty.

Kant's first version of the categorical imperative, is enunciated in the following principle:

An action is morally right for a person in a certain situation if, and only if, the person's reason for carrying out the action is a reason that he or she would be willing to have every person act on, in any similar situation.

The first formulation of the categorical imperative, then, incorporates two criteria for determining moral right and wrong:

- Universalizability: Where the person's reasons for acting must be reasons that others can act upon, at least in principle.
- Reversibility: The principle of reversibility implies that the person's reasons for acting must be the reason he/she would be willing to accept when applied to his/her own self.

Unlike the principle of utilitarianism, Kant's categorical imperative focuses on a person's interior motivations and not on the consequences of an individual's external actions. Moral right and wrong, according to the Kantanian theory, are distinguished not by what a person accomplishes, but by the reasons a person gives for what he tries to do.

The second formulation Kant gives of the categorical imperative is, 'treating humanity as an end', which means that one should treat each person as a being whose existence as a free rational person should be promoted. For Kant, this meant two things: (*a*) respecting each person's freedom by treating others only as they have freely consented to be treated beforehand, and (*b*) developing each person's capacity to freely choose for him or herself the aims he or she will pursue. On the other hand, to treat a person only as a means, is to use the person only as an instrument for advancing one's own interests and involves neither respect for, nor development of, the person's capacity to choose freely. Kant's second version of the categorical imperative can be expressed in the following principle:

> An action is morally right for a person if, and only if, in performing the action, the person does not use others merely as a means for advancing his or her own interests, but also both respects and develops their capacity to choose freely for themselves.

This version of the categorical imperative implies that human beings each have an equal dignity that sets them apart from tools or machines that is incompatible with their being manipulated, deceived, or otherwise unwillingly exploited to satisfy the self-interest of another.

The other popular deontology theories as described by Cavanagh et al., (1981) are related to the notion of justice and rights. The theory of justice requires the decision-maker to be guided by equity, fairness, and impartiality, i.e., the comparative treatment given to the members of a group when benefits and burdens are distributed, when rules and laws are administered, when members of a group coordinate or compete with each other, and when people are punished for the wrong they have done or been compensated for the wrong they have suffered.

The theory of rights asserts that human beings have certain fundamental rights and should be respected for all their decisions. In general, a right is an individual's entitlement to something. A person has a right when that person is entitled to act a certain way, or is entitled to have others act in a certain way towards him or her. The entitlement may derive from a *legal* system that permits or empowers the person to act in a specified way, or that require others to act in certain ways towards that person; the entitlement is then called a *legal right.* The entitlement can also derive from a system of *moral* standards independently of any legal system. Such rights, which are called moral rights or human rights, are based on moral norms and principles that specify that all human beings are permitted or empowered to do something, or are entitled to have something done for them.

So far, we have focused on pragmatic theories of the present, which are rooted in the logic of the existent world. Although these theories provide a good basis for ethical decision making, there are other mechanisms that govern ethical ideology. One such obvious source of morality is thought to lie in religion. After all, if a God exists, who better than God himself to decide what is right and wrong? If God is omniscient, then surely he must be the best authority on matters of ethics. Thus, for a Christian, the ethical rule book is the *Bible*, for a Muslim it is the *Quran,* for Jews it is the *Torah* (the first five books of the Christian's old testament interpreted by Talmud), and for Hindus the various scripts from the *Upanishads* to the *Bhagwad Gita*. We next explore some of the Indian philosophical theories that can be used for ethical decision making.

INDIAN ETHICAL PHILOSOPHY

Moral and ethical values are embedded in the ethos of civilization. The ancient philosophy of any civilization is manifested in our value system and becomes reflected in our behaviour. Although Indian ethics does not exist as a separate subject, the ethical aspect of Indian philosophy is centuries old and is referred to in rich historical as well as contemporary literature, such as the *Vedas, Upanishads* and the *Bhagavad Gita*. Modern philosophers like Ravindranath Tagore, Mahatma Gandhi and Swami Dayanand, have also contributed to this rich literature.

Some of the historical influences that have shaped Indian ethical philosophy are given below:

1. Rule books such as the *Thirukural;* Bhartrihari's *Nitishthaka* (sixth century AD); *Arthashastra* (fourth century BC); *Manusmriti* (fifth century BC); and *Patanjali's Yoga Shastra* (second century BC).

2. Ethical discourses, which are not explicitly didactic and are experiential-cum-analytical, such as the *Bhagwad Gita* (second century BC); and the *Vedantic Upanishads* (fourth century BC).
3. Epic and literature, which are fashioned with elegance, such as the *Ramayana, Mahabharata, Bhagavatham, Panchatantra, Naganandham,* and the *Jataka* tales. The epics were translated in all the regional languages. Each of these translations was modified from the original Sanskrit version and provided a distinct ethical message.
4. Regional works from the medieval period, such as those of Kabir from Uttar Pradesh (fifteenth century AD); Nanak from Punjab (fifteenth century AD); Alvars and Nayanmars of Tamil Nadu (eighth century AD); and Basaveswara of Karnataka (twelfth century AD) (Sekhar, 1998).

Among various schools of Indian philosophy, some of the common fundamental points of agreement are the theory of karma, the doctrine of the soul, and the doctrine of *mukti* (freedom).

Almost all the Indian systems agree in the belief that an individual's actions leave behind some sort of potency, which have the power to ordain joy or sorrow in the future accordingly. When the fruits of the action are such that they cannot be enjoyed in the present life, it is believed that the benefits will be reaped in the individual's next birth, as a human or any other being. It was also believed that the unseen (*adrsta*) potency of the action generally required some time before it could give the doer the merited punishment or enjoyment. These would accumulate and set the basis for suffering and enjoyment for the doer in his/her next life. Only the extreme fruits of those actions, good or bad, can be reaped in this life. Thus, the nature of an individual's next birth is determined by the pleasurable or painful experiences that have been made ready for him by his maturing actions in this life. The *Bhagwad Gita* also advocates that a person has a choice in his/her action, but never in the results. The results are determined the moment the action is performed—the fruits of the action cannot be avoided. The results of taking action are not under our control. Therefore, individuals should only concentrate on their actions without worrying about the results they will bring (Swami Dayanand, 1999).

Almost all the Indian systems admit the existence of a permanent entity called *atman* (the soul). There are divergent views as to the exact nature of this soul. Vedanta says that it is that fundamental point of unity implied in pure consciousness (*chit*); pure bliss (*ananda*); and pure being (*sat*) (Parthasarthy, 1984). It is unanimously agreed that it is pure and unsullied in its nature, and that all impurities of action or passion do not form a real part of it.

When a man attains a very high degree of moral greatness, he has to strengthen and prepare his mind for further purifying and steadying it for the attainment of his ideals, and most of the Indian systems are unanimous with regard to the means to be employed for this purpose. There are indeed differences in certain details, but the means to be adopted for purification is essentially the same in all of them.

Not only do the Indian systems agree to the cause of inequalities in the share of grief and joy for different persons, and the cycle of births and rebirths from time immemorial, they also agree in believing that this timeless chain of *karma* and its fruits ends somewhere. This end was not to be attained at some distant time or in some distant kingdom, but was to be sought within us. Karma leads us to this endless cycle, and if we could divest ourselves of such emotions, ideas or desires as lead us to action, we should find within us the actionless self which neither suffers or enjoys, neither works, nor undergoes rebirth (Dasgupta, 1957; Sharma, 1965).

As might be expected, Indian systems all agree on the general principles of ethical conduct that must be followed for the attainment of salvation. Controlling all passions, no injury to life in any form, and a check on all desires for pleasure, are principles which are almost universally acknowledged. Thus, the Indian philosophy provides a rich basis for ethical theories. Having glimpsed the theories, let us analyze how the study of ethics has been approached over the years.

APPROACHES TO STUDY ETHICS

The field of ethics is usually broken down into two different ways of thinking about the subject: descriptive and normative. Descriptive ethics explains how things are, whereas normative or prescriptive theory tells us how things ought to be. It is not unusual for disagreements in debates over ethics to arise because people view the subject from different perspectives (i.e., one of these two categories).

NORMATIVE ETHICS

This view attempts to answer specific moral questions concerning what people should do or believe. The word 'normative' refers to guidelines or norms, and is often used interchangeably with the word 'prescriptive'. Normative ethics involves arriving at moral standards that regulate right and wrong conduct. In a sense, it is a search for an ideal litmus test of proper behaviour. Thus, it is an attempt to analyze what people should do, or whether their current moral behaviour is reasonable. Traditionally, most of the fields of moral philosophy have involved normative ethics. Philosophers have critically investigated the nature and grounds of moral standards, moral principles, moral rules, and moral conduct. The ethical theories discussed in the previous section delineate what could be the norm for deciding what is ethical and what is not.

The category of normative ethics also includes the entire field of Applied Ethics. This field is the attempt to take insights from the work of philosophers and theologians, and apply them to real-world situations. For example, bioethics is an important and growing aspect of applied ethics, which involves people taking moral decisions regarding issues like organ transplants, genetic engineering and cloning. Business ethics is another such applied field.

DESCRIPTIVE ETHICS

The category of descriptive ethics is the easiest to understand—it simply involves describing how people behave and/or what sort of moral standards they claim to follow. Descriptive ethics incorporates research from the fields of anthropology, psychology, sociology and history, as part of the process of understanding what people do, or have believed about moral norms.

Anthropologists and sociologists can provide us with all sorts of information about how societies, both past and present, have structured moral standards, and how they have expected people to behave. Psychologists can study how a person's conscience develops and how that person actually makes moral choices in real or hypothetical situations. Descriptive ethics also studies the codes of conduct created by professional organizations to regulate the conduct of members.

Descriptive ethics is sometimes referred to as comparative ethics because it often involves comparing ethical systems: comparing the ethics of the past to the present; comparing the ethics of one society to another; and comparing the ethics which people claim to follow with the actual rules of conduct which do describe their actions.

Strictly speaking, then, descriptive ethics is not entirely a field within philosophy—rather, it is more a speciality, which involves many different fields within the social sciences. It is not designed to provide guidance to people in making moral decisions, nor is it designed to evaluate the reasonableness of moral norms. Nevertheless, actual work in moral philosophy cannot proceed very far without the knowledge gained from descriptive ethics.

In short, descriptive ethics asks these two questions:

1. What do people claim as their moral norms?
2. How do people actually behave when it comes to moral problems?

FOCUS OF THE BOOK

In this book, the descriptive approach to understand individual ethics is being followed.

For ethics to be applied and for action to be taken, it is very important to study the descriptive aspect of ethics. It provides insight into how individuals perceive ethical situations, and how they act in those situations. Identifying normative moral standards is one thing, but how it is used by individuals is yet another.

Over the years, business ethics has been analyzed from a number of perspectives. Some researchers focused on the organization, considering issues such as the impact of social, economic and political environment on organizations, the social responsibilities of the organization towards its customers, employees, other stakeholders, as well as the environment. When the individual is the focus of the research, the issues studied are individual and situational variables and their influence on his/her ethical ideology.

From the above discussion, three ethical foci emerge. Which combine dynamically with each other. They concern ethics from:

- The personal standpoint.
- Ethics from the organizational or enterprise standpoint.
- Ethics of the system in which the enterprise operates, i.e., society as a whole.

These foci have been referred to as the micro, macro and meta levels of ethics.

To introduce some order into this variety, it will help if we distinguish three different kinds of issues that business ethics investigates: systemic, corporate, and individual. Systemic issues in business ethics are ethical questions raised about the economic, political, legal, and other social systems within which businesses operate. These include questions about morality of capitalism or of the law, regulations, industrial structures, and social practices within which any business operates. The corporate issues in business ethics are ethical questions raised about a particular company. These include questions about the morality of the activities, policies, or organizational structure of an individual company that is viewed as a whole. Finally, individual issues in business ethics are ethical questions raised about a particular individual or individuals within a company. These include the questions about the morality of the decision, actions or character of an individual manager.

The research carried out on ethical behaviour of the managers at the workplace was of great importance for the following reasons.

As a part of their jobs, all managers have to make decisions. Further, although their objectives, intentions and actions are generally related to technical, economic or human resource factors, they directly or indirectly affect the welfare of a number of people in the society. They influence the future, not only for their organizations, but also for the people who work for them, the consumers who use their products, stockholders who invest their savings in the company, and for the society as a whole. All these people should be able to trust the managers' judgments. Since the manager is the link between labour, shareholders, suppliers and customers, the ethical actions of managers directly affect the ethical direction and health of the organization (Hyman et al., 1990). Ethics has to be considered an inextricable part of the managerial decision process, and it is essential for managers to maintain a concern for ethical integrity (Gupta and Sulaiman, 1996). This implies that each manager has to become his or her own moral philosopher, and apply moral thinking to the decisions he makes, and the actions he takes in his daily life as a manager (Buchholz, 1989).

While business organizations have made abundance of wealth possible on the one hand, at the same time these organizations have also created some of the many crises of our century. Crises that professional managers are forced to face and resolve. Every now and then, these managers face situations of ethical dilemmas. According to

Velasquez (1992), the kind of dilemmas faced by these managers may be the moral issues raised by the 'external' effects that businesses have on society. These include consumer groups that accuse businesses of inflicting dangerous products on an unsuspecting public, of unethical sale practices, and of using advertising to manipulate vulnerable groups, such as children. This mainly concerns the impact of businesses on external stakeholders.

Another kind of ethical dilemma that managers often face, is concerned with the 'internal' conflicts that business organizations create among their own members and constituencies, including managers, employees and stockholders. Employees accuse managers of being negligent in their moral duty to care for the safety of their employees, and of recklessly exposing them to hazardous chemical substances. Stockholders file resolutions charging that officers and directors of corporations make unethical use of their funds, or engage in unethical operations. Thus, tragic dilemmas arise when the values and policies of an organization is in conflict with the employee's own aims and values.

Ethics is related to the personal success of the professional manager himself, which includes job satisfaction Otherwise, stress at the workplace is inevitable, while a professional manager may be clever enough to hide his unethical behaviour for sometime, it will eventually be noticed. A company can build and state its core ethical values, which should become part of the way of corporate life and be internalized and reflected in the behaviour of each manager.

Thus, the ethical dilemmas that business organizations often present for their managers are not trivial, nor are they avoidable. Managers have no choice but to face the ethical issues raised by their business institutions, and attempt to deal with them. Every manager makes his/her ethical judgment based upon his/her moral standards. Moral standards differ between individuals because the ethical systems of belief—the values or priorities, the convictions that people think are truly important, and upon which their moral standards are based— also differ. These beliefs depend upon each person's family background, cultural heritage, religious association, educational experience, and other factors. The understanding of these differences may have implications for the individuals as well as for the organizations.

Despite the interest, concern, and a number of public prescriptions to deal with ethical decision making in organizations, little empirical investigation has been undertaken. However, the paucity of research is not surprising, given the delicate nature and complexity of this area. Managers are not likely to allow their 'ethics' to be directly observed or measured. Nor would it be acceptable to attempt to manipulate ethical decision making in the field. Their decisions and acts can produce tremendous social consequences, particularly in the realms of health, safety, and welfare of consumers, employees, and the community. If ethics is so important and its influence so widespread, it is imperative to study the dynamics or logics used in ethical decision making.

This provides the backdrop and motivation for the present book, which explores some issues related to decision making by managers in situations of ethical dilemma. Though the concept of ethics has been greatly debated, there is a dearth of fundamental research in the area. This book provides a descriptive look at ethical decision making by Indian managers. The lack of empirical work in the area was one of the biggest challenges we faced and was the motivation for this book. It addresses the issue of ethics at the level of the individual, through systematic research. It also identifies the personal and situational issues that affect ethical decision making and ethical logic that people use in the workplace.

2

INVESTIGATING ETHICAL ORIENTATION

This book focuses on the actual perceptions and beliefs of Indian managers, as well as their ideal normative prescriptions for ethical behaviour. The beliefs are assessed through quantitative and qualitative techniques. Since the major findings and the contribution of the book are based on the data gathered, it is important that readers are made aware of the methodology that we have followed for the collection and analysis of the data, and our subsequent conclusions. Hence, this chapter presents the details of the methodology followed and discusses these issues at length, as they are important for and central to the book. The focus of the book is the individual and therefore most of the variables used in the study are at the individual level. However, individuals do not work in isolation, thus the organizational influence on their behaviour also needs to be taken into account. Thus, case studies were developed for two organizations; one from the public sector and the other from the private sector. The predominant methodology was a questionnaire-based survey. Due to the non-availability of any psychometrically sound measures to access the individual cognitive ethical frameworks and decision-making behaviour (particularly in Indian situations), a preliminary study was conducted to test, develop and validate the measures of ethical decision making and ethical frameworks, the results of which are reported in Chapter 3. A pilot study was conducted to validate the measures used before conducting the final survey.

This chapter is divided into four sections. Section one contains the details of the pilot study that includes the procedure of the pilot study, sampling, instruments used for data collection, results and the evolution of the final questionnaire used in the main study. Section two contains details of the methodology used in the main study and includes details like sampling, research site, the measures used and their psychometric properties. Methodological details of case studies developed are included in section three of the chapter. The last section contains details of the statistical procedures used for the analysis of the data. It should be noted here, that this chapter reports in detail all the variables used in the study except ethical decision making and ethical frameworks, which are discussed at length in Chapter 3. Chapter 3 describes in detail the procedure followed for the development of the instruments used for assessing individual ethical decision-making behaviour, and cognitive ethical frameworks used by Indian managers while making decisions in situations of ethical dilemma.

PILOT STUDY

As stated earlier, the present study is an exploratory study in Indian situations. Therefore, it becomes important that before applying the measures chosen for the study straight to the targetted sample, they be validated, refined and tested for their reliability and validity. Thus, with these two objectives in mind a pilot study was conducted using part-time MBA students at the Indian Institute of Technology (IIT), Delhi (92 working executives) as a sample.

SAMPLING

The data was collected on a structured questionnaire (details follow) which was distributed to the students after classes. They were asked to return the filled questionnaires the next day, before class started. It took around 10 days to receive 92 complete questionnaires from two batches of part-time MBA students. The profile of the sample is given in Table A.1 (Annexure I).

INSTRUMENTS USED

A structured questionnaire containing the measures of the study variables was used; these variables and their instruments are discussed in the subsequent sections. Annexure II contains the questionnaire used in the pilot study. All the scales were subjected to factor analysis as a partial test of construct validity. The main applications of factor analytic techniques are: (a) to *reduce* the number of variables; and (b) to *detect structure* in the relationships between variables, that is, to *classify variables*.

An item was included in the factor when the loading of that item was above .55 and cross loading below .35. Cronbach's coefficient alpha was conducted to test the internal consistency and reliability of the scales. A scale having a reliability coefficient of .5 and above was included in the study (Nunnally, 1978).

The different measures used in the study are described in the following section.

Guna

This refers to a construct from Indian philosophy. In the present study, it is viewed as an Indian equivalent of personality, represented by three constituents, namely *Sattwa*, *Rajas*, and *Tamas*. The conceptual details of this construct are given in Chapter 5. Some of the adjectives from the English language, which defines these three *Guna* to the nearest meaning possible, are given below in Figure 2.1.

Figure 2.1

Some Adjectives Defining the Three *Guna*s*

Sattwa	Rajas	Tamas
Patience	Love of fame	Ignorance
Poise	Passion	Greed
Self-control	Power	Anger
Serenity	Strife	Brutality
Altruism	Unrest	Confusion
Compassion	Impatience	Resistant
Contentment	Jealousy	Inertness
Goodness	Pride	Unsteadiness

* This philosophy believes that the predominance of one character over the other two accounts for the dissimilarities observed among people. For example, a person in whom *Sattwa* is predominant will be contemplative, for it means that the individual is peace-loving, knowledgeable, has an inquiry mind, and is clear thinking. *Rajas Guna* refers to activity, meaning one who is hyperactive, and ambitious. On the other hand, if a person is generally dull and inactive, his/her predominant quality is *Tamas*. See Chapter 5 for more details.

This scale is adopted from Chakraborty (1985); Sastry (1981); and Kaur (1992). The scale had 30 items, 10 for each *Guna*, placed in a Likert format. The respondents were asked as to what extent they possessed the characteristics given therein. The score varied from one to five (1=very low, 2=low, 3=average, 4=high, 5=very high).

A factor analysis of data for the construct of *Guna*s disclosed three common factors Table A.2 (Annexure I).

In the first factor, all the five characteristics corresponded to the *Sattwa Guna* of the original scale and therefore, was named *Sattwa*. They were: patience, self-control, serenity, altruism, and goodness. Out of the four characteristics in the second factor, three corresponded to the *Tamas Guna* of the original scale and only one was from *Rajas Guna*, hence, this scale was named *Tamas*. The items under this factor were strife, confusion, inertness, and unsteadiness. The third factor comprised five items, three corresponding to the *Rajas Guna* of the original scale, and two to the *Tamas Guna*. They were love of fame, jealousy, pride, anger and brutality. After examining these and noting their factor loading, it was decided to call this factor *Rajas*.

These 14 items were then included in the final questionnaire used in the main study.

Machiavellianism

An individual who has a Machiavellian personality believes that it is appropriate to further his/her ends using any means required. The concept is discussed at length in Chapter 5. The focus is on obtaining and using power to further one's own end, regardless of the impact on others. This personality trait is measured on a continuous scale. Items were taken from the original scale (of a pool of 71 items) developed by Christie (Christie and Geis, 1970). Out of 71 items, 20 statements indicated as positive were included in the questionnaire. These 20 items were placed in a Likert format. Respondents' opinion about each item varied from one to five, where 1 = strong disagreement; 2 = some disagreement; 3 = indifference or inability to make up one's mind; 4 = some agreement and 5 = strong agreement.

The analysis of the data obtained from the pilot study for the Machiavellianism measure disclosed only one common factor (Table A.3 Annexure I). A total of 17.7 per cent of the variance was accounted for by the seven items loaded on this factor in the factor matrix. The eigen-value for the factor was higher than one (3.53157), and the reliability alpha was .6855 (i.e., much higher than the set criteria). The seven statements representing the construct of Machiavellianism under this single factor were:

1. If there is any chance that a recommendation might backfire, be very cautious in recommending anyone.
2. It is wise to flatter important people.

3. It is better to *Compromise* with existing evil than to go out on a limb in attacking such individuals.
4. The best way to handle people is to tell them what they want to hear.
5. One should upset as few people as possible.
6. Practically anything can be justified after it is done.
7. Never tell anyone the real reason you did something unless it is useful.

These seven items were included as a measure of Machiavellianism in the final questionnaire used for the main study.

Leadership Style

The issue of ethics and leadership is dealt with at length in Chapter 7 of this book. For the present research, the following three leadership styles are included for investigation (Sinha, 1995).

Authoritative: These leaders make all the decisions for the group and provide detailed step-by-step directions to their subordinates. They keep information to themselves, maintain a distance from group members, and praise or rebuke them according to their personal whims.

Participative: A participative leader is characterized by three features: (a) he/she believes that all group members have resources which are important and can be utilized by facilitating frank discussions and joint decisions; (b) he/she creates a situation in which group members maintain ego-supportive (rather than an ego-deflative) relationships; and (c) he/she sets high performance standards.

Nurturant-Task: These leaders are nurturant to those subordinates who work hard and with sincerity they are reinforcers, and believe in rewarding subordinates for the quality and quantity of their performance.

The analysis of the data disclosed three common factors (Table A.4, Annexure I). All the three factors had eigen value and reliability coefficient alpha which was higher than the set criteria. A total of 37.3 per cent variance was accounted for these 13 significant items in the factor matrix. The extracted factors are described below.

In the first factor, all the five items corresponded to the participative style of leadership style of the original scale. The five statements under this factor were:

1. I allow my subordinates to solve problems together.
2. I mix freely with my subordinates.
3. I treat my subordinates as equals.

4. I encourage frank discussions whenever a situation arises.
5. I am informal with my subordinates.

The second and third factors had four items each, corresponding to the Nurturant-task and Authoritative styles of leadership respectively. Therefore, factor two and three were called Nurturant Leadership style and Authoritative Leadership Style respectively. The statements under factor two, representing the nurturant type of leadership were:

1. I allow my subordinates to solve problems jointly and I mix freely with my subordinates.
2. I treat my subordinates as equals.
3. I encourage frank discussions whenever a situation arises.
4. I am informal with my subordinates.

The third factor had the following statements representing the Authoritative Leadership:

1. I behave as if power and prestige are necessary for demanding compliance from my subordinates.
2. I make it clear to my subordinates that personal loyalty is an important virtue.
3. I do not tolerate any interference from my subordinates.
4. I believe that if I am not always alert, there are people who may pull me down.

All the 13 items, as a measure of leadership styles, were included in the final questionnaire used in the main study.

MAIN STUDY

The questionnaire finalized as a result of the pilot study was used in the main study to collect the individual responses (for details see Annexure III). For in-depth analysis of the impact of organizational culture (related to ethical decision making) on the individual's ethical framework, case studies of two organizations (one from the public sector and one from the private sector) were also undertaken.

RESEARCH SITE

The study was carried out in 10 organizations located in and around Delhi. A purposive sampling technique was followed. A major factor that was considered critical was the ownership of the organization. Keeping this in mind, five organizations chosen were from the public sector (government owned) and five were privately managed.

Only large organizations with a turnover of over 10 billion and employing more than 500 people, were included in the sample. A brief description of the organizations is given in the following subsection. The details of the research sites are also given below.

Public Organization 1: was established in 1965 to provide engineering and related technical services for petroleum refineries, oil and gas pipelines, and petrochemical industry projects. Since its formation, the company has been responsible for implementing a large number of projects. In addition to petroleum refineries, with which it initially started, it has diversified into other fields, such as pipelines, petrochemicals, oil and gas processing, offshore structures and platforms, fertilizers, metallurgy and power. Today, it provides a complete range of project services in these fields. This organization has one of the most diversely skilled engineering workforces in this part of the world. It employs engineers, technologists and specialists having graduate and higher qualifications in various disciplines of engineering, technology, business administration, etc. The company has about five million man-hours available annually in its design offices, along with about 10,000 man-months of construction management services per annum. The total employee strength of the company is around 3,500.

Public Organization 2: is the oldest and largest commercial bank in India, with a history that is 189 years old. The bank was nationalized in 1955. It has a network which extends all over India, with a spread of nearly 8,888 offices across the country. It's overseas network comprises 52 offices in 35 countries. This bank has continued to maintain its position as India's premier commercial bank, and the driving force behind rural development, industrial diversification and technology upgradation in India. It pioneered the financing of small-scale industries and was the first to begin agricultural financing in India. Keeping pace with financial sector reforms in India, it introduced merchant banking, mutual funds, factoring services, home finance, etc., by forming separate subsidiaries for these activities. Almost 47 per cent of all transactions relating to India's foreign trade are routed through this bank. It has a 20 per cent share in the total deposits and 22 per cent share in the total advances of all scheduled commercial banks in India. It has a market share of 32 per cent in NRI deposits. The bank has a consistent, unbroken record of profits throughout its history and has steadily increased its profits every year. For the year 1997 ending in March, the profit was $370m. It has a predominant market share in both wholesale banking and retail banking in India.

Private Organization 3: has specialized in water and waste-water treatment for over three decades. A pioneer in the field in India, and one of the few in the world with a complete range of water and waste-water technologies, product and services. The company was formed as a subsidy to a British company in 1964. The company has its business spread all over India, and even in international markets, such as Russia, South east Asia, Japan, Africa, Egypt, the Middle East, the US and the UK, as well as neighbouring countries like Bangladesh, Nepal, Mauritius and Sri Lanka.

Public Organization 4: the first plant of this company was established nearly 39 years ago at Bhopal, and was the genesis of the heavy electrical equipment industry in India. Today, it is the largest engineering enterprise of its kind in India, with a well-recognized track record of performance, making profits continuously since 1971–1972. The company catered to core sectors of the Indian economy viz., power, industry, transportation, transmission, and defense. The company's wide network (14 manufacturing divisions, nine service centres and four power sector regional centres, and about 150 project sites) enables it to be closer to its customers to provide them with suitable products, systems, and services at competitive prices.

Private Organization 5: manufactures and markets automotive and industrial lubes. With a market share of 20 per cent, it is a dominant private sector player in the lubes market. The company commenced operations in India in 1919, with four regional offices in Bombay, Delhi, Calcutta and Madras. The company, which is a part of a multinational organization, has a strong presence outside its home country. The group is focused on the lubes business and its global competitors are mainly integrated oil companies. Over 40 per cent of its turnover is from the Asian subcontinent. The company has a worldwide market share of about 12 per cent. The parent company has a portfolio of 5,000 products. The company has seven blending plants, at geographically dispersed locations. Of these, two plants are located in Maharashtra (Mumbai and Patalganga), one in the east (Pahapur, West Bengal), one in Silvasa, two in the south (Tamil Nadu and Karnataka); and one in North India.

Public Organization 6: is one of the jewels of the public sector. It has almost one-fifth of the total power-generating capacity of the country in all the combined sectors. It is also one of the few highly profitable public sector companies. The top officials in the company state that the key to its excellence lies in the quality of the manpower employed to achieve it. More details about this organization are given in Chapter 5.

Private Organization 7: is a software organization with operations all over the world. Its products include software, services, and document processing systems. The other agencies with which the company interacts are Unisys, Microsoft, SCO, Uniplex, AST, and Compaq. It has around 2,270 employees with its head office in Mumbai and 20 branch offices all over the country. Since its new CEO was appointed in 1999, the organization has undergone major changes.

Private Organization 8: is the second largest cigarette company in India. Currently, the market share of the company is about 13 per cent. In North India and *Rajas* than, it is the market leader. The organization has completed 50 years of operations in India. It was established in 1936 at Calcutta and was a subsidiary of the parent company in the UK. Its first factory was established in 1944 at Bombay. In 1979, its management was taken over by one of the large Industrial houses of India. The current turnover of the company is around Rs 100 billion and its current sales turnover is around Rs 13,500 million. It has three factories located at Mumbai, Ghaziabad and Hyderabad.

Private Organization 9: is the largest commercial undertaking in India, and the only Indian company in Fortune's 'Global 500' listing of the world's largest industrial and service companies, with a ranking of 287 for the fiscal year 1997. Among the petroleum refining companies, it is ranked at twentieth by sales as well as profits. Incorporated in 1959 as a private limited company, it became a corporation in 1964. It owns and operates six of the country's 14 refineries, with a refining share of over 40 per cent. Its seventh refinery with a capacity of six million tonnes per annum will be commissioned shortly at Panipat in north-west India. Another grassroots refinery is planned on the east coast as a joint venture. This Organization meets 55 per cent of the petroleum products' consumption of India. It is also the canalizing agency for the import of crude oil and major petroleum products.

Private Organization 10: was incorporated in 1962 and went public in 1973. The company employs over 5,000 people and manufactures branded generic pharmaceuticals, bulk activities and intermediates. The company's turnover in 1998–1999 was over $ 425 million. Its products are sold in over 40 countries and it has manufacturing operations in seven countries. The company has a 13 per cent share in India's pharmaceutical export. A significant fact about the company is that its profile is quite unlike that of a typical generic company. The company has manufacturing operations in seven countries and spends a reasonable proportion of its revenues on research. The company operates as autonomous profit centres spread across the world, rather than using a typical 'domestic' vs 'international' approach.

RESPONDENTS

Altogether, 319 executives from 10 different organizations constituted the sample for the study. Care was taken to include executives from different divisions and different levels of the organizations. An effort was made to include enough women executives, because gender was one of the variables of the study. However, due to the fewer number of women in managerial positions and their relative non availability, only a small number of women executives could be included in the sample. Organization type and gender-wise split of the sample can be seen in Table A.5 (see Annexure I). Any age group-wise split of the sample is given in Table A.6 (see Annexure I).

INSTRUMENTS USED

Details of some of the instruments used, with their reliability test and validation, are given in the previous section under pilot study results. Other measures used in the study were locus of control, job satisfaction, ethical decision-making scale and ethical frameworks. The instruments, of locus of control and job satisfaction were not included in the pilot study, because these instruments have been well tested and standardized. Further, their inclusion in the pilot study was making the questionnaire too lengthy. The measures for locus of control and job satisfaction are described below. For the measurement of ethical decision making and ethical frameworks, new instruments were constructed especially for the present study. These new constructs form the core of the study. Since any work of a similar nature in the Indian context could not be found, it became important to develop a new measure in the specific cultural context, validate it and test its reliability before actually putting it to use in the main study. Due to the importance of the issue, a separate chapter has been included to deal with the issues of ethical decision making and ethical framework (see Chapter 3).

Locus of Control

Locus of control represents an individual's perception of being able or unable to control what happens to him (Rotter, 1966) or the degree to which one believes that one's actions influence the outcome one experiences in life. Individuals who believe that they have direct control over events are said to have an internal locus of control, and are termed 'internals'. In contrast, people who ascribe the control of events outside forces beyond their own control, are said to have external locus of control and are referred to as 'externals'.

The Adult-Nowicki-Strickland Internal-External control scale (Nowicki and Duke, 1983) was used to measure this construct of locus of control. This scale had 40 statements to be answered in a yes/no format. Some of the research references in support of the reliability of this scale are given in Table A.7 (Annexure I). Due to the high reliability of the scale, it was not included in the pilot study.

Job Satisfaction

A 7-item scale used in Tandon (1990), to measure job satisfaction taking into account different aspects of the job, was used for this study. The respondents were asked to indicate how satisfied they were with these aspects on a 5-point scale (1=very dissatisfied, 2=dissatisfied, 3=neutral, 4=satisfied, 5=very satisfied). The results of the factor analysis of the data obtained from the main study are reported here.

The factor analysis yielded two neat factors. The results are reported in Table A.8 (Annexure I). The two factors together explained a total of 52.2 per cent of variance. The first factor contained items reflecting growth opportunity, challenge and advancement on the job, and was called Intrinsic Satisfaction. The second factor had elements of friendliness, respect received and job security, and was labelled Extrinsic Satisfaction. The reliability coefficient of this factor was .53, despite the factor loadings being fairly high. The inter-item correlations of item 61 with item 62 and 66 were .24 and .38 respectively, and these between 62 and 66 were .26, which might be the cause of lower reliability. The intrinsic and extrinsic satisfaction scales showed an adequate reliability coefficient of .67 and .53 respectively. The means and standard deviation (SDS) of the two factors can also be referred to in Table A.8 (Annexure I). The scale characteristics obtained of all the measures used in the study are given in Table A.9 (Annexure I).

The final questionnaire was divided into three sections (see Annexure III). Section 1 contains items on individual personality variables, namely *Guna*, locus of control, and Machiavellianism. Section 2 has items on outcome variables viz. leadership style and job satisfaction. Section 3 contains items on ethical decision making and cognitive frameworks (described in Chapter 3) of decision making in situations of ethical dilemma.

Qualitative Study

In the main study, individual respondents were asked to give their perception of the organizational culture related to decision making in the situation of ethical dilemma on two scales—ethical decision-making frameworks and ethical decision-making situations. For the purpose of validation of these results, it was decided to conduct a case study of at least two organizations. These case studies also aimed at highlighting the influence of the organizational ethical decision-making culture on individuals working in these organizations. Keeping the above two objectives in mind, two case studies were carried out, and two organizations, one from the public sector and the other from the private sector, were selected. The case studies included observations of the real-life practices, analysis of some records and interviews with key people. Since the objective was to study the ethical components of culture, the symbols, language and ideal workers of the organization were analyzed keeping in mind the ethical component. Further, certain real-life decisions taken in the organization were analyzed, and care was taken to choose situations that involved ethical dilemmas. For this purpose, four or five top executives of these two organizations were interviewed (with the assumption that the opinion of the top executives in the organizations reflects the overall philosophy of the organization). The schedule was non-structured. During the interview, the respondents were asked to cite any real incidence of their company, which they remembered, related to marketing, finance or human resource management. Care was taken not to reveal the real interest of the researcher in matters related to ethical decision making, to avoid any kind of social desirability bias (for details see Chapter 8).

ANALYSIS

The present work aimed at investigating some antecedents as well as consequences of ethical frameworks. The antecedents of ethical frameworks are hypothesized to be the interaction of some individual-related variables. Besides this, the independent effects of the study variables are hypothesized. Thus, we have two sets of analyses—one for investigating the interaction effects, and the other for main effects. For main effects, we have used one-way Analysis of Variance (ANOVA), correlations and t-tests.

INTERACTION EFFECTS

As already mentioned, the interaction effects were hypothesized for some relationships.

The algebraic or statistical interaction has been largely analyzed with two techniques: ANOVA and multiple regression analysis. Different researchers have used varying techniques (either ANOVA or multiple regression). 'This difference in analytic preference fits (well) with underlying assumptions about causes of behaviour' (Schneider, 1983: 8). It needs to be mentioned here, that the key construct of the present work—ethical frameworks—is theoretically conceived of as a continuous variable. Since the multiple regression analysis preserves the continuous nature of the variables, it should be a preferred technique. Hence, in most cases, multiple regression analysis was used to study the interactions. However, in some interactions that involved discreet variables, ANOVA was used. The methodology followed for hierarchical regression needs to be explained here.

Some of the interaction hypotheses were tested through a hierarchical multiple regression analysis. For each interaction term, the variables were first converted to z-scores to give the scores equivalence, as they all roughly fall into the normal curve. Finally, the interaction term was taken as the product of these z-scores. Instead of determining the incremental contribution of each variable by assuming it was added last, the hierarchical method requires the researcher to specify the order of inclusion. In the present study, the interaction terms were included in the independent (or main) effects of the two at the third step. The increment in R^2 at each step was taken as the component of variation. Thus, by taking the interaction terms at the third place, the confounding effects of the main effects were controlled. For an interaction hypothesis to be significant, the beta weights of the product term had to be significant. The significance of beta weights was tested through F-ratios. Significant interactions were further analyzed graphically. Scores with $\pm$ one standard deviation from the means were plotted (Hunt et al. 1975). While plotting the curves, the mean scores were each divided by the number of items in order to maintain consistency across the figures. It needs to be mentioned here, that the graphical representations show the direction of the interaction effects, which is not shown by the beta weights. For the purpose of graphical representation, the data is grouped into qualitative categories (Low and High in the present study). Thus, it is possible that despite the beta weights being significant, the graphs of the same interaction might not appear significant. This should not be a cause of undue worry, as the interaction is not a 'discontinuous qualitative variable that differentiates subgroups of individuals who are qualitatively different but is a continuous quantitative variable' (Zedeck, 1971: 305).

CHAPTER OVERVIEW

As has been mentioned, our predominant focus is on the perception of people. For this, it is important that the readers are aware of how these perceptions were assessed. This chapter was an effort in that direction. The sample details, along with details of the process and questionnaire, are present in this chapter. The predominant methodology was a questionnaire-based survey. A preliminary study was conducted to test, develop and validate the measure of ethical frameworks, the results of which are contained in Chapter 3. A pilot study was conducted to validate the measures used before conducting the final survey. This chapter is divided into four sections. Section one of the chapters contains the details of the pilot study that includes the procedure of the pilot study, sampling, instruments used for data collection, results and the evolution of the final questionnaire used in the main study. Section two contains details of the methodology used in the main study. The contents of this section include details of the questionnaire-based study, like sampling, research site, the measures used and their psychometric properties. The measures used in the study, besides ethical decision-making and ethical framework scales (see Chapter 3) are *Guna*, locus of control, Machiavellianism, leadership style, job satisfaction and ethical decision making. The final questionnaire was divided into three sections (see Annexure III). Section 1 contains items on individual personality variables, namely *Guna*, locus of control, and Machiavellianism. Section 2 has items on outcome variables viz. leadership style and job satisfaction. Section 3 of the questionnaire contains items on ethical decision-making and cognitive frameworks (described in Chapter 4) of decision making in situations of ethical dilemma. The methodology followed in undertaking the qualitative study (case studies of the two organizations) are also provided in brief. The details are available in Chapter 8. This chapter also gives details of the important statistical analysis methods used in the study, such as Interaction Effects and Hierarchical Regression.

3

ETHICAL DECISION MAKING AND COGNITIVE FRAMEWORKS

Managers in organizations face situations of ethical dilemmas every day. The issues could range from the use of office means for personal use, to those of corporate social responsibilities. In the present business scenario, with the opening up of the market and increasing national and international competition, both the opportunities for, as well as the strict surveillance on unethical conduct, are on the increase. In such situations, the question of how managers behave (ethically or unethically) when faced with situations of ethical dilemma, is more important than it was ever before. Do the situational characteristics play any role in influencing individual decisions? Does the same individual behave differently in different situations? If two individuals take the same decision in an ethical or unethical situation, is there any difference in their reasoning? Are there different cognitive frameworks to explain the logic behind individual decisions in situations of ethical dilemma? These are some of the questions which arise while focussing on an individual and his/her ethical behaviour. In this chapter, an attempt has been made to develop the instruments for assessing individual decision making in different situations of ethical dilemmas, and also to identify the cognitive frameworks used by them in taking such decisions. Before presenting the details of the procedure followed during the development of the measures of ethical decision making and cognitive ethical frameworks, a brief review of the literature regarding operationalization of the measurement of ethical decision-making behaviour is presented here.

ETHICAL DECISION MAKING

The operationalization of different ethical perspectives for empirical studies has been varied. Some have used response categories and quantified data to interpret the results (Galbraith and Stephenson, 1993; Harris and Sutton, 1995; Brady and Wheeler, 1996; Schminke et al. 1997), while others have used open-ended responses to infer qualitative results (Fritzsche and Becker, 1984; Premeaux and Mondy, 1993). A brief review of the methodology followed for the operationalization and measurement of ethical frameworks in various studies indicates a lack of consistency and standardization.

Fritzsche and Becker (1984) in their investigation studied the extent to which ethical theories influence behaviour. They made an assumption that the influence of ethical theory upon behaviour was reflected in respondents' open-ended responses to vignettes, inviting an expression of a rationale for action. There were five vignettes used to collect data, describing a decision containing potential ethical dilemma. The respondents were asked to indicate the likelihood of behaving in an unethical manner in a given situation. A Likert scale ranging from 0 to 10 points, anchored with 'definitely would not' (0) and 'definitely would' (10) phrases was used. After making a decision, the respondents were asked to give reasons as to why they made that decision. The responses to open-ended questions were aggregated into common response categories. These categories were named after four ethical theories—act utilitarianism, rule utilitarianism, theory of right and theory of justice. It was concluded that practitioners relied almost totally on utilitarian philosophy.

While trying to link management behaviour to ethical philosophy, Premeaux and Mondy (1993) used the same vignettes and methodology that was followed by Fritzsche and Becker (1984) in their study. The findings of the investigation also matched with the results of the original study.

Many researchers have used more qualitative data to assess the framework used. Harris and Sutton (1995) compared the ethical values measures of MBA students and Fortune 1000 executives. A questionnaire developed by Harris (1990), that contained 15 short scenarios was used to measure ethics in a multi-domain manner. The instrument was designed to measure five domains of ethical values. These domains or constructs were labelled by Harris (1990) as: (a) fraud; (b) coercive power; (c) influence dealing; (d) self-interest; and (e) deceit. These domains were measured along a five-point Likert-type scale, with 1 as the anchor for the greatest degree of approval of the described action, and 5 as the opposite action. Respondents were also asked to indicate which of the four descriptive statements representative of four ethical maxims (egoism, utilitarianism, golden rule and Kant's categorical imperative) best described their reasoning process, and used a forced choice self-reporting method of collecting data.

In another study by Brady and Wheeler (1996) on ethical predispositions, an instrument having eight vignettes with ethical content was used. Following each vignette were four statements (two statements supported utilitarian solution and utilitarian rationale each, and two statements supported formalist solution and formalist rationale each). The term formalist here represented the human tendency to assess ethical situations in terms of their consistent conformity to the pattern of rules, or some other formal features. It does not specify whether those patterns are laws, ideals, principles, customs, mores or anything else. Respondents were asked to rate each statement on a scale (1 to 7), indicating the extent to which the statement would fit (or would not) their way of thinking. Each of the four statements was constructed to represent one of four options (i.e., four for each vignette), both utilitarian and formalist solutions, and utilitarian and formalist rationale was possible. Respondents' utilitarian and formalist scores were calculated by averaging responses to the appropriate items. The results of the study showed that consistent and correlated results are achieved whether ethical predispositions are measured with responses to vignettes, or with preferences for character traits, implying that the measurement of ethical predisposition was method-independent.

Later, Schminke et al. (1997) also used the scale developed by Brady and Wheeler (1996). They conducted a study to examine the influence of an individual's ethical frameworks on his/her perception of organizational, procedural and distributive justice. The scale, as mentioned earlier, measured the extent to which respondents displayed utilitarian and formalist ethical predispositions. There were four scenarios (representing procedurally just and distributively just; procedurally just and distributively unjust; procedurally unjust and distributively just; and procedurally unjust and distributively unjust situations) that were used to assess the individual's perception of procedural or distributive justice. It was found that ethical formalists were more sensitive to procedural justice issues, and that utilitarians were more sensitive to distributive justice issues.

McDonald and Pak (1996) investigated cognitive frameworks in the form of a questionnaire, along with 14 ethical scenarios. Each framework was represented in the framework questionnaire instrument by four representative statements. The five-point Likert-type scale ('indicating strongly agree to strongly disagree') was used for each scenario, and the respondents were asked to tick the statements they would consider in making their decision, in the scenarios given in the questionnaire.

The above review of literature revealed that researchers follow a variety of methods, procedures and questionnaires. However, one common point followed by almost all the researchers in their investigations was the use of vignettes involving ethical components (the nature of vignettes also varied across studies). It was felt that in order to understand and describe the decision-making behaviour of Indian managers in different situations of ethical dilemma, a decision-making scale based on vignettes representing the different situations of ethical dilemma needed to be developed for the study. The detailed procedure of development of this scale is described here.

DEVELOPMENT OF THE INSTRUMENT FOR
ETHICAL DECISION MAKING

An ethical decision-making measure is defined in the present context as decision making in a situation of ethical dilemma. An ethical dilemma is a situation where more than one alternative is possible as a solution of a problem that has an ethical component.

Besides defining the framework, there was a need to design an instrument to assess which evaluative framework(s) are typically used by Indian managers in general, as well as in particular situations. It is realistic to assume that the framework utilized by the decision-maker will vary according to the circumstances of the decision. Therefore, it was felt that the respondents should be exposed to different situations by asking them to respond to vignettes containing ethical dilemmas. The responses to these vignettes could help in analyzing the individual's choice of ethical frameworks, against a common background.

The present study focused on the behaviour of individuals in situations of ethical dilemma related to his/her workplace. Therefore, vignettes having a component of ethical dilemma and related to workplace situations in organizations had to be identified for the study. Given below is the procedure that was followed to make the selection of the vignettes for the questionnaire.

Based on the literature review (published cases) and informal discussions with practising managers (MBA part-time students at IIT, New Delhi), 20 vignettes of ethical dilemmas representing everyday situations faced by managers were developed. These 20 situations were given to five experts (three academicians and two practitioners) to review. As a result of the discussion, 14 situations were finally selected to be included in the pilot study questionnaire.

These situations were shared with the respondents and they were asked a question towards the end for each situation, as to how he/she would behave if found in the same situation. The question was kept open-ended and respondents were asked to answer in the space provided after each situation. The responses to the questionnaire were then analyzed. Given below is an example of a situation and the possible responses to it:

Situation–

Your product has good potential for sale in institutions. However, in institutional sales, due to the high cost of your product the whole procedure of selling and then collecting the payment is quite long and time-consuming. To deal with this problem, a proposal is made for appointing a sub agent to handle market development, necessary gift giving and money transfers. How do you react to the proposal?

The response categories were–
1. The proposal is acceptable. An increase in sales means an increase in profit, and thereby greater benefits to the employees.
2. I would never agree to such a proposal. Such short cuts are not desirable in the long run.
3. There is no harm in accepting the proposal.
4. The acceptability of the proposal depends upon many other factors.
5. I will agree to this proposal only if there is no other solution.

Only those vignettes that had extreme responses were considered situations of ethical dilemma. The vignettes with responses clustering at any one end were dropped. It was also found that ethical frameworks used by organizations were equally important, as they provided the backdrop against which individual behaviour tools were placed. Therefore, out of the vignettes selected, only nine vignettes where individual as well as organizational responses were possible were included in the study.

As a result of the above selection criteria, five vignettes were finally selected to be included in the study (see Annexure III).

Scale Construction

Each vignette was followed by a five-point scale, wherein responses at the lower end of the scale were termed (by five experts) as *Values* (ethical) and the responses at the higher end were termed *Compromise* (unethical).

The term *Compromise* was defined here as the response to a situation of ethical dilemma, where the individual takes a decision based upon the need of the situation, rather than adhering to rigid principles, or morally correct behaviour in society.

Values was defined as the response to a situation of ethical dilemma, which is socially considered morally correct.

The respondents were asked to give their answers against column 'a' and column 'b', where column 'a' was meant for individual decisions, and column 'b' was meant for measuring the individual perception of the organizational response in the given situation of ethical dilemma. The five situations included in the questionnaire were: (*a*) 'new and improved marketing strategy'; (*b*) 'gifts and bribes'; (*c*) 'padding up the expense bills'; (*d*) 'nepotism'; and (*e*) 'insider trading' (see Annexure III).

For the purpose of establishing that all the five vignettes included in the measure were different from each other, i.e., represented five different work situations and individuals' responses varied for each one, a t-test was conducted for the responses obtained for these vignettes in the main study. Table A.10 (Annexure I) reports the results of the t-test.

It can be inferred from Table A.10 that barring one, the rest of the values for t were highly significant, suggesting that responses made in all the vignettes were different from the others. The findings highlight the significance of situational factors in influencing the process of decision making in situations of ethical dilemma. It implies that different individuals in similar situations and the same person in different situations would make different decisions. It was also felt important to analyze if there existed any generic difference between the situations leading towards a pattern of response exhibited by the majority of the respondents. For this purpose, one sample t-test with a test value of 2.5 (the mean value of the possible range of scores) was conducted on the scores obtained on these situations. The results are represented in Table 3.1. The t values were significant in four out of five situations.

Table 3.1
Sample T-Test for the Five Vignettes of Ethical Decision-Making Dilemmas

Decision making	Test Value = 2.5			
	t	*mean*	*Standard Deviation*	*Direction of decision making*
Vignette 1	−3.489**	2.2444	1.2919	*Value*
Vignette 2	19.989**	3.7443	1.0943	*Compromise*
Vignette 3	1.038	2.5714	1.2072	*Neutral*
Vignette 4	−3.201**	2.2787	1.2076	*Value*
Vignette 5	8.135**	3.0782	1.2187	*Compromise*

From the results given in Table 3.1, it can be inferred that in the four out of five of the given situations, the results of the ethical decision making scale were significantly different from the average score of 2.5, i.e., either in the *Compromise* or *Value* direction. This means that in four out of five situations, people made clear decisions either towards a *Compromise* or a *Value* direction.

In the case of Vignette 1, which was regarding the 'new and improved' marketing gimmick, it can be inferred from that the mean and t value that the majority of respondents took a decision in the *Value* direction i.e., made an ethical decision. In this situation, a suggestion was made about placing a false 'new and improved' tag on the product package and advertising it to improve the product's sale in the market. Therefore, in the process the customer was likely to be cheated, as he would purchase the same old product falsely advertised to be new and improved.

In case of Vignette 2, the majority of the responses were in the *Compromise* direction, i.e., an unethical decision. The mean value of the response of the total sample was significantly higher than the average possible score. The situation was about the use of gifts and bribes to obtain a business favour. The consequence of the *Compromise* decision in this situation would be the smooth functioning of business procedures and more profit expected for the organization. It appears that the use of gifts and bribes in business has become quite acceptable.

In Vignette 3, the difference was not significant, i.e., the respondents in this situation were not clearly on one side. The situation was about inflating expense bills by an otherwise high performing executive. The respondents were asked to take decisions whether the company should fire such a person or keep him despite his dishonesty. The response was mixed.

Vignette 4 was about 'nepotism'. The general response was significantly greater towards the *Value* direction, i.e., an ethical decision and did not advocate any favour in the selection process of a candidate. The consequences of the unethical decision in this case would be disadvantageous to the most deserving candidate and a direct and indirect long-term loss to the organization.

Vignette 5 discusses the issue of 'insider trading'. Observing the t value and the mean value in Table 3.1 for this situation, it can be inferred that the response was significantly high towards the *Compromise* direction, i.e., an unethical decision of using confidential information of the company for personal gain. However, as a result of this decision, no visible harm was caused to the company or any other person.

The content analysis of the five vignettes along with the pattern of responses in each case, leads to two points of conclusion, i.e., people at the workplace generally take unethical decisions or use wrong means where:

- the end result is good and does not cause any harm to the other stakeholders; and,
- when the consequence of the decision is not harmful, though not beneficial either, to the majority of the stakeholders.

This scale of ethical decision making was able to generate some information about the decisions people make in different situations of ethical dilemmas. However, as mentioned earlier, it is the cognitive process and the reasoning used by the individual in such situations which is more important than the end result. It is quite likely that two people take the same decision, but their logic or justification for the process is totally different. For example, two persons may notice a hundred rupee note lying on the street, and both of them decide not to pick it up because of two different reasons. The first person may think that if somebody notices the action and makes it public, it would harm his/her reputation, and the other may think that it is wrong to pick up something that does not belong to him/her. Therefore, it also becomes important to see what cognitive ethical framework people use while making decisions in situations of ethical dilemmas.

COGNITIVE ETHICAL FRAMEWORKS

Based on the various prevailing theories, some of which are discussed in Chapter 2, in the field of ethical decision making, different researchers have identified and used various frameworks (for example, concepts of Utilitarianism, Justice, Kant Imperative and Duty), which can be used to explain and guide an individual's ethical decision-making process. It needs to be mentioned here, that philosophers have traditionally identified the normative or ideal logic for ethical decision making and they are likely to form a part of an individual's cognitive processes. However, they do not take into account only the ideal but other logic too, that works as psychological defenses. Thus, a descriptive work like this one will not only focus on the ideals but the actual and practical logic too.

A variety of ethical frameworks have been used in the past. Arthur (1984) has provided an extensive list of frameworks of moral reasoning, which include: *hedonism*—extreme selfishness; *utilitarianism*—the greatest good for the greatest number; *pragmatism*—whatever minimizes conflict; *salvation (a)*—good work to earn redemption; *salvation (b)*—isolation, mediation and devotion; *golden rule*—based on faith, charity and reciprocity; *divine right*—maintenance of the 'pecking-order'; *egalitarianism*—suppress the rich, encourage the poor; *paternalism*—maintaining the sanctity of the natural process (nature).

While suggesting a contingency model of ethical decision making, Ferrel and Gresham (1985) discussed ethical frameworks as individual variable factors. They followed the classification of ethical frameworks based upon the basic philosophy of teleological and deontological approaches, where the teleological approach included *utilitarian* philosophy, and deontological philosophies included the *right and justice principle*.

Some of the frameworks studied directly in the context of business include the *doctrine of the mean,* where the decision-maker seeks the mean, or the moderate course of action between the extreme behaviours known as *intuition ethics*. Hence, the decision-maker is guided by simply what he/she feels or understands to be the right course of action. In *conventionalist ethics*, the decision-maker is permitted to participate in unethical actions in business because it is assumed that business is like a game and therefore, has its own set of rules, supporting the statement that all is fair in love, war and business (Steiner and Steiner, 1988). *Professional ethics* refers to situations where one is guided to only take the action, that would be viewed as correct by a panel of professionals and/or colleagues. Under the *categorical imperative,* individuals act in such a way that the action taken under those circumstances could be deemed as the universal law of behaviour for others who face the same circumstances. The *TV test* is where individuals act in such a way that one would be comfortable explaining his/her action on T.V to the general public (Laczniak and Murphy, 1991).

In an exploratory study, McDonald and Pak (1996), while investigating the cognitive frameworks used by business managers, identified eight frameworks viz., self-interest, utilitarian, categorical imperative, duty, justice, neutralization, religious conviction, and light of the day.

Clearly, the studies indicate that ethical frameworks have been conceptualized in a variety of ways. At this early stage of ethical framework research, often a variety of frameworks is used, wherein the problems in consistency and terminology are apparent. We are still at an early stage of ethical framework from the above review. Problems with the consistency of terminology are to be expected when a number of researchers enter a new area of study. Besides terminology, the other equally important issue is that of measurement.

Further, Indian religious tradition is rich in delineating the values systems and ethical standards. The review in Chapter 2 revealed that there were no systematic studies to translate this tradition into the cognitive frameworks used by the individual/managers. Hence, this chapter reports the outcome of developing a new psychometrically sound multi-dimensional measure of cognitive frameworks used by managers, while making decisions in situations of ethical dilemma. This is intended to address, along with the above mentioned frameworks, logic based on Indian ethical philosophies.

INDIAN ETHICAL PHILOSOPHIES

These studies and theories provide the possible ethical frameworks that managers may use. This chapter attempts to pinpoint how managers organize them in their mental framework. An empirical basis (through a study) has been used to identify these frameworks.

This chapter contains details of the process of development of the measure of ethical frameworks that Indian managers use. This includes the details of item development process, followed by refinement of the measure and content validity. The construct validity of the measure is established through factor analysis for individual ethical frameworks. A factor analysis for public and private sector respondents was also conducted to further test the cross validity of the construct. The results of the factor analysis for the organizational ethical frameworks are also reported in this section. Organizational ethical frameworks were the perception of the individuals about the framework (ethical logic) used by the organizations.

ETHICAL FRAMEWORK MEASURE

Item Development Process

Keeping in view the issues raised during the review of literature, we began with two sets of frameworks. The first one contained sub frameworks that are used in every day life. The frameworks were: self-interest, utilitarianism, categorical imperative, duty, justice, neutralization, and light of the day. The second set of frameworks was based on religious beliefs in general, with some concepts emanating from Indian philosophy in particular. Hence, the frameworks that emerged from religious prescriptions and Indian scriptures was included in the study to observe their use by modern managers. For this purpose, a few Indian religious concepts like karma*, moksh* and sreyas* (discussed subsequently), along with the framework of religious convictions, were included. Thus, the process of framework development started with two broad categories of frameworks viz. practical or operational frameworks, that are based upon every day operational life, which are essentially amenable to a logical analysis rooted in the here and now, and a religious framework, which is based upon the religious or mythological prescriptions, involving an element of faith. The definitions of these frameworks are given ahead.

---

*Karma: where the only concern is duty without worrying about the results; moksh: means breaking the cycle of birth and rebirth; and sreyas: refers to an individual's long-term perspective concerning not only this life but also the next.

Practical Framework

Self-interest: In this framework, during the decision process the principal evaluation concern is only the selfish gain of the greatest degree of personal satisfaction. Therefore, the decision is made in such a way that it ensures the best interest, or self-promotion of the individual decision-maker. If the decision is an organizational one, then the corporate entity is considered to be the moral agent and the same rule applies.

Utilitarianism: When the decision is taken under this framework, the emphasis is on balancing the costs and benefits, or good and bad, in an effort to maximize utility. Utilitarianism asserts that the decision-maker should always act in order to produce the greatest ratio of good over bad for everyone. The focus of the decision-maker in this framework is on the consequences of his her decision, and the impact of these consequences on those concerned with it.

Categorical Imperative: This framework is based on the principle that an action is either morally right or wrong, regardless of the consequences. This framework consists of two formulations, which are simplistically referred to as the universal rule and the means-ends rule. The universal rule is concerned with whether the decision-maker would be willing to have others act in this way to him/herself. The means-end rule is concerned with whether the individuals concerned are being treated as an 'end in themselves', i.e., respected and in possession of their rights, or are they being treated as a 'means' and utilized purely for the sole achievement of a specific objective?

Duty: An action may be inherently right because of the duty that one has. In an organizational context, a decision would involve considerations of whether the action of interest was in keeping with, or violated any prescribed rule of duty. For example, the framework of duty would approve actions that were observed to be aligned with one's fiduciary relationships, but would disapprove of an action that would violate that obligation.

Justice: This framework is concerned with the 'fairness' of a decision and whether there has been a just distribution of benefits and burdens among all those concerned with it, despite factors like age, sex, religion, interests, income, personal characteristics, social and occupational positions. It is based on the pre-existing notion of freedom, equality and concern for the disadvantaged, although it has been suggested that most adult individuals do possess an intuitive sense of fairness, based on natural justice. The description of the ethical frameworks is given in Figure 3.1.

Figure 3.1

Two Sets of Ethical Frameworks

Practical Framework	Religious Framework
Self-interest: selfishly gaining the greatest degree of personal satisfaction.	Religious Conviction:
Utilitarianism: to produce the greatest ratio of good over bad for everyone.	Moksh: breaking the cycle of birth and rebirth.
Categorical Imperative: would the decision-maker be willing to have others act in this way to him/herself? Are the individuals concerned being treated as an end in themselves, or are they being treated as a 'means' and thus utilized?	Sreyas: long-term perspective with concerns not only for this life but also for the next.
Duty: an action may be inherently right because of the duty that one has.	Karma: only concern is duty without worrying about the results.
Justice: 'fairness' of the decision.	
Neutralization: a rationalization tactic involving (a) denial of the victim; (b) denial of injury; and (c) appeal to higher loyalties.	
The light of day: what if this information went public?	

Neutralization: Individuals often use the neutralization framework as a technique, to reduce the possible impact of norm-violating behaviours upon their self-concept and their social relationships. More than an ethical framework, this is a rationalization technique. The most common perceptual components of neutralization are: (a) denial of responsibility—where individuals argue that they are not personally accountable for their actions due to circumstances beyond their control; (b) denial of injury—where the individual is not important and could be an acceptable violation of normative behaviour since no one suffered; (c) denial of victim—where individuals condone their actions by arguing that the violated party deserved whatever happened, i.e., a form of retributive justice is evoked; (d) condemning the condemner—where the individual points out that he/she is not alone in the unethical action and that others have behaved in the same manner i.e., condoning by majority action; (e) appeal to higher loyalties—where individuals propose that the norm violation action is required in order to achieve a higher ideal of values, i.e., for the benefit of the organization or the society.

The light of day: This principle suggests that during the decision-making process, the most salient factor that is taken into consideration by the decision-maker is in connection with the question, 'what if this information went public'. The decision-maker is consciously aware of what might be the reaction of family, friends and associates if the details relating to the circumstances under which the decision was taken are revealed and received extensive publicity.

Religious Framework

Religious Conviction: Under the ethical framework of religious conviction, the decision-makers will refer to their religious convictions and the decision is likely to be based on the directions of their religious faith.

Moksh: This framework is based on the belief that the present life is a block in the cycle of birth and rebirth. The individual is keen to obtain *moksh* (the liberation which is eternal happiness) from the cycle of birth and rebirth (*puner Janma*). It is believed that the present life is an outcome of the actions in one's previous life, and that the actions in the present one will decide your next life. Hence, every action is judged in terms of its impact on the next life. Therefore, it is alright to undertake activities that lead to the liberation and/or improvement of our next life.

Sreyas: This framework emphasizes the preference for long-term benefits over short-term gains, i.e., having a future orientation to life. Life is treated as one long journey, wherein what an individual does at any given point of time impacts not only at that point of time, but also the future. Here, the future is not limited to the present life, but may be seen as extending to different lives that a soul may take. Hence, every activity has to be assessed in terms of its long-term impact.

Karma: In this framework, the decision-makers consider every action as their duty, detached from the fruits of the action. They believe that their jurisdiction is restricted to the work performance, and that the results are not under their control. *Karma* thus, is paramount and is detached from the results that it may yield.

These definitions of the 11 frameworks and 60 statements representing these frameworks (taken from the literature as well as generated on the basis of the definitions of the frameworks) were given to a panel of experts for discussion (three academicians and two practising managers). From the discussion, the following issues were raised and addressed:

1. The framework of *karma* often overlapped with the framework of duty. Therefore, a decision was taken to dissolve the framework of duty and broaden the definition of karma, so that it included the concept of duty in it.

2. Due to the lack of consensus on the framework of neutralization among the experts, it was dropped. The concern was that it would be used for justifying an act after it was committed, instead of being a guiding framework for ethical decision making.

3. The experts also felt that the framework of categorical imperative overlapped in parts with the framework of justice. Therefore, a decision was taken to combine the two and broaden the definition of justice to include the components of categorical imperative in it.

4. The experts were of the opinion that the framework of *sreyas* was an important one, but that it needed to focus more on the practical aspects instead of the religious ones. Hence, the items concerning its impact on the next life were dropped. It was also felt that if the name of this framework was changed to 'long-term perspective', it would have more practical appeal. Therefore a decision was taken to change the name accordingly and include it as a part of the practical framework.

The 60 statements (representing the frameworks) given to the experts were reduced to 50 after reviewing their content, leaving out the ambiguous and unclear statements.

Refinement of the Measure and Content Validation

Thus, five sub frameworks (self-interest, utilitarianism, justice, long-term perspective and light of the day) were identified as pragmatic and three (religious conviction, *moksh* and *karma*) as religious frameworks. The revised definitions of *karma* and justice are given below.

Karma: An action may be inherently right because of the duty that one is obliged to feel. In an organizational context, a decision would involve considerations of whether the action of interest was in keeping with, or violated any prescribed rule of duty. At the same time, in this framework, the decision-maker considers every action as his/her duty—without any attachment to the fruits of action. He/she believes that his/her jurisdiction is restricted to performing or not performing the work/action, or performing it in a different way, and that results are not under his/her control.

Justice: This framework is concerned with the 'fairness' of a decision, and whether there has been a just distribution of benefits and burdens among all those concerned with it, despite their age, sex, religion, interests, income, personal characteristics, social and occupational positions. It is based on the pre-existence of, concepts like freedom, equality, and concern for the disadvantaged, in the mind of the decision-maker. This framework also comprises two formulations of categorical imperative, which is simplistically referred to as the concept of justice based on the universal rule and the means-ends rule (discussed in the earlier section).

For further refinement, an exercise was also conducted with working executives (40 MBA part-time students). The 50 selected statements were randomly arranged and the respondents were asked to categorize these statements under various frameworks based on the definitions of the frameworks given to them. The results of the exercise were analyzed using the criteria of 80 per cent consensus i.e., only those items were included in a framework that were placed in one category by at least 32 respondents. This resulted in 39 statements belonging to the above-mentioned eight frameworks. These 39 statements were included in the final questionnaire used for the main study. Table 3.2 gives the details of the items under each framework.

Table 3.2
Items of Ethical Frameworks

Self-interest
- Do something that is in your best interest.
- In today's business world you must look after yourself and your own interests.
- Ultimately, you should ask whether these actions are consistent with your own goals and do what is good for yourself.
- That you cannot be expected to be responsible for everyone and everything and you have to keep in mind your own interest.
- Interest of the individual and organizations cannot be paramount in all decision making.
- We cannot always look at selfish interests.

Utilitarianism

- It should secure the benefit of the larger number.
- The decision should produce the greatest net value to all the parties.
- The results should benefit a large number of people.
- The action should serve the purpose of the majority.

Karma

- It is a waste of energy worrying about the effect that an action might have; you should just do what you have to.
- The results of the duties that we perform are not under our control.
- The only thing that is in our control is the performance of our duties.

Justice

- An unethical action is fair if it is directed towards an unethical individual or organization.
- It is important that justice is seen to be done.
- It should be the most equitable decision.
- People must be treated fairly.
- The consequences of the decision should affect the majority in a positive way.
- It is important that discriminatory practices be avoided.
- It is not fair to treat people as a means to an end.
- Justice must prevail in all circumstances.
- Some things in life are definitely right or wrong, thus, there is a natural justice which must be followed.

Religious Conviction

- What is the right thing to do under your religious beliefs.
- It is in line with the advice from a religious source.
- Your religious faith must permit such an action.

Moksh *

- It should not have a bad effect on your next life (Janma).
- It should help in improving your next life (Janma).
- Every action is judged in terms of its impact on the next life.
- Whatever is happening with you, now is the result of your action in your previous life.
- You consider your next life while making a decision.

Long-term Perspective

- Immediate goals are not the only concern; you must also keep in mind the future.
- Unethical business practices are not beneficial in the long run.
- Having an eye on the future is important.
- What would be the best outcome in the long run?
- Long-term goals are more important than short-term ones.

The light of day

- What effects the action might have on you/your organization's personal reputation if it becomes public.

- What would be the reaction of your family and friends/peers if the details of this action were revealed?
- You or your organization would lose, if your or the organization's involvement in this decision were publicized.
- 'I would feel embarrassed if people found out what I had decided to do'.

* *Moksh* items were not considered for organizational ethical frameworks.

Methodology

The ethical framework measure finalized as a result of the above exercise was used in a study to collect the individual responses (see Annexure III). A survey through a structured questionnaire developed for the purpose was conducted to collect the data.

Organization, gender and age-wise split of the sample can be seen in Tables A.5 and A.6 (Annexure I). The respondents were asked to reply on a five-point scale as to what extent they consider each factor (represented by each statement) while making the decisions regarding the given situations in the questionnaire. There were two columns given after each statement (column *a* and *b*). Column *a* was for the respondents themselves and column *b* was for the respondents to express their perception of the same for the organization, i.e., how would the organization react in the given situation. Some of the items in the scale were not relevant in the context of an organization. In such cases **0** was marked against such items in column *b* (see Annexure III).

Results

Individual Ethical Frameworks

The data received from the survey was subjected to a varimax rotated factor analysis as a partial test of construct validity. The results of the factor analysis for ethical frameworks for individuals are given in column 1 of Table A.11 (Annexure I). Only those items which had a factor loading greater than .5 and cross loading below .35, were selected as representing the factor. The analysis of data for individual ethical frameworks revealed two factors that met the criteria of eigen value greater than one and loading of at least three items on the factor. The factors are described as follows.

The first factor had eight items. Of these, three belonged to the long-term perspective; four to justice and one to the utilitarian framework. The content analysis of the items revealed that these items together had ideas of long-term focus for justice. It was concluded that these items reflected a pragmatic orientation, and therefore, this framework was named Pragmatic Framework.

The second factor also had eight items. Of these, five items were from the framework *moksh* and three belonged to the religious conviction framework. A content analysis of the items revealed that they reflected the religious orientation of the individuals therefore, the factor was named Religious Framework. The clustering of the *moksh* and religious conviction items suggested that in the Indian context, *moksh* is an important belief among Hindus.

To check for cross validity and factor stability of the construct, a factor analysis was also conducted for the responses of the private and public sector separately. This is in line with the recommendations of Schwab (1980) and DeVellis (1991), that for cross validation, researchers collect data on different samples. This also addresses the issue of sample specificity. The results of the factor analysis for the private and public sector are given in column 2 and column 3 respectively, of Table A.11 (Annexure I). The results reveal that the same factors, by and large, emerged from both the perspectives. These results further establish the cross validity of the construct. The factor analysis revealed that from all the three perspectives, the first factor (pragmatic framework) explained the maximum percentage variance. This indicates that the pragmatic framework is the predominant factor and is used more frequently by managers as compared to the religious framework.

Scale Characteristics

Table A.11 (Annexure I) lists the descriptive statistics of the items, inter-item and item test correlation of the scale. It can be seen from the table that the items within the factor show a fairly high correlation, as opposed to the items across factors.

Reliability and Validity: The reliabilities (Cronbach's alpha), mean and standard deviations of the sub scales for the total sample, as well as for the public and private sectors separately, are given in Table 3.3. As can be seen, the scale showed high reliability coefficients in all the three cases.

Moksh may be considered to be a culture-specific construct, thus, to check for universal applicability, the reliability of the second factor was calculated with only three items of religious conviction (removing the ones related to *moksh*). The reliability obtained was .75, establishing the fact that even without the items related to *moksh,* the factor can be used for measuring ethical frameworks.

Table 3.3
Mean, Standard Deviations and Alpha Coefficients of the Ethical Framework Scale

	Total Sample		Private Sector		Public Sector	
	F I	F II	F I	F II	F I	F II
Reliability Alpha	0.72	0.85	0.82	0.86	0.79	0.85
Mean	31.5	19.5	41.07	18.49	38.16	17.84
Standard Deviation	4.8	7.8	5.5	7.8	6.6	7.1

For further validation of the scale on ethical frameworks, criterion related to the scale was also assessed. Criterion validity would mean that it should be able to predict certain behavioural outcomes on the job. Ethical decision-making, leadership styles and job satisfaction may be considered as important criteria variables for ethical frameworks. The relationship of ethical decision making with ethical frameworks is discussed with ethical frameworks in the last part of this chapter.

The emergence of the two distinct logics for ethical decision making needs to be explored. To begin with, many logics and frameworks as identified by philosophers in the west, as well as Indian philosophies were included. For theoreticians, each of these logics are independent in their own right. However, the Indian manager's cognitive frameworks do not perceive them as numerous and distinct frameworks. In their view, they are all clubbed under two heads: one emanating from practical and logical realities based on the here and now, the other based on religious philosophies that need not be governed by the realities of the perceptible and logical world.

This has yielded an insight into what the Indian manager perceives and how his/her perception becomes influenced by often seemingly conflicting frameworks. The universal practical frameworks would focus on logic, rationality and data, while the religious framework may be based on faith in a religious philosophy.

The Indian manager is thus on the crossroads of two ethical logics and appears to use both of them. However, because of the characteristics of business organizations, it is likely that the present-day manager shows a greater use of practical and pragmatic frameworks.

Organizational Ethical Frameworks

Table A.12 (Annexure I) presents the factors obtained after an analysis of the data for organizational ethical decision-making frameworks. The analysis of the data revealed two neat factors. The first factor had seven items; two were from the framework of justice, three from long-term perspective and two from utilitarianism. Some of the items were the same as those of the individual framework factor. Therefore, keeping the same considerations in mind, this factor was called the Organizational Pragmatic Framework.

Table 3.4
Individual and Organizational Ethical Frameworks with their Item Statements.

Individual Ethical Frameworks	Organizational Ethical Frameworks
Pragmatic Ethical Framework	
Ultimately, one should ask whether the actions are consistent with one's own goals and do what is right for oneself.	It is important that justice is seen to be done.
Immediate goals are not the only concern; one must also keep in mind the future.	Having an eye on the future is important.
What would be the best outcome in the long run?	What would be the best outcome in the long run?
People must be treated fairly.	People must be treated fairly.
The consequences of the decision should affect the majority in a positive way.	Long-term goals are more important than short-term ones.
Long-term goals are more important than short-term ones.	We cannot always look at selfish interests.
It is important that discriminatory practices be avoided.	
It is not fair to treat people as a means to an end.	
Some things in life are definitely right or wrong; there is a natural justice, which must be followed.	
Religious Framework	
It should not have an adverse effect on my next life (*janma*).	What is the right thing to do according to my religious beliefs?
It should help in improving my next life (*janma*).	It is in line with the advice from a religious source.
Every action is judged in terms of its impact on the next life.	My religious faith must permit such an action.

(Table 3.4 contd...)

What is the right thing to do according to my
religious beliefs?

It is in line with the advice from a religious
source.

Whatever is happening with me now, is the
result of my actions in a previous life.

My religious faith must permit such an action.

I consider my next life too while making
decisions.

The second factor had only three items and all of them belonged to
religious conviction. Therefore, according to the considerations of the
second factor of the individual framework, this factor was called Organizational Religious Framework. Items with regard to *moksh* were
not considered relevant from the organizational perspective and hence,
were deleted for this analysis.

ETHICAL FRAMEWORKS AND ETHICAL DECISION MAKING

An individual's ethical ideology (studied through the concept of ethical frameworks) was expected to influence individual decisions when
faced with a situation of ethical dilemma. Forsyth and Berger (1982)
have also warned that the variations in ethical ideologies can be used
to predict individual differences in moral behaviour. At the same time,
situational factors also influence the individual decisions when faced
with ethical dilemma. From this perspective, individuals are expected
to apply different ethical frameworks when facing different situations
of ethical dilemmas. Current behavioural research strongly supports
a person-situation interactive explanation of human behaviour, in
which both individual and situational factors influence the behaviour
choice made by individuals (Jones, 1985; Luthans and Kreitner, 1985;
Trevino, 1986). Therefore, different situations of ethical dilemma were
used (to provide variations in situations) to study ethical decision
making and other behavioural outcomes.

First of all, the relationship between individual ethical frameworks
and decision-making behaviour in given situations of ethical dilemma
was ascertained using correlations. The results are reported in Table
A.13 (Annexure I).

In three out of five vignettes of ethical dilemma, individual ethical frameworks had a significant correlation with the nature of decision making. In the first situation ('new and improved marketing strategy') both the religious and pragmatic frameworks showed a significant relationship with ethical decision making. To investigate which out of the two frameworks is the better predictor in the case of the first vignette, a regression analysis was conducted. The results are given in Table A.14 (Annexure I). From Table A.14, it is evident that the beta value for both the frameworks was significant, but from the t value it can be concluded that the individual pragmatic framework is a better predictor of the nature of decisions in given situations of ethical dilemma.

For the third situation ('padding up of the expense bills'), the religious framework showed a highly significant positive relationship. This means that a person with a stronger religious framework would be more prone to taking a decision towards the *Compromise* dimension of ethical decision-making behaviour. Similarly, in the fourth situation ('nepotism'), it was the pragmatic framework that significantly correlated with the nature of decision making. However, the negative and highly significant relationship suggested that individuals higher on the pragmatic framework would score towards the *Values* dimension of ethical decision making.

In light of the research, it was felt that the effect of organizational factors could not be ignored while studying the decision-making behaviour of individuals in given situations of ethical dilemmas. Stead et al., (1990) clearly indicated that the ethical ideologies of management have a major impact on the ethical behaviour of the employees. There are several other researchers who support this conclusion (Arlow and Ulrich, 1980; Baumhart, 1961; Brenner and Molander, 1977; Carroll, 1978; Hegarty and Sims, 1978, 1979; Posner and Schmidt, 1984; Vitell and Festvand, 1987).

Therefore, to understand what predicts individual ethical behaviour accurately, both the individual and organizational ethical frameworks were put forward as predictors of ethical decision making in each situation. A significant influence of either the individual ethical framework or organizational framework was observed in the case of three vignettes i.e., vignette one, three and five. Results are reported in Tables A.15, A.16 and A.17 (Annexure I).

Table A.15 indicates the regression analysis results for the first vignette ('new and improved marketing strategy'). From this table it can be concluded that the most accurate predictor of ethical decision behaviour in the given situation was the organizational pragmatic framework. It can be observed from Table 3.8 that in case of this vignette, both the individual ethical frameworks were operative in influencing the individual decision. However, Table A.14 clearly indicated that when taken together, out of all the four frameworks the organizational pragmatic ethical framework was the best predictor of decisions in the given situation. If the content of this vignette were to be analyzed (Annexure III) it would be revealed that the final decision taken in the given situation may reflect the organizational ethical ideology.

Table A.16 (Annexure I) gives the results of the regression analysis for the third vignette ('padding up of the expense bills'). In this situation, individual religious ethical frameworks was found to be the best predictor of the nature of the decision. The content of the situation (Annexure III) also indicated that if the management was not involved or was not aware of the situation then it was the individual ethical ideology that would guide the behaviour in such a situation.

Similarly, the individual behaviour in case of the fifth vignette ('insider trading') was found to be guided by individual pragmatic framework. i.e., it was found to be the best predictor of individual behaviour in the given situation. Regression results for this vignette are given in Table A.17 (Annexure I).

The overall results of the analysis discussed above are summarized in Table 3.5. The results show that both the frameworks identified in the study, i.e., Pragmatic and Religious Frameworks, are found to be operative in the ethical decision-making process. Both these frameworks are of significant importance. The pragmatic framework is grounded in reality and the religious framework represents the faith of the individual in a higher power. At this point it may be relevant to briefly discuss Protestant ethics, which is considered the western equivalent of religious ethics.

The Protestant ethic, is a code of morals based on the principles of thrift, discipline, hard work, and individualism. The adjective 'Protestant' is explained by the fact that these qualities were seen to have been especially encouraged by the Protestant religion. The major formulators of the concept of the Protestant ethic were the German political philosopher and sociologist, Max Weber and the English historian, Richard H. Tawney. Both men saw a close relationship between the Protestant ethic and the rise of capitalism.

Weber was impressed by the seeming fact that modern capitalism had developed mainly in those areas of Europe where Calvinistic Protestantism had taken root early in the Protestant Reformation. In *The Protestant Ethic* and the *Spirit of Capitalism* (1905; revised 1920; English translation, 1930), Weber argued that a causal connection existed between the two; his concern was with the effect of religion on economic life, but he claimed that the reverse influences were equally important. Weber held that the doctrine of predestination, and the remote and unknowable Protestant God created intense anxieties in the individual regarding that person's state of grace. A practical means of reducing those anxieties took the form of a systematic commitment to a calling, that is, to hard work, thrift, and self-discipline, the material rewards of which were not consumed personally, but saved and reinvested. Since these qualities were also those required for success in the newly emerging capitalist economy, it followed that those who practiced them also formed the nucleus of the new capitalist class. Furthermore, success in the commercial world tended to assure the individual, that he or she was, in fact, in a state of grace, because God had smiled on his or her endeavours. Weber theorized that with the waning of a religious world view, the Protestant ethic remained 'the spirit of capitalism'.

Table 3.5
The Ethical Decisions and Ethical Frameworks and their Coexistence

	Direction of Decision Making	Coexisting Framework	The Framework Best Predictor of the Decision
Vignette 1 *'new and improved'*	*Value*	Both pragmatic as well as religious	Organizational Pragmatic
Vignette 2 *'gifts and bribes'*	*Compromise*		
Vignette 3 *'padding up of the expense bills'*	*Neutral*	Religious	Individual Religious
Vignette 4 *'nepotism'*	*Value*	Pragmatic	
Vignette 5 *'insider trading'*	*Compromise*		Individual Pragmatic

This means that even in western ethical philosophy, religion and business pragmatism go hand in hand. The religious belief of the individual helps him/her develop discipline in life. This Implies that these two frameworks are not mutually exclusive, but compliment each other and that either of the two dominates depending on the situation. It is also evident from other findings that the situational component plays a very significant role in influencing the choice of ethical frameworks, as well as the final decision in the case of an ethical dilemma.

CHAPTER OVERVIEW

The main focus of this chapter was to see what decisions managers take in situations of ethical dilemmas, and what ethical ideologies (measured through cognitive ethical frameworks) they follow while taking these decisions. Efforts were made to develop psychometrically sound, multi-dimensional measures of ethical decision making and ethical frameworks. The two dimensions of ethical decision behaviour identified and used in the scale for ethical decision making were *Compromise* and *Values*. These two dimensions formed two poles of a continuum. Here, *Compromise* was defined as the response of an individual to a situation of ethical dilemma, where the decision is taken based upon the need of the situation, rather than adhering to rigid principles irrespective of what is considered morally correct in society. *Values* was defined as the response that is socially considered morally correct. The scale consisted of five situations of ethical dilemma often faced by the managers in work situations. These were: (*a*) 'new and improved marketing strategy'; (*b*) 'Gifts and bribes'; (*c*) 'Padding up the expense bills'; (*d*) 'Nepotism'; (*e*) 'Insider trading'. The response to this scale highlighted the importance of situational factors in influencing decisions in case of ethical dilemma.

The process of the development of the ethical framework measure began by choosing 11 frameworks from the literature. Out of the 11, eight were taken from the existing literature on ethics (self-interest, utilitarianism, categorical imperative, duty, justice, neutralization, religious conviction and the light of day), and three were taken from the Indian religious literature (*moksh, karma, sreyas*). A series of exercises and input from the experts finally led to eight frameworks and 40 statements. The frameworks were self-interest, utilitarianism, *karma*, justice, religious conviction, *moksh*, long-term perspective and the light of day. The factor analysis of the responses gave the following results, wherein two dominating ethical frameworks emerged, called Pragmatic and Religious Frameworks (Bhal and Sharma, 2001a). The components of this pragmatic framework included utilitarianism, long-term perspective and justice. The religious framework however, consisted of items of religious conviction and *moksh*. This shows that the respondents had a simpler conceptualization of the frameworks than anticipated, as the sub-categories of frameworks did not emerge as separate categories. Further, the emergence of the same two factors in cross validation for the private and public sector separately provided additional evidence of the stability of factor structures of the sub scales. The first factor in all the three samples, i.e., the total sample, the public sector sample and the private sector sample, was the pragmatic framework, explaining a greater percentage variance in all the three cases. This indicates that though the managers may use religious frameworks, they predominantly use a pragmatic framework in making every day decisions. Although the results showed a strong reliability. It would be prudent to mention that the size of the sample is not very large (especially when it is divided between public and private sector organizations). Second, although the scale is expected to be culturally free since most of the dimensions considered were taken from the review of literature, based upon its popularity and universality, the sample consisted of respondents from only one culture. Hence, further research across cultures is required to establish the cross-cultural validity of the scale. The results of the relationship between individual ethical frameworks and ethical decision-making behaviour in the given five situations showed that for different situations, different frameworks were operative.

4

AGE, GENDER AND ETHICAL CONDUCT

As has been discussed in the previous chapter, a holistic understanding of the issue of ethics at the workplace highlights the importance of both the individual and situational factors and their integration. Individual differences in ethical ideology are explained mainly through differences in the process of socialization, along with other demographic variables. Our beliefs, attitudes and values are formulated through the process of socialization, which is different for different individuals. Everything that we do is based consciously or unconsciously on these factors. The values that we hold are essentially established in our early years, absorbed from parents, teachers, friends and others. Our early ideas of what is right or wrong were probably formulated from the views expressed by our parents. Interestingly, the values inculcated are relatively stable and enduring.

Sekhar (1997), in his book *Ethical Choices in Business*, gave a causal chain in ethics.

Values $\longrightarrow$ Intentions $\longrightarrow$ Behaviour $\longrightarrow$ Consequences

He emphasized that our behaviour is a reflection of our intentions and that these intentions are a manifestation of our value system.

Values are a conception of what is good and desirable. They are our notion of what *ought to be*. Our idea of what is the right thing to do in a situation, comes from our values. They are like our own internal mode of reality, similar to the operating system of a computer. Therefore, an individual's ethical ideology cannot be understood without understanding the individual differences in terms of both the demographic and psychological variables. The most important demographic variables which have been frequently considered by researchers, are age and gender. This chapter discusses how age and gender have been important factors in studying ethics and its applications.

AGE AND ETHICS

The issue of age and experience is crucial to an employee, as well as to the organization he/she works with. Age and experience are considered from the date of appointment to promotion and then retirement. There is a vast body of literature based on the research which seeks to analyze the relationship between age and experience, and individual behaviour in an organization. Usually, age and experience are not taken as two separate variables because it is difficult to separate the effect of one from other, as experience comes only with age.

Some potential implications of the research evaluating the effect of age on an individual's behaviour as given by Bruce and Waldman (1990) are: the avoidance of workers obsolescence, developing job retaining programme for improving cognitive abilities, and optimizing, the fit between individual abilities and the task requirement to maintain an individual's cognitive abilities during his/her life span. A number of cross-sectional and longitudinal research studies have focused on differences in cognitive test performance across the life span of individuals.

Since the mid-1960s, the primary focus in the developmental life span literature has been on the distinction between changes with age that occur with crystallized versus fluid intellectual abilities (Horn, 1967; Horn and Cattell, 1966). This distinction represents two overlapping categories of cognitive abilities: one primarily based on accumulated knowledge and experience (*crystallized*), and the other on more basic or inherent cognitive abilities (*fluid*). Discrepancies have been reported in the literature concerning the relationship between age and cognitive test performance for both crystal and fluid abilities. One of the studies has produced results that have supported age-related stability, as well as increases in cognitive test performance for crystallized measures of cognitive abilities at more advanced ages (Salthouse, 1988). However, for measures tapping into fluid-type abilities, the general pattern of the performance has been marked by some decline with increasing age (Horn, 1982; Salthouse, 1988).

Research on adult moral development has found that some adults continue their cognitive moral development beyond formal schooling (Colby, et al. 1983). If years at work play a significant role in continued adult moral development (Trevino, 1986), then age, as a surrogate, would be expected to be positively related to ethical thinking and behaviour.

The literature suggests that age or career stage is a factor in determining values, as younger managers tend to assign less importance to trust and honour, and more importance to money and advancement than older executives (England, 1978).

A numbers of studies have compared the ethical value measures of students and practitioners, to analyze the effect of age and experience on ethical behaviour. A majority of these studies (Arlow and Ulrich, 1980; Bellizzi and Hite, 1989; Kreitner and Reif, 1980; Singhapakdi, 1990) show business professionals to be significantly less tolerant of questionable business practices than students.

Barnett and Karson's (1989) study of 513 executives analyzed decisions involving ethics, relationships and results. The career stage was viewed as a surrogate for age in this study. Respondents early in their careers acted significantly less ethically in the 'expense fund' scenario than those respondents who were at a later stage in their careers and generally found to act more ethically in all situations.

Age was found to be negatively related to one's Machiavellian orientation in a study by Arlow (1991). The measure used to access the business ethics of 138 college students was based on the work of Miesing and Preble (1985). It was found that those under the age of 24 had a significantly higher Machiavellian score than those aged 24 or above, supporting the findings of Miesing and Preble (1985).

Ruegger and King (1992) surveyed 2,196 students enrolled in business courses with the intent to determine whether or not age played a role in the person's perception of proper ethical conduct. Students were asked to evaluate the ethical acceptability of 10 hypothetical situations. This study found that those students falling in the 40-plus age group were the most ethical, followed by the 31–40 age group, the 22–30 age group and those who were 21 years and under. Although only 40 students were tested in the 40-plus group, age did appear to have a significant effect upon how people viewed business ethics.

Serwienk (1992), in a sample of 421 employees of small insurance agencies, found that older workers had a stricter interpretation of ethical standards in two of four indices used in the study.

Premeaux and Mondy (1993) found that segments of the group who were five years or less from retirement' were much more likely to act in accordance with a 'rule' or 'right' philosophy. They also explain that possibly, after an extensive business career, these individuals either realize that long-term benefits of acting more ethically outweighed the possible short-term gain, or were never keen to jeopardize their retirement benefits, earned through many years of service.

Hunt and Vitell (1986) suggest that these findings are due to differences in perceptions of reality and the way in which individuals actually process or make ethical decisions. They propose that individuals' ethical perceptions are influenced by environmental and experiential factors, as well as by the nature of the situation itself. At the same time, Callan (1992), in a study of 226 state employees, found that age did not significantly influence the attitude of respondents towards ethics. Again the view is mixed as ethical positions change with age, but no single factor can be identified as causing this change. College freshmen and juniors, for example, were found to be more justice oriented (fairness and equality) than business management students, who tended to be more utilitarian (maximize benefit/minimize costs) in their approach to ethical dilemmas (Borkowski and Ugras, 1992). The author concluded that this difference might be due to idealism on the part of the former group, and experience from the employment for the latter. It is possible that as one matures, there is less emphasis on selfish interest and an increase in concern for others. It is not certain however, whether it is age or the accumulating work experience associated with age, that causes individuals to modify their ethical positions as they move towards different stages of life.

According to Glover et al. (1997), age was not a predictor of ethical decision making.

Further, the reaction as to whether age can be a determining factor for commenting upon the ethical standards of an individual is mixed and needs further probing. A small attempt was made here to study these differences empirically. The results are reported below.

EMPIRICAL FINDINGS

For the present analysis, age was categorized as follows:

Up to 35   = Young
36 to 45   = Middle
46 and above = Old

To explore the relationship of age (a demographic variable) with ethical framework, one-way ANOVA was performed. The results of the test are given in Table 4.1.

Table 4.1 indicates that there were highly significant differences among the three age groups in the case of the Religious framework, but this difference was not so significant in the case of the Pragmatic framework.

Table 4.1
One-way ANOVA: Ethical Frameworks as a Function of Different Age Groups (Young, Middle and Old).

		Sum of Squares	df	Mean Square	F
Individual Religious Ethical Framework	Between groups	9.731	2	4.866	5.287 **
	Within groups	276.072	300	.920	
	Total	**285.803**	**302**		
Individual Pragmatic Ethical Framework	Between groups	1.950	2	.975	2.694
	Within groups	108.946	301	.362	
	Total	**110.896**	**303**		

Note: ** = $\underline{P}$ < .01

To see how these three age groups vary in their choice of ethical frameworks, a further analysis to compare the different means was conducted. The results are presented in Table A.18 (Annexure I). The differences were significant between the young and old age group and they were also significant in case of both the frameworks, i.e., the individual Religious, as well as the individual Pragmatic ethical framework. In the case of the Religious framework, it was observed that managers belonging to the older age group scored higher on the Religious framework, compared with younger managers. It was further confirmed when the significant positive difference between the two groups were observed in the Religious framework. However, in the Pragmatic ethical framework, the reverse was true, i.e., the younger group of managers (respondents) scored higher in their choices, as compared with older group respondents.

Between the middle and young age groups also, people belonging to the young age group scored higher on the Pragmatic framework than the Religious framework, where even though the middle age group scored high, the differences were not significant. Between the middle and old age groups, respondents belonging to middle age group scored higher on the Pragmatic framework than the respondents of the older age group; in the Religious framework, older respondents scored higher than the middle age respondents. However, none of these differences were significant.

Therefore, it can be concluded that in all the three groups, the respondents belonging to the lower age groups scored higher in their choice of Pragmatic frameworks, than their older counterparts, who were higher scorers in the Religious framework.

Table 4.2 depicts the relationship between age and ethical decision making. It is evident that the age groups significantly differed from one another in three out of five vignettes. To see how the age groups differed from each other, a comparison of the means analysis was also conducted (see Table A.19 Annexure I).

In Vignette 1 i.e., 'new and improved marketing strategy,' there was a significant difference between the middle and old age groups. From a comparison of the two groups, it can be inferred that for the older age group, the choice was towards *Compromise,* as compared with the middle age group. The middle age group respondents scored lower for this particular situation (i.e., towards *Values*) than the old age group.

Table 4.2
One-way ANOVA: Ethical Decision Making as a Function
of Different Age Groups (Young, Middle and Old).

		Sum of Squares	df	Mean Square	F
	Between groups	12.831	2	6.416	3.916 *
Vignette 1	Within groups	504.596	308	1.638	
	Total	**517.428**	**310**		
	Between groups	5.377	2	2.688	2.264 **
Vignette 2	Within groups	363.426	306	1.188	
	Total	**368.803**	**308**		
	Between groups	15.651	2	7.826	5.528
Vignette 3	Within groups	431.777	305	1.416	
	Total	**447.429**	**307**		
	Between groups	3.649	2	1.824	1.253 **
Vignette 4	Within groups	439.663	302	1.456	
	Total	**443.311**	**304**		

(Table 4.2 contd..)

	Between groups	18.270	2	9.135	6.376
Vignette 5	Within groups	416.931	291	1.433	
	Total	**435.201**	**293**		

Note: ** = $P < .01$,   * = $P < .05$

For situation three, i.e., 'padding up of the expense bills', the differences were significant in the case of young and old, and middle and old age groups. For both groups (i.e., young/old and middle/old), it was observed that the old age group leaned towards *Compromise*. The decision choice of the young and middle age groups were more towards *Values* as compared with the old age group. Vignette 5 was a situation related to 'insider trading' and significant differences in the choice of ethical decision making were found between the young-middle and old-middle age groups. In both the cases, it was observed that the middle age group scored towards *Values,* whereas both the young and old age groups scored towards *Compromise*. It can be concluded from the results, that in the given situations, individuals in the old age group were more in favour of a *Compromise* as decision, compared with other age groups. This could be due to the fact that over the years, the people in this category who are wiser and more experienced have learned what works better in a given situation. On the other hand, it is apparent that the new breed of managers is still experimenting with their ideologies.

GENDER AND ETHICS

Whether men and women are different in their perception of ethical dilemma and social issues has been a matter of much debate in the literature and otherwise.

In the present scenario, with more women managers in the workplace, the issue of difference in the ethical ideology of men and women is also gaining momentum. A recent debate* on the topic 'Are Women CEOs More Ethical than their Male Counterparts?', is an example of the increasing interest on this issue.

As described earlier, Kohlberg (1969) suggested a stage theory of moral development with three main stages and six substages i.e.:

---

* A part of the BT-Electolux 'Managing Tomorrow' series event, held at Delhi, Hyatt Regency on 6 November 2003.

(*a*) Pre-conventional Morality—punishment obedience and personal reward orientation; (*b*) Conventional Morality—the 'good boy/nice girl' orientation, and the 'law and order' orientation; (*c*) Post-conventional Morality—social contract orientation and universal ethical principle orientation.

In order to determine which stage of moral development a person was at, Kohlberg presented the person with moral dilemmas. Moral dilemmas were judged, not according to the respondent's position (to steal the drug or not), but on the basis of the kind of reasoning the answer exhibited. Initially, Kohlberg administered his test to people all over the world, being careful to include all races, and rural as well as urban dwellers. There was only one thing he forgot: he only administered his test on males! When Kohlberg's instrument was administered on a large scale, it was discovered that females often scored a full stage below their male counterparts. The moral reasoning of women and girls was more likely to focus on maintaining connectivity and emotional bonding. This often looked like the 'good girl' orientation.

In light of the differences between the scores on the Kohlberg scale, one could draw either of two conclusions:

–females are less morally developed than males, or
–something is wrong with Kohlberg's framework.

Gilligan's (1982) research began with an interest in moral development. She was particularly interested in the issue Kohlberg raised: why do some individuals recognize a higher moral law, while others simply are content to obey the rules without question? Later, Gilligan began to look more closely at the responses she was receiving in her work, and began to suspect that Kohlberg's framework did not illuminate the responses she encountered. It was almost like trying to place round pegs into square holes. Thus, she suggested that there are differences between the moral voices of men and women.

Gilligan concluded that men and women have a distinctly different moral orientation and argued that whereas women perceive moral questions as problems of care involving empathy and compassion, men appear to conceptualize them as problems of right, justice and fairness (Figure 4.1).

Figure 4.1

The Difference between Male and Female Moral Voices according to Gilligan

Men	Women
Justice	Care
Rights	Responsibility
Treating everyone fairly and in the same way	Caring about everyone's suffering
Apply rules impartially to everyone	Preserve emotional connectedness
Responsibility toward abstract codes of conduct	Responsibility toward real individuals

Gillian also suggested that differences exist between male and female views of the Self (Figure 4.2).

Figure 4.2

Male and Female Views of Self according to Gilligan

Men	Women
Autonomy	Relatedness
Freedom	Interdependence
Independence	Emotional connectedness
Separateness	Responsiveness to needs of others
Hierarchy	Web of relationships
Rules guide interactions	Empathy and connectedness guide interactions
Roles establish places in the hierarchy	Roles are secondary to connections

Gilligan's seminal research (1982,1987) focuses on the moral and ethical dimensions of gender socialization. She asserts that at maturity, men and women differ markedly in their ethical orientations. She further adds that women's conception of morality is concerned with the activity of care and centres moral development around the understanding of responsibilities and relationships, just as men's conception of morality as fairness ties moral development to the understanding of rights and rules. Lyons (1983) supported Gilligan's thesis that these two distinct moral orientations are significantly related to gender. Lyons (ibid.) expands on this theme, suggesting that the focus of men's and women's sense of what is or is not moral is not the only difference. She hypothesizes that the fundamental processes by which men and women make moral choices are different. Men are more immersed in an ongoing ethical consciousness which is not limited to discrete events and situations.

Hinman (1977) suggested four models to explain the place of gender in ethics. They are presented in Figure 4.3 along with their propositions and criticism.

Figure 4.3

Four Models to Explain the Place of Gender in Ethics

Model I   *The Separate but Equal Thesis*
- Men and women have different but equally valuable moral voices
- Criticisms:
  - Reinforces traditional stereotypes
  - Hard to retain the '...but equal' part
  - Suggests that men and women have nothing to learn from one another, since each have their own exclusive moral voice
  - Devalues men with a 'female voice' and women with a 'male voice'

Model II   *The Superiority Thesis*
- Women's moral voices are superior
- Criticisms
  - Inversion of traditional claims of male superiority
  - Exclusionary
  - Demands that one side of the comparison be the loser

Model III   *The Integrationist Thesis*
- Only one moral voice, same for both men and women morality is androgynous
- Criticisms
  - Loses richness of diversity
  - Tends to be assimilationist in practice, reducing other voices to the voice of the powerful majority

Model IV   *The Diversity Thesis*
- Suggests that there are different moral voices
  Sees this as a source of richness and growth in moral life external diversity
- Criticisms
  - Different individuals have different, sex-based moral voices—internal diversity
  - All of us have both masculine and feminine moral voices within us
  - Minimizes gender stereotyping

Hinmen (1977) further tried to explain the issue by saying that there are two ways of thinking about the relationship between masculinity and femininity within each individual i.e., exclusive and inclusive. This can be understood by the following two models of gender diversity (Figures 4.4 and 4.5).

Figure 4.4

Exclusive Models of Internal Gender Diversity

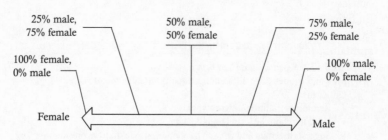

In this model, which is the most common traditional model, an increase in masculinity is bought at the price of a decrease in femininity, and vice versa.

The other model is based on Sandra Bem's (1974) conceptualization of gender, which submits that an increase in femininity is not bought at the price of a decrease in masculinity, and vice versa.

Figure 4.5

The Bem Scale

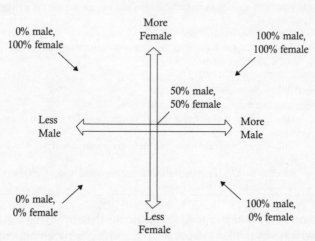

Hinman concluded that perceiving the concept of gender according to Bem's framework allows us to appreciate both the feminine and the masculine moral voices within each of us and avoid traditional stereotypes.

There is a great deal of empirical research into the differences between men and women. These studies have been conducted at various levels of the population, and each level has produced conflicting findings. For example; women have been found more concerned, sensitive and critical of ethical issues (Beltramini, et. al., 1984; Chonko and Hunt, 1985; Ferrell and Skinner, 1988; Jones and Gautschi, 1988; Wipple and Swords, 1992); they have been found to be more ethical in their decisions than their male counterparts (Betz, et al., 1989; Glover, et al., 1997; Ruegger and King, 1992). Significant differences in the ethical values, decision process, moral reasoning and ethical judgment has been observed between men and women (Harris,1990; Freeman and Giebink, 1979); situational differences have also been observed between men's and women's ethical decision choices (Dawson, 1997).

Men and women have also been found to differ in the use of ethical frameworks for example, Schminke (1997) studied the gender differences in ethical decision making among 75 managers. He used Brady's (1990) classification of ethical framework i.e., *formalist* and *utilitarianism*.

A Survey of Ethical Theoretic Aptitudes (SETA) (Brady, 1990), along with three vignettes (each one rated as neutral, utilitarian and formalist by trained raters), was used in this study. The results showed that men and women did not differ on the ethical models to which they personally subscribed. Further, they responded to ethical dilemmas faced by others in a manner consistent with their own ethical aptitudes. Finally, gender differences played a role in how they responded to ethical dilemmas faced by others. In particular, women were harsher on women than on men, and men were harsher on men than on women. In none of the three scenarios did men or women evaluate the opposite gender's actions negatively.

Gender differences in the use of ethical frameworks were also confirmed by Harris (1989), in his study of four ethical maxims. The responses of men showed a decisive preference for an *egoist* (self-interest)-based decision approach. Women, in contrast, professed the use of a *utilitarian* approach. The findings were supported by a replication study in which Galbraith and Stephenson (1993), concluded, using the same ethical maxims as Harris (1989), that men and women use different decision rules when making ethical evaluations (male-egoist and female-utilitarian) and that no one particular decision rule is used by the majority of either men or women in different types of ethical judgments.

At the same time, there is a strong body of literature suggesting that there is no difference between men and women in their ethical behaviour (Fritzsche, 1988; Hegarty and Sims, 1978; Singhpakdi and Vitell, 1990); no difference in their moral reasoning (Derry, 1989; Lifton, 1985; Walker, 1984); no difference in their ethical perception (Davis and Welton, 1991; Kidwell, et al., 1987); no difference in their ethical attitudes and values (Shukla and Costa, 1994); and no difference in the ethical beliefs and ethical judgements (McNichols and Zimmerer, 1985; Stanga and Turpen, 1991; Tsalikis and Oritz-Buonafina, 1990).

Studies on gender leadership also show contradictory results, for example, in a study on gender differences among leadership, Rice, et al. (1984) concluded that there were relatively few significant differences in the measures of either leadership success or leadership processes, a function of either leader-sex or leader-sex follower-sex combinations, despite scattered significant leader-sex effects. The more general pattern indicated that male and female leaders were equally successful and that they engaged in similar leadership processes.

Most reviews of men and women leadership have concluded that empirical studies show weaker and fewer leader-sex differences than would be expected on the basis of sex-role stereotypes (Bartol, 1978).

On the other hand, the international women's forum in 1982 conducted a survey of men and women leaders and some of their findings as reported by Rosener (1990), were that the women were more likely to use transformational leadership—motivating others by transforming their self-interest into the goals of the organization, and that women are much more likely than men to use power based on charisma, work record, and contacts (personal power), as opposed to power based on organizational position, title and the ability to reward and punish (structural power).

Hence, an overall conclusion drawn based upon the above review, was that the evidence on whether men and women managers differ—especially with respect to their ethical propensities—is mixed.

There are some popular theories, which try to explain the research findings. Some of these theories are explained as follows:

Self-selection theories as stated by Dobbins and Platz (1986) assert that who choose business careers have traits different from those typical of their gender. This proposition could account for observed differences in the ethical attitude or behaviour of women in the general population, compared to those in the work environment. There is also no difference in the behaviour of men and women at their workplace.

The *Structural* theory holds that differences between the sexes due to early socialization will be overridden in the work environment by the perceived costs and rewards associated with occupational goals; thus, while women may enter a business career with values different from men, they will respond similarly to the same training and occupational environment, and become more like men in their actions and perceptions (Derry, 1989). This theory would suggest that observed ethical differences between the sexes might be a function of variables other than gender.

The *Situational* theory suggests that ethical differences between men and women may be context-specific; stemming from a scenario type of research that has found that gender differences exist in some situations, but not in others (Barnett and Karson, 1989; Tansey et al., 1994).

The *Gender Socialization Theory* postulates a separate and distinct 'feminist ethics', which has its origin in gender socialization theory. This theory holds that general and nearly universal differences that characterize masculine and feminine personalities are formed during childhood and are incontrovertible; these in turn differentially shape the work-related interests, concerns, and value of the sexes (Dawson, 1997). As quoted by Dawson (ibid.) the roots of the gender socialization theory are traced to the work of Freud (1925); Piaget (1932); and Mead (1934).

Extending the analysis of these early scientists in modern writings, Stoller (1964) and Chodorow (1978) maintained that gender identity was established by about the age of three years through the mother–child relationship, which is experienced by boys and girls. Gender identity, the core of personality, is thereafter irreversible and unchanging.

Lever (1978), explains that sex differences in personality formation of infancy are reinforced in middle childhood by the pattern of children's games—'The crucible of social development'. Whereas traditional girls' games are turn taking where competition is indirect, traditional boys' games are more complex and competitive, requiring adjudication of disputes. Thus, girls learn respect for inclusion and avoiding hurt, while boys learn respect for rules and fairness. Through these influences, boys and girls reach puberty with different interpersonal orientation and a different range of social experiences.

Larwood and Wood (1977) also emphasize the importance of gender socialization when they comment that one of the reason for women's disadvantage relative to their male counterpart may be due to early socialization experiences and their resulting personal characteristics. Boldizar, et al. (1989) showed that the process by which men's and women's education, occupation, and marital status interact to affect their adult moral development, differ considerably.

The phenomenon of women joining the corporate work force is relatively new and there exist stereotypes of both men and women, for example, men are generally thought to be independent, objective, assertive, unemotional and active, whereas women are generally perceived as dependent, subjective, passive and emotional (Broverman, et al., 1972). Further, Schein (1975) demonstrated that the stereotype of an effective manager has more in common with the male stereotype than with the female stereotype.

It is also observed that professional women may be subject to assumptions in the workplace: as women, they are presumed to be less career oriented and less committed to their organizations than are men (Morrison, et al. 1987) and they continue to suffer from pervasive stereotyping (Auster, 1993).

The role gender plays in organizational processes has received substantial attention. Much recent gender research examined differences in management styles and approaches and two contradictory positions emerge. The first suggests that women bring a unique set of managerial qualities and skills, and a unique feminine managerial style to the organization (Grant, 1988; Loden, 1985). This approach contends that women managers will, and should, operate differently in managerial decision-making, leadership, and problem-solving situations, than her male counterparts, and that these traits make women especially well-suited as managers, albeit in a non-traditional style.

Given below are some of the opinions voiced by eminent business women during their participation in a debate on the topic 'Are Women CEOs More Ethical than their Male Counterparts?' (Business Today, 2003).

Renuka Ramnath, CEO, ICICI Ventures, said that the ethical practices come intuitively to women. 'Men tend to adopt the principle of justice when looking at issues, while women follow the principle of care—much the same way a mother cares for a child'. She argued that 'women by nature are cooperative and men competitive', and that it all comes down to one's personal values. 'Women operate from the platform of relationships', Ramnath concluded.

Ranjana Kumar, Chairperson and Managing Director, Indian Bank, argued that since women donned so many hats, it left them with too little time to be crooked. 'Men have enough time to relax and contemplate. Women don't have that luxury'. A disadvantage to women managers, she felt, was the lack of role models. 'Being pioneers, we have to be extra careful. A single slip can put us in awkward position', said Kumar. The bottom line: women had too much in hand to be unethical.

Renu Karnad, Executive Director, HDFC said 'We have always been the nurturers, transferring civilizational values. What you teach your children at home is what you practice at the office. For us, the office is an extension of home'. Karnad insisted that women in general displayed a greater sense of responsibility.

Swati Piramal, Director (Strategic Alliances), Nicholas Piramal contended that, 'Men have created a civilization that follows their own tendencies. Women have to work within the narrow confines of this sphere', She, however, agreed with the other panelists that women were far better at long-term relationships than men.

Meenakshi Madhavani, CEO, Spatial Access Solution, pushed the point further, saying: 'It pleased me no end to see that not a single woman was involved in the recent 20 big scandals around the world. In India too, no women CEO or managers were involved in any corporate scam', she said. 'That is because women tend to be as concerned about the means as the ends'.

The above review suggest that these gender differences may carry over to male and female underlying moral structures, value systems, and ethical frameworks.

In all, whether men and women managers share equal managerial skills and ethical orientations is not really the critical point; what matters is understanding any differences that may exist and achieving symmetric perceptions of the way each approaches the business environment (Schminke, 1997). Therefore gender is a very important variable to be studied in the context of ethics in general and ethics at the workplace in particular. Hence, the gender differences in ethics have been empirically tested and the results are reported in the next subsection.

EMPIRICAL FINDINGS

A t-test was conducted to observe the relationship of gender variables on a selection of the ethical frameworks by individuals in situations of ethical dilemma. Levene's test of equality of variance was also performed before conducting the t-test to confirm the homogeneity between the two samples. The result showed no significant differences in the variance of the two samples and a t-test for equal variance was performed to see the relationship of gender with ethical frameworks. The results of the t-test are given in Table 4.3.

Table 4.3
T-test: Mean Difference between Genders for Ethical Frameworks

Framework	Gender	N	Mean	Standard Deviation	t
Individual Religious Framework	Men Women	276 25	2.5333 1.9481	.9675 .8934	2.913 **
Individual Pragmatic Framework	Men Women	277 25	3.9151 4.1700	.6032 .6069	−2.022*

Note: ** = $P < .01$ * = $P < .05$

From Table 4.3, it is evident that the difference between men and women on the choice of ethical frameworks was significant in case of both the ethical frameworks i.e., Religious and Pragmatic. The direction of the differences implied that men showed a greater use of the Religious framework and women followed the Pragmatic framework.

The difference between men and women on ethical decision choices was found significant only in one case, i.e., Vignette 1 ('new and improved marketing strategy'). The results can be seen in Table A.20 (Annexure I). The details about the five situations used in the study are given in Chapter 3 and also in Annexure III. The difference between men and women suggested that for particular situations men scored significantly higher than women. Higher scores by male respondents here would mean a choice towards the *Compromise* dimension of ethical decision making and a lower score by women would mean a decision choice towards *Values*. There are many empirical findings where similar results were obtained and women were found to be more ethical in their decisions than men (Akaah, 1989; Arlow,

1991; Betz, et al., 1989; Bhal and Sharma, 2001b; Borkowski and Ugras, 1992; Glover, et al., 1997; Ricklets, 1983; Ruegger and King, 1992). At the same time, the fact that the significant difference between male and female decision-making behaviour in a situation of ethical dilemma occurred in only one out of five situations, supports the view that while women may enter business careers with values different from men, they will respond similarly to the same training and occupational environment and become more like men in their actions and perceptions (Derry, 1989). It is important here to add a word of caution in the interpretation of the results for gender difference as the sample size of women was too small in comparison to the male respondents included in the present study.

From the above results we can conclude that women managers were found to use more Pragmatic ethical frameworks in decision making and Religious framework was more frequently used by the male managers. In situations of ethical dilemma, women were found to make more ethical decisions than their male counterparts.

CHAPTER OVERVIEW

Age and gender are two very important individual variables in the context of ethical behaviour at the work place. The issue of age and experience is crucial to an employee as well as to the organization he/she works with. Age and experience are considered from the date of appointment to promotion and then retirement. There is a vast body of literature based on the research findings which try to analyze the relationship between age and experience and the individual's, behaviour in the organization. There were significant differences in the choice of ethical framework among three age groups. The respondents were divided into three age group categories; young (up to 35 years of age), middle (36 to 45 years) and old (46 years and above). Among all the three pairs i.e., young-old, middle-young and middle-old, the respondents of younger age group categories scored higher in their choice for Pragmatic framework than their older age group counterparts, who had higher scores on Religious frameworks. Significant differences were also observed in the decision-making behaviour among the three age group categories in the five given situations of ethical dilemmas. It was observed that in all the three pairs, i.e., young-middle, young-old, middle-old, people in the older age group were more in favour of *Compromise* decisions as compared to their younger counterpart age groups, who scored high on the *Value* direction of ethical decision making.

There is a long tradition of empirical research into the differences between men and women. These studies have been conducted at various levels of the population, and at each level has produced conflicting findings. For example, women have been found more concerned, sensitive and critical of ethical issues (Beltramini, et al., 1984; Chonko and Hunt, 1985; Ferrell and Skinner, 1988; Jones and Gautschi, 1988; Whipple and Swords, 1992); they have been found to be more ethical in their decision than their male counterparts (Betz, et al., 1989; Glover, et al., 1997; Ruegger and King, 1992). Significant differences in the ethical values, decision process, moral reasoning and ethical judgment has been observed between men and women (Harris,1990; Freeman and Giebink, 1979); situational differences have been observed between men's and women's ethical decision choice (Dawson, 1997). Men and women have also been found to differ in the use of ethical frameworks, for example, Schminke (1997) studied gender differences in ethical decision making among 75 managers. He used Brady's (1990) classification of ethical framework i.e., *formalist* and *utilitarianism*.

There are some popular theories, which try to explain the research findings. Some of these theories are explained as follows: 'Self-selection' theories as stated by Dobbins and Platz (1986) assert that who choose business careers have traits different from those typical of their gender. The 'Structural' theory holds that differences between the sexes due to early socialization will be overridden in the work environment by the perceived costs and rewards associated with occupational goals; and the 'Situational' theory suggests that ethical differences between men and women may be context-specific.

Therefore, gender is a very important variable to be studies in the context of ethics in general and at the workplace in particular.

5

GUNAS AND ETHICAL CONDUCT

Understanding ethics from the perspective of virtues requires that the character of human beings be taken as a prime indicator of ethical conduct. Aristotle, the main propounder of this theory recommended a balanced person, not given to extremes, as the virtuous person. St Thomas Acquinas, a philosopher of the Middle Ages, went one step beyond logic and reason, and added the theological or Christian virtues of faith, hope and charity, as the virtues that enable a person to achieve a union with God. Ethical and spiritual philosophy in India has a rich element of virtues. Interestingly though the virtues identified in the *Gita*, have a spiritual objective (of union with God), they are reflected in the thoughts, feelings and behaviour of people, and are referred to as *Gunas*. The subsequent interpretation of these virtues, make it an eminent object of study in the context of ethics.

A construct of Indian origin, which is quite close to the concept of personality and thus considered relevant, were *Gunas*. When translated, they refer to the characteristics of people. The *Sankhya* school of Indian philosophy says that the entire physical universe, including the human mind, is a manifestation of *mula-prakriti* (basic nature) or primordial *prakriti* (nature) (Hiriyanna, in Chakraborty, 1987: 76). This *prakriti* (basic nature) has three constituents, namely *Sattwa, Rajas* and *Tamas*. All matters and empirical phenomena, including the mind, are matter-manifest in endless combinations of these three *Gunas* (ibid.). As such, there is no direct work that establishes a relationship between *Gunas* and ethical behaviour, however, there is a direct link between the two. *Guna* is the only concept, which discusses the basic nature of a human being. While the western concept of personality emphasizes the development of various attributes as a manifestation of environmental influence during the process of socialization, the concept of *Guna* goes much deeper. It would be interesting to see if this basic nature (*Guna*) influences the individual ethical ideology and decision choice in situations of ethical dilemma. This requires a better understanding of the concept of *Guna*. In essence, *Guna*s can be understood as personality attributes of individuals which are deep rooted.

THE CONCEPT OF *GUNA*

*Guna*s are the preponderance of a given type of temperament in an individual's inner nature. The human mind and intellect function constantly, but they always appear to function under the different 'climatic conditions' within our mind. These varying climates of the mind are called the three *Guna*s: the good (*Sattwa*), the passionate (*Rajas*) and the dull (*Tamas*). The human personality behaves differently under each of these temperaments. Therefore, their combinations result in an infinite variety of personalities in the world. Further, an individual personality has different moods and behaviours at different periods of time, during different situations, problems and challenges.

According to Morales (1998) the empirical reality that we perceive around us is composed of matter. Whether we are referring to the buildings we reside in, the many possessions we strive for, or the very bodies with which we identify so intimately, all objects are composed of the *prakriti*, or the prime material energy, of God. Of the many qualities that are discernible in *prakriti*, the essential feature encountered is that of transience. Matter is in a constant state of flux, a continual cycle of becoming, being and dissolution. Thus, everything that we perceive around us, though seemingly stable, ultimately is destined to cease existing. *Prakriti* itself is not a purely undifferentiated field of substance. It consists of a substratum of three different modes, each one dependent upon the other two for their mutual existence and proper functioning. These three modes of *prakriti*, or material energy, are also known as the three *Guna*s, which in Sanskrit means 'qualities' or 'modes'. These three interdependent strands of the material substance are different aspects of the same energy, which in turn is under the full control of the Supreme. *Sattwa* is the finest frequency that *prakriti* adopts. *Rajas* is the intermediate catalytic energy source. *Tamas* is the resting place, the dullest mode of material energy. The qualitative hierarchy of the three *Guna*s can be visually represented in this way: *Sattwa* = spiritual, *Rajas* = energy to act, *Tamas* = matter.

Chinmayananda (1992), while clarifying the understanding of the concept of *Guna* expressed that spiritual teachers uniformly believe that the vitalizing principle in matter is the Spirit, which is universally the same everywhere. In science it is well known that the world of matter is the same everywhere. The one eternal principle, or the Spirit, expresses itself as different individuals, even though the elements that constitute matter are one and same everywhere—due to the *Guna* born of *Prakriti*. Chinmayananda further added that the term *Guna* does not indicate the properties of a material but the 'attitude' with which the mind functions. The psychological being in every one of us comes under the influence of three different 'climatic conditions' prevalent in our body: unactivity (*Sattwa*), activity (*Rajas*) and inactivity (*Tamas*). These three in different proportions, influence the mental and the intellectual calibre of every individual, and provide the distinct flavour in each personality. All three are always present in every individual, but from person to person their proportion slightly differs; hence the differences in the character, conduct and behaviour of each individual. In short, *Gunas,* are the three different influences which every individual has to balance in such an endless variety at different moments of time. It can also be said that there are a variety of different mental climates in which our minds behave so differently from each other, according to their given moods, governed by the predominating *Guna* at any particular moment of observation.

Chinmayananda (1992: 875) further adds that when *Sattwa* begins to dominate as the most important influence in our thought life, due to its purity, it is ever luminous—it has neither the dull colours of *Rajas*, nor the dark impurities of *Tamas*. Under the *Sattwa* influence, the mind is steady, reflecting ever faithfully, the consiousness, or the Self. He further says that 'once the individual has come under the influence of *Rajas*, he expresses innumerable desires, and bound in his own attachments, he lives in the world manifesting a variety of passions'. Thus, it is believed that, under the influence of *Tamas,* man's intellectual capacity to discriminate between the right and wrong becomes blurred.

In the fourteenth chapter of the *Gita*, there is a very detailed description and definition of the three *Gunas*. The use of the words *Sattwa, Rajas* and *Tamas* is intended to point out the diversity, the names and the number of the *Gunas*. They are called *Prakriti-Sambhava* (born of nature), in order to show that they all evolve from *Prakriti,* and that the material creation is an amplification of these three *Gunas*. Of these

Sattwa, being immaculate, is illuminating and flawless (14.6); *Rajas,* which is of the nature of passion (14.7); and *Tamas* signifies dullness (14.8). The characteristics associated with the three *Guna*s are mutually different.

SATTWA (ILLUMINATION)

The quality of *Sattwa* is absolutely pure in character and untainted by any form of evil; hence it is illuminating and free from morbidity of any kind. It lends illumination to the mind and the senses, uprooting sorrow, distraction, depravities, evil propensities and vices (14.6, The *Bhagwad Gita*). Evil actions are recognized when we try to satisfy the appetites of the flesh, the selfish agitations of the mind and the egocentric desires of the head. Illumination is a state of knowledge and peace, where the mind is purified from all its agitations and the intellect is cleansed of passions and criminal lust. There is inward peace and happiness and the individual enjoys a greater share of subtle understanding and intellectual comprehension. The ego is dissolved and the actions are purely for the sake of actions. When an individual has experienced the thrilling joys of creative thinking and inspiring life of goodness and wisdom, he becomes so attached to them that he will thereafter sacrifice anything around in order to constantly experience that subtle joy. A scientist working in his laboratory, a painter working in his canvas, a poet seeking his own joys in his vision are all examples of Illumination, which sets in when the work itself becomes inherently satisfying. The mind itself is called *Sattwa,* as its basic nature is clear in quality. Like a computer hard drive that is yet to be programmed, it is free from any cultural input. Although the mind is by nature naturally pure and clear, it is darkened by negative thoughts and emotions. People who are *Sattwic* in their mental nature possess good intellects and memory, they have an inherent instinct for cleanliness. They are drawn to higher learnings, have a good will and are unselfish and kind. They have a devotion to doing the right thing throughout their life. This *Guna* denotes such qualities as purity, brightness and essence. It is also light—both in the lustre of its radiance and in terms of its actual weight in terms of physics. Thus, individuals who are of a spiritual, clean (both physically and mentally) and peaceful nature are said to be living a *Sattwic* existence; they are residing in goodness. *Sattwa* is the quality most sought by all spiritual practitioners. Change happens in an orderly manner. Every effect is proportional to and consistent with its cause and, therefore, predictable. Peace, quiet and order prevail. There is no resistance to change and change causes no confusion. Agitation and volatility are completely absent where this attribute predominates. This attribute is characteristic of light, knowledge and consciousness. There is absence of darkness, ignorance, sloth, and confusion in entities where *Sattwa Guna* is the dominant attribute.

At the subjective level, cognition, knowledge and understanding feed *sat*. *Sat*, in turn, leads to the lack of ill will and evil feelings, peace, painlessness, and feelings of happiness leading to further knowledge and understanding. This too, is a vicious circle of feelings of peace and happiness, knowledge, and understanding.

RAJAS (PASSION)

Desire is the hallmark of passion, as the name indicates. Such a person looks for the satisfaction of all his/her desires. Desire is our mental relationship towards objects which have not yet been acquired by us. A strong attachment binds the person to the objects acquired. These two—desire for the acquisition of things and the creation and attachment to the things so acquired—characterize a person with passion. Such a person is constantly guided by a desire for things not acquired and becomes entangled in the joys of his successes. *Rajas* creates distraction or turbulence in the mind that causes us to look outward and seek fulfillment in the external world. It is the mind agitated by desire, which when frustrated creates anger. *Rajas* is disturbed thoughts and imaginings. It includes willfulness, manipulativeness and ego. It involves power seeking, stimulation and entertainment. *Rajasic* types have a nature that tries to overpower others. They manifest a propulsive and dynamic energy. They are always dissatisfied with the positions and possessions they have and always want more. They are ambitious and industrious to climb to a higher status in life at every opportunity. *Rajas* denotes activity and movement. It is the mediator between the other two *Gunas*, as well as their empowerer. For, without the kinetic assistance of *Rajas*, neither *Sattwa* nor *Tamas* can act. It is *Rajas* which motivates the individual to labour and inspires work. Those persons in whom *Rajas* predominates tend to be of a fiery and passionate disposition. While a certain degree of *Rajas* is always necessary in order to facilitate any sort of activity, too much of this quality makes one restless, thus hampering meditation and other forms of disciplined spiritual pursuits. The entities with *Rajas* as the dominant attribute can be said to be in a state of unstable equilibrium. Their behaviour is rather unpredictable. This attribute is accompanied by lack of peace, disorder, confusion, agitation and volatility.

At the subjective level, attachment and desire are the cause of *Rajas*. *Rajas*, in turn, results in greed, ambition, motivation that cause activity, and sensual enjoyment leading to further attachment and desire. A *Rajasic* human being is thus caught in a vicious circle of attachment, desire, activity, and its fruit. Actions and their fruit cause further desire, including greed and a longing to hold on to the hard-earned fruit of actions. Fruit of actions and their attachment become a cause of bondage that keeps the human being incessantly involved in listless activity. Thinking is seldom tried. Understanding remains confused. Value systems and world-views are unclear and doubts abound. Thus, *Rajas* is characterized by greed, worldly ambition, motivation, activity, fruit of activity, attachment and desire.

TAMAS (DULLNESS)

Tamas is dullness, darkness and the inability to perceive. It is the mind clouded by ignorance and fear. *Tamas* creates laziness, sleep and inattention. It involves lack of mental activity, insensitivity and domination of the mind by external or subconscious forces. *Tamasic* people are lazy and ignorant, they lack intelligence and prefer to just sleep and eat. They have many fears and do not instigate anything useful by themselves. They lack basic cleanliness and do not take care of themselves. *Tamas* is the source of obstacles, resistance and obstructions. *Tamas* brings about cessation. Those who are of a *Tamasic* nature tend toward lethargy, procrastination and self-destructive behaviour. It is the end point of the descent and de-evolution of *prakriti*. It is, thus, the very antithesis of *Sattwa*. This attribute is possessed by entities that are highly resistant to change. The rate of change in entities with dominance of this attribute is either so slow that they appear not to change at all, or they may change their state beyond recognition under extreme conditions. *Tamasic* entities are more like things than beings, as they appear lifeless because of their static nature. *Tamas* is characterized by lack of motivation and ambition, apathy, neglect, and sloth. A *Tamasic* human being is caught in a vicious circle of delusion, sloth, and sleepiness. It is easy for the body to get used to sloth and sleepiness. They become a cause of bondage that hinders human development and keep the human being focused primarily on the body.

Such a person has a very narrow world-view, and a value system that is totally materialistic and body centred.

The consequences of all the three *Gunas* are also different. The *Sattwa*, *Rajas*, and *Tamas* correspond to *sukha* (happiness), *duhkha* (agony), and *moha* (attachment) respectively (Chakraborty, 1987: 78). The *Bhagwad Gita* (Chapter 14, *shloka* 16) suggests that the fruit of good action is *Sattwic* and pure, the fruit of *Rajas* is pain, and fruit of *Tamas* is ignorance. It also says (*shloka* 18) that those who follow *Sattwa* go upwards, the *Rajasic* remain in the middle, and the *Tamasic* who follow the course of the lowest *Guna*, go downwards (Sastry, 1981). Thus, *Sattwa* is superior to *Rajas*, and *Rajas* to *Tamas* in terms of their aid to the mind for a true understanding of facts and events (ibid.: 76).

Chakraborty (ibid.: 79) also observed that a correspondence could be seen between the attitude of the modern man towards life and some of the characteristics of *Rajas*. These include love of fame, pride, and display of power.

The different characteristics of these three *Gunas* can be summarized in the following Figure 5.1.

Figure 5.1

Characteristics of the Three *Guna*s

Sattwa	Raja	Tamas
Truth	Activity	Inertia
Light/illumination	Passion/desire	Darkness
Essence	Energy	Mass/matter
Upward flow	Expansion	Downward flow
Intelligence	Movement	Sloth/dullness
Binds by means of attachment to knowledge and joy.	Binds by passion born of craving and attachment.	Binds by means of ignorance and obstruction.
Is the ruling trait when the light of knowledge shines forth.	Is the ruling trait when greed, excessive projects, cravings and restlessness arise.	Is the ruling trait when darkness, dullness, stagnation, indolence, confusion, torpor, and inertia appear.

Another perspective on these three *Gunas* compare the three in the following manner[*] (Figure 5.2).

---

[*] http://www.susankezios.com

Figure 5.2

Comparison of the Characteristics of the Three *Guna*s

Tamasic—Animal	*Rajasic*—Human	*Sattvic*—Angelic Human
Split Personality	Aligned Personality	Personality United to Spirit
Angry, Confused, Stupid	Demanding, Positive, Active	Graceful, Peaceful, Disciplined
Impulsive	Emotional, Commotional	Intuitive, Sensitive
God as Existence	God as Companion	God as Personal and Present

Based on the work of Vamadeva (David Frawley)*. *Prakriti* itself is said to be a composite of the three prime qualities of *Sattwa*, *Rajas* and *Tamas*.

Sattwa is the power of harmony, balance, light and intelligence— the higher or spiritual potential.

Rajas is the power of energy, action, change and movement—the intermediate or life potential.

Tamas is the power of darkness, inertia form and materiality—the lower or material potential.

Perhaps the simplest way to understand the *Guna*s for the modern mind is as matter (*Tamas*), energy (*Rajas*) and light (*Sattwa*), the main factors of our physical universe.

The three *Guna*s reflect the three worlds of Vedic thought.

The earth is the realm of *Tamas*, or darkness, and physical matter. The atmosphere, also called *Rajas* in Vedic thought, is the realm of action and change symbolized by the storm with its process of light-ning, thunder and rain, but it indicates energy or subtle matter on all levels. Heaven is the realm of harmony and light, *Sattwa*. It indicates light as a universal principle, which is the causal or original form be-hind the gross and subtle elements or forms of matter and energy.

The entire universe consists of light that moves in the form of en-ergy and becomes densified in the form of matter. The three great lights of *Agni*, *Vayu* and *Surya* energize these three worlds as the spirit within them. The first is *Agni*, or fire. Fire is hidden in our bodies, in plants, in the rocks, and in the very core of the earth itself. The second is *Vayu*, or lightning. The power of the wind, which creates lightning,

---

* from the Web page of the American Institute of Vedic Studies, *Vedic Yoga and the Three Gunas*, by Vamadeva (David Frawley) in press.

circulates through the atmosphere. The third is *Surya*, or the sun. The sun represents the cosmic light of the stars that pervades the great space beyond this world. These three lights are interrelated. It could be said that lightning is the fire in the atmosphere and the sun is the fire in heaven. Or, fire is the sun on earth and lightning represents the solar force in the atmosphere. Or even, lightning on earth creates fire and in heaven it energizes the sun.

These three lights also reflect the three *Gunas*. *Agni* is the *Tamasic* form of light; the fire that is hidden in darkness. *Vayu* is the *Rajasic* form of light; light in its active and energetic mode as lightning or electrical force. *Surya* is the *Sattwic* form of light; light as pure illumination (*prakasha*).

The movement from *Tamas* to *Sattwa* is a movement from earth to heaven. It occurs through bringing the light out of the earth (*Agni*) and raising it to heaven (*Surya*). This requires crossing the atmosphere through using its forces (*Vayu*).

BEHAVIOURAL MANIFESTATION OF *GUNAS*

In the seventeenth and eighteenth chapters of the *Bhagvad Gita,* the manifestation of these three *Gunas* is described by taking different behavioural dimensions. Some of these dimensions relevant to the present context as interpreted by Chinmayananda (1992) and Radhakrishnan (1948) are presented here.

SACRIFICE

It is sacrificial action in general by which an individual dedicates his wealth and deeds to the service of others. In other words, when a person uses his resources to help others fulfill their aim and objectives, it is called sacrifice.

That sacrifice which is offered, according to the scriptural law, by those who expect no reward and believe firmly that it is their duty to offer the sacrifice, is 'good' (*Sattwic*) (17.11). When we extend a helping hand to others without any expectations for any kind of return it is called a *Sattwic* sacrifice. Individuals dominated by this *Guna* indulge in such sacrifices.

Sacrifice which is offered in expectation of reward or for the sake of display are to be understood as 'passionate' (*Rajasic*) (17.12) i.e., people having dominance of *Rajas Guna* would help others only with some ulterior motive in mind.

The sacrifice which is not in conformity with the law, in which no food is distributed, no hymns are chanted and no fees are paid, which is empty of faith, are declared to be 'dull' (*Tamasic*) (17.13). The distribution of food and payment of fees are symbolic of help to others without which all work is self-regarding.

It implies that those who expect no rewards do the right thing, but are indifferent to the consequences. A Socrates or a Gandhi is concerned only whether he is doing right or wrong, acting the part of a good or a bad man, and not whether he has a chance of living or dying.

AUSTERITY

Austerity (*tapas*) is an intelligent method of living in a balanced relationship with the world of objects, thereby avoiding all unnecessary dissipations of our vital energies. The energies that are so economized and conserved are thereafter directed and employed in cultivating creative fields i.e., in simple world optimum utilization of the scarce resources towards constructive purposes.

There are three types of austerities described in the *Bhagwad Gita:* austerity of deed, speech and thought.

The worship of *Devas, Brahmana, Guru,* and the wise; purity, honesty, celibacy, and non-violence; these are said to be the *austerity of deed* (17.14). To maintain an attitude of attunement with a higher ideal, whereby the meditator develops in himself the qualities of the meditated, is called 'worship'. All the cultural development, moral growth and ethical unfoldment can be accomplished only through these processes implied in 'worship'. Speech that is not offensive, but is truthful, pleasant, beneficial and is used for the regular reading of the scriptures, is called the *austerity of speech* (17.15). Speech is a powerful vehicle in a man and it reflects the intellectual calibre, the mental discipline and the physical self-control of the speaker. Unless he is well formed at all these levels, his words will have no force. To control and conserve this wealth of energy would constitute a great inner wealth indeed for the speaker. An individual' s speech should be honest and agreeable, as well as beneficial. Speech should not be wasted. Control of speech does not mean entering into a state of inert and lifeless silence. Investing the energies of speech in self-profiting and self-creative channels of endeavour is considered to be austerity of speech. The serenity of mind, kindness, silence, self-restraint, and the purity of mind are called the *austerity of thought* (17.16). Serenity of mind can be gained only when our relationship with the world at large is placed on a healthier platform of understanding, tolerance, and love. The warm feeling of affection for others, which readily rises in a heart of true devotion and love, is kindness. Silence of speech must arise from the relative silence of the mind. Thus, it means that noiseless inner calm, which one comes to experience when corroding passions and exhausting desires do not build up in one's mind. All this is impossible unless we are able to control our inner nature deliberately (self-control), which is not possible unless our motives are pure and unselfish.

Three-fold austerity of deed, speech and thought practiced by yogis with supreme faith, without a desire for fruit, is said to be *Sattwic* austerity.

Austerity that is done for gaining respect, honour, reverence and for show, is said to be *Rajasic*, unsteady and impermanent.

Austerity performed without proper understanding, or with self torture, or for harming others, is declared to be *Tamasic* austerity—twisted and torn into a disfigured personality, perverted in its emotion and unclean in its ideals. This alone can be the outcome of any unintelligent austerity.

CHARITY

Charity that is given as a matter of duty, to a deserving candidate who does nothing in return, at the right place and time is called *Sattwic* charity (17.20).

Charity that is given unwillingly, or to get something in return or looking for some fruit, is called *Rajasic* charity (17.21). Charity is performed reluctantly, not conscientiously. In our everyday worldly activities, many of our gifts fall under this category.

Charity that is given at the wrong place and time, to unworthy persons, without paying respect or with contempt, is said to be *Tamasic* charity (17.22).

The *Gita* insists that we must use the faculty of discrimination to see whether the charity reaches the deserving members of the community. Charity must come from within, as an expression of an irrepressible urge of one's heart.

ABANDONMENT (*TYAGA*)

Abandonment refers to 'giving up of all anxieties for enjoying the fruits of action'. All desires are always for the fruits of our actions. Action is an effort made in the present, which, in its own time, will, it is hoped, fulfill itself into the desired fruit, and the fruit is what we will reap later on as a result of the present action. Through the process of abandonment (*Tyaga*) our momentary anxiety to enjoy the fruits is overcome. It implies that desire and agitation bring about restlessness, and the deeper the desire, the greater is the amount of dissipation of our energies within. A dissipated individual cannot execute any piece of work with steady efficiency and true ardour. Abandonment (*Tyaga*) this means disciplines in our activities.

Obligatory work performed as duty, or renouncing attachment to the fruit, is alone regarded as *Sattwic Tyaga* (17.16). Thus, abandonment (*Tyaga*) of the good (*Sattwics*), or real abandonment (*Tyaga*), means 'doing the actions with the correct mental attitude'. Abandonment (*Tyaga*) is the subjective renunciation of all inner selfishness and desire, which limits the freedom of the individual in his field of activity. An individual established in *Sattwic* abandonment never hates, nor does he/she ever feel attached to the circumstances and schemes of things which are agreeable to his/her taste. He/she is overwhelmed neither by extreme joy, nor by extreme sorrow. When to such individuals of *Sattwic* abandonment (*Tyaga*), impulses such as jealously, anger, passion and, greed, arise, he/she does not get involved in those impulses, as we do in our attachments and identifications with them.

Renunciation (*Tyaga*) refers to one who abandons duty merely because it is difficult, or because of fear of physical hardship is known as *Rajasic* renunciation (*Tyaga*) (17.15). By performing such *Rajasic Tyaga*, one does not get any benefits. This is clearly seen in its unsaid suggestions, that a man of action and passion (*Rajas*) will readily undertake to act and fulfill his obligatory duties if they are not painful, and are not too fatiguing. Thus, to become a man of action, fulfilling all obligations and performing all duties without sacrificing one's own personal comforts, is no heroic life at all.

Renunciation (*Tyaga*) of obligatory work—the abandonment of duty is due to delusion, and is declared to be *Tamasic* renunciation (*Tyaga*) (17.14). Every individual has his/her own obligations to himself/herself and to others in the society. They include both the unavoidable daily duties, as well as the special duties that arise on special occasions in the life of an individual, and in the present society. Therefore, as long as the individual is a member of the society, enjoying the social life, and demanding protection and profit from the society, he/she has no right according to the Hindu code of living, to abandon his 'obligatory duties'. Even if one abandons one's moral duties in ignorance, one is not excused; for, as in the civil law of the modern world and in the physical laws of phenomenal world, so in the spiritual kingdom also, 'ignorance of law is no excuse'. If an individual ignores his/her obligation out of ignorance and lack of proper thinking, and refuses to serve the world he/she is living in, that 'abandonment' is considered as 'dull' (*Tamasic*).

In conclusion about abandonment it can be said that according to the *Gita* performance of one's obligatory duties is itself the most glorious of all forms of 'abandonment' (*Tyaga*), and it can be considered doubly so, when it involves a certain amount of sacrifice of one's own personal convenience and bodily comfort.

KNOWLEDGE

The term knowledge here is used in a broader sense; it does not mean intellectual knowledge, instead refers to the spiritual knowledge of the divine. This knowledge pertains to the knowledge of *atman* and *parmatman* and the essential unity of the two.

Knowledge by which one perceives a single imperishable reality in all beings as undivided in the divided, is considered to be *Sattwic* (18.20). For these individuals one life exists in all, expressing itself differently as its different manifestations, because of the different constitution in the matter arrangements. The 'knowledge' that can recognize the play of this one principle of consciousness in and through all the different equipments, is fully *Sattwic*.

Knowledge by which one sees different realities of various types among all beings as separate from one another, is considered as to be *Rajasic* knowledge (18.21). The intellect of such a person perceives distinctions among the living creatures, and divides them into different classes—as the animal, the vegetable and the human kingdoms—as men of different castes, creeds, races, nationality, etc.

Knowledge by which one clings to one single effect as if it is everything, which is irrational, baseless, and worthless is declared to be *Tamasic* (18.22).

Such individuals are generally fanatic in their faith and devotion, in their views and values in life. They never enquire into, and try to discover, the cause of things and happenings; they are unreasonable. Looking through such a confused intellect loaded with fixed ideas, the dull not only fail to see things as they are, but invariably project their own ideas upon the world and judge them wrongly. The 'knowledge' of the *Tamasic* individual is circumscribed by its own concept of self-importance, and thus its vision becomes narrow and limited.

To summarize, the 'knowledge' of the good (*Sattwic*) perceives the oneness underlying the universe; the comprehension of the passionate (*Rajasic*) recognizes the plurality of the world; and the understanding of the dull (*Tamasic*) indicates a highly crystallized, self-centred ego in him, and view of the world is always perverted and ever false.

Duty

Obligatory duty performed without likes, dislikes, and attachment by the one who does not desire fruit is said to be *Sattwic*. (18.23). For such a person, 'action' itself is its fulfillment. A *Sattwic* individual acts, because to remain without doing service is a choking death to him/her. Such an individual serves the world in a sense of self-fulfillment and inspired joy.

Action performed with ego, selfish motives, and with too much effort; is declared to be *Rajasic*. (18.24). Such undertakings are always works of heavy toil involving great strain, all the consequent physical fatigue and mental exhaustion. Such a person is constantly exhausted with his/her own anxieties and fears at the thought of whether his goal will ever be achieved, if at all. Chinmayananda says all the activities of political leaders, social workers, great industrialists, over-anxious parents, fanatic preachers, prosyletizing missionaries and blind money makers, when they are at their best[*], are examples of this type.

Action that is undertaken because of delusion; disregarding consequences, loss or injury to others, as well as one's own ability, is said to be *Tamasic* action. (18.25). *Tamasic* behaviour includes all such careless and irresponsible 'actions' undertaken merely because of some delusory misconception of the goal type. Drinking, reckless gambling,

---

[*]For even these can easily fall into the type of the 'dull' (*tamasic*). Hence, we specifically refer to them as 'when they are at their best'.

corruption, etc., are all examples of *Tamasic* actions. Such people surrender their dignity and status, their capabilities and sublet faculties—all for the sake of the pursuit of a certain delusory goal in life.

Actions of this type (*Tamasic*) immediately provide the performer with a substantial dividend of sorrow. *Rajasic* 'actions' take comparatively longer time to deliver its quota of disappointments and sorrows, while *Sattwic* 'action' is always steady and blissful.

ACTOR (DOER)

So far, a description of the three types refers to 'Knowledge' and 'Action' have been presented. The third type of constituents that go into the makeup of an action the 'doer', the ego that has the desire to act. Since the three *Gunas* to influence the psychological life and the intellectual perception of every individual, the doer personality in each one of us must also change its moods and temperaments according to the preponderant *Gunas* that rules the individual at any given moment of time. Consequently the 'ego' is also classified under three kinds.

The agent who is free from attachment, is non-egoistic, endowed with resolve and enthusiasm, and unperturbed in success or failure, is called *Sattwic*. (18.26). Such an individual sincerely feels that he/she has not done anything spectacular even when he has done the greatest good to mankind, because he surrenders his egocentric individuality.

An individual who is passionate, desires the fruits of work, who is greedy, violent, impure, and is affected by joy and sorrow; is proclaimed to be *Rajasic*. (18.27). Such a person is full of desires, passions, and attachments and tenaciously clings to some desired gain or goal. He/she is swayed by passion and eagerly seeks the fruit of his/her work. He/she is ever greedy in the sense that such a 'doer' (*Rajasic*) is never satisfied with what he/she gains and greedily thirsts for more. His/her thirst is insatiable because his/her desires constantly appear to multiply. He/she never hesitates to injure another, if such injury were to win his/her end. He/she is blind to the amount of sorrow he might bring to others; and is concerned only with the realization of ulterior motives.

Undisciplined, vulgar, stubborn, wicked, malicious, lazy, depressed, and procrastinating; such an agent is called a *Tamasic* agent. (18.28).

UNDERSTANDING (INTELLECT)

According to the predominating *Gunas*, 'Understanding' (Intellect) and 'Fortitude' also can fall under a three-fold classification. *Buddhi* or 'Understanding', refers to the individual's intellectual capacity to grasp what is occurring around him. The intellect has various functions like observing, analyzing, classifying, willing, wishing and remembering, etc. Yet, the most essential faculty out of all these is the power of discrimination. Without discrimination, neither observation nor classification, neither understanding nor judgement, is ever possible. Essentially therefore, the function of the intellect is 'discrimination', which is otherwise called the faculty of 'right understanding'.

The *Buddhi* or intellect, by which one understands the path of work and the path of renunciation, right and wrong action, fear and fearlessness, bondage and liberation, is *Sattwic*. (18.30). *Sattwic Buddhi* is defined as that which makes known to us what type of work is to be done, and what type of work is to be renounced; which distinguishes the right from the wrong, which knows what to be feared and what to be faced fearlessly; which shows us the cause of the present ugliness in our life and explains to us remedies for the same.

Rajasic is the intellect by which one incorrectly distinguishes between *Dharma* (righteous) and *Adharma* (unrighteous), and right and wrong action. (18.31). Such a *Rajasic* understanding cannot reach high judgement, because it is invariably coloured by its own preconceived notions and powerful likes and dislikes.

Tamasic is the intellect which is obscured by ignorance, accepts *Adharma* (unrighteousness) as *Dharma* (righteous) and imagines everything to be which it is not. (18.32). In fact, it is not understanding at all. At best, it can be called only a chronic bundle of misunderstandings. Such an intellect runs into its own conclusions, but unfortunately, it always end up with the wrong conclusions ones.

FORTITUDE (*DHRITI*)

Fortitude is the faculty of constantly keeping one idea in the mind and consistently working it öut to its logical end. It means consistency of purpose and self-application, without allowing oneself to waver in decision making.

The unwavering resolve by which one regulates the activities of the mind, and senses; that resolve is *Sattwic* (18.33). The constancy with which one steadily controls one's mind and sense-organs and their activities, through single-pointed attention and faithful concentration upon a given point of contemplation is the fortitude of a *Sattwic*. Constancy in endeavour and consistency of purpose or, fortitude that is expressed in any field of activity, becomes *Sattwic* fortitude.

The resolve by which a person, craving for the fruits of his work, clings to *Dharma* or righteous deeds, *artha* or accumulation of wealth, and *kama* or enjoyment of sensual pleasures with great attachment; that resolve is *Rajasic* (18.34). The constancy of pursuit of such an individual will be in these three fields of duty, wealth and pleasure, and he will be pursuing one or the other of them with an extreme desire to enjoy the resultant satisfaction.

The resolve by which a dull person does not give up sleep, fear, grief, despair, and arrogance; that resolve is *Tamasic* (18.35). This is also reflected in a lack of resolve or fortitude.

PLEASURE (HAPPINESS)

Pleasure also is three-fold, according to the predominant *Gunas* in the individual. The joy arising out of inner self-control and the consequent sense of self-perfection, is no cheap gratification. In the beginning, its practice is certainly very painful and extremely arduous. However, an individual who has discovered the necessary courage and heroism to walk the precipitous 'path' of self-purification and inward balance, comes to enjoy the subtlest of happiness and the all-fulfilling sense of inward peace. In short, the sense of fulfillment and the gladness of heart that well up in the individual, as result of his balanced and self-disciplined life of high ideals and divine values of life, are the enduring happiness of a *Sattwic* person (18.37).

Sensual pleasures appear as nectar in the beginning, but become poison in the end; such pleasures are called *Rajasic* pleasures (18.38). *Rajasic* happiness arises only when the sense organs are actually in contact with the sense-objects. Unfortunately this cannot be permanently established; for the objects are always variable. Further, the subjective mind and intellect, the instruments that come in contact with the objects, are also variable and changing.

Pleasure that deludes a person in the beginning and in the end; which comes from sleep, laziness, and confusion; such pleasure is called *Tamasic* (18.39).

According to Morales (1998) there are several lifestyle choices that are recommended in order to make one's life more *Sattwic*. This programme includes the following:

1. Practising the philosophy and disciplines of yoga on a daily basis. This includes following the ethical virtues taught in yoga (such as non-violence, not stealing or lying, as well as the *asanas*, or psycho-physical exercises of yoga).

2. Having a purely vegetarian, healthy and organic diet. A purely *Sattwic* diet is lacto-vegetarian, that is, avoidance of all meat, fish and eggs (dairy products such as milk, yoghurt and cheese are acceptable). Such a diet will increase one's health, stamina, intelligence and bring about peace of mind.

3. Ridding one's mind of all negative, violent and disturbing thoughts and images. This is done, for example, by avoiding violent entertainment, ridding oneself of feelings of vengeance and hatred, and filling one's mind with thoughts of God instead. The music we hear also affects our consciousness. We want to avoid music that is charged with explicitly sexual (*Tamasic*) or violent (*Rajasic*) lyrics.

4. Meditating daily. In order to have a *Sattwic* existence, we need to purify and still the mind. This is best achieved by having a daily practice of meditation and prayer.

5. Associating with others who are also leading a *Sattwic* lifestyle. We are all consciously and unconsciously influenced by the nature of the company we keep. If we associate with *Tamasic* or *Rajasic* people, we in turn become *Tamasic* or *Rajasic*. However, if we associate with those who are *Sattwic* by nature, then we cannot help but be positively influenced by them.

By strictly and enthusiastically following this Programme, we can gradually transform our conciousness from one of self-destructiveness into one of positive spiritual attainment.

The *Gita* points out that it is possible to go beyond the *Gunas*, to transcend their characteristics. He who endeavours to do so creates ultimate freedom.

In the *Bhagavad Gita*, Arjuna asks Krishna how he can recognize the man who has gone beyond the three *Gunas*, and what has he done to have gone beyond them? Krishna replies by listing the characteristics of such a person and by reiterating the central theme in the *Gita*:

non-attachment to the fruits of one's labour: Whatever quality arises—light (*Sattwa*), activity (*Rajas*), delusion (*Tamas*)—such an individual neither dislikes its presence, nor desires it when it is not there. The person who is unattached, who is not disturbed by the *Gunas*, who is firmly rooted and knows that only the *Gunas* are acting, who is equally self-contained in pain or pleasure, in happiness or sorrow, who is content with whatever happens, who sees dirt, rocks, and gold as equal, who is unperturbed amid praise or blame of himself, indifferent to honour and to disgrace, serene in success and failure, impartial to friend and foe, unattached to action—that individual has gone beyond the three *Gunas*.

The mention of the theoretical concept of *Guna* is available in the writings of great philosophers like Aurobindo (1977) and Swami Vivekananda (1976). There is almost no systematic account of any empirical work in the organizational setting available that is particularly related to the concept of ethics. The present work is a beginning in this direction.

The little empirical literature available on the construct of *Guna* suggests some probable relationships between the *Guna* and other organizationally relevant variables. Chakraborty (1985) suggested a relationship between *Guna* and leadership. It has been argued that to be effective, it is necessary for a leader to develop an integrated personality, which is possible by acquiring more *Sattwa*, with a progressive diminution of *Tamas*, and an increasing discipline of *Rajas*. Likert's (1961, 1967) system-4 leadership style, which has been deemed to be strongly associated with higher productivity, cannot be generated by the predominance of *Rajas* and *Tamas Gunas*.

GUNA, ETHICAL FRAMEWORKS AND ETHICAL DECISION MAKING

To empirically understand the influence of these three *Gunas* on individual ethical ideologies and ethical decision-making behaviour it was important to first identify their *Guna* characteristics. The measure used for this purpose is described in Chapter 2.

Before proceeding further it was felt important to observe if there existed any mutual relationship among the characteristics of these three *Gunas* measured here. Therefore, a statistical correlation was calculated. The results are given in Table 5.1.

Table 5.1
Correlation among Different Personality Variables

	Rajas Guna	Sattwa Guna
Sattwa Guna	−.108 (318)	–
Tamas Guna	.361 ** (317)	−.147 ** (318)

Note: Figures in parenthesis represent N (the sample size).
    ** = P < .01 * = P < .05.

Among the three possible relationships, only two were found significantly correlated. These two significantly correlated pairs are described below:

These two *Gunas* were found to be positively and highly correlated. As mentioned earlier the literature shows a correspondence drawn between the attitudes of modern men/women towards life and some of the characteristics of *Rajas Guna*. These include love of fame, pride and display of power (Kaur, 1992). At the same time, *Tamas* was equated with *moha*. *Moha* could be defined as close attachment to your belongings and your relationships. Therefore, *moha* could also be associated with modern day men/women who are neck deep in competition. This correlation between the two *Gunas*, i.e., *Tamas* and *Rajas* may be a manifestation of all that discussed above about their co-existence.

Tamas and *Sattwa Guna* were significantly correlated, but in a negative direction. As explained before, *Tamas* was characterized by anger, greed, ignorance, brutality etc., whereas *Sattwa* is characterized by purity, security, poise, calmness, altruism and contentment (Chakraborty, 1985: 187–188). Therefore, no correspondence or overlap was observed between the two (*Sattwa* and *Tamas*), rather they appeared to be opposite to each other, i.e., strengthening of *Sattwa* hastens our approach towards a pure mind, taking it closer to the *pursha* or *purna* (complete) aspects of our being (Chakraborty, 1987: 78), which means reducing or moving away from *Tamas*—possibly explaining the negative relationship between the two (*Sattwa* and *Tamas*).

The correlations found between the three *Gunas* might help in explaining the relationship of *Guna* with ethical frameworks and ethical decision making.

GUNA AND INDIVIDUAL ETHICAL FRAMEWORKS

To find out the relationship among ethical frameworks and different *Guna,* the correlation of the *Gunas* with the two ethical frameworks was explored. The results are shown in Table 5.2.

Table 5.2
Correlation among Ethical Framework and Different *Gunas*

	Individual Religious Framework	Individual Pragmatic Framework
Rajas Guna	−.004 (302)	−.018 (303)
Sattwa Guna	.031 (303)	.047 (304)
Tamas Guna	−.058 (303)	.027 (304)

Note: Figures in parenthesis represent $\underline{N}$ (sample size).

There was no significant result observed in this correlation. In the beginning of this chapter, it was discussed that these three *Gunas* co-exist in every individual. However, there can be predominance of either of the three. So, it was felt that in addition to correlating the individual *Guna* with the ethical frameworks, the influence of their interaction on the choice of ethical frameworks should also be observed. Therefore, the effects of interaction between different *Gunas* on ethical frameworks was observed through hierarchical regression. The results are depicted in Table 5.3.

Table 5.3
Results of Hierarchical Regression:
Interaction Effect of *Gunas* on Ethical Framework

	β *Coefficient*	
	Individual Religious Framework	Individual Pragmatic Framework
Rajas and **Tamas**	−0.125* (0.012)	−0.0075 (0.002)
Rajas and **Sattwa**	0.138 (0.012)	−0.0095 (0.003)
Tamas and **Sattwa**	0.190* (0.037)	0.0132 (0.003)

Note: * = $\underline{P} < 0.05$, Figures in parenthesis represents 'R' squares change values and figures not in parenthesis represents 'β' values.

There were two significant relationships observed in the interaction of *Gunas* on ethical frameworks. In the individual religious framework, two interactions, i.e., between *Rajas* and *Tamas,* and *Tamas* and *Sattwa* were found to be significant. It implied that these two interactions could predict the individual religious framework. Figures 5.3 and 5.4 also represent this relationship of the religious framework and the interaction between *Rajas* and *Tamas* and *Tamas* and *Sattwa* respectively.

Figure 5.3

Interaction Effect of *Rajas* and *Tamas* on Religious Framework

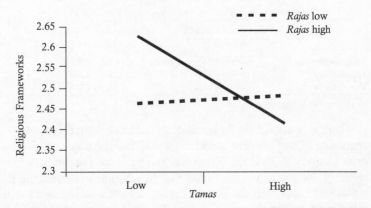

It is evident from Figure 5.3 that an individual with high *Rajas* but low *Tamas* would score highest on the religious framework, whereas scores on the religious framework would be lowest in the case of individuals with high *Rajas* and high *Tamas*.

Figure 5.4

Interaction Effect of *Tamas* and *Sattwa* on Religious Framework

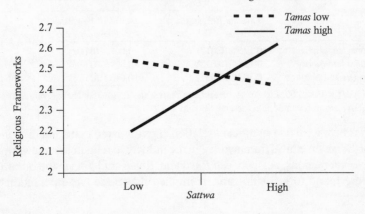

Similarly, from Figure 5.4 it is visible that high scores on the religious framework could also be predicted in the case of interaction between the *Tamas* and *Sattwa Guna* combination. In the case of high *Tamas* but low *Sattwa,* individual scores on the religious framework would be lowest. Highest scores on religious framework could be predicted with high *Tamas* and high *Sattwa.*

GUNA AND ETHICAL DECISION-MAKING BEHAVIOUR

In order to understand the manifestation of *Guna*s on the ethical decision-making behaviour of the Indian managers, statistical correlations (Table 5.4) of these three *Guna*s were calculated with scores on decision-making behaviour (for details see Chapter 2).

Table 5.4
Correlation between Ethical Decision Making and Different
*Guna*s for Different Situations

Decision Making	Vignette 1	Vignette 2	Vignette 3	Vignette 4	Vignette 5
Rajas Guna	.106 (310)	−.005 (308)	.116* (307)	.110 (304)	.118 * (293)
Sattwa Guna	.024 (311)	.007 (309)	−.005 (308)	.005 (305)	−.046 (294)
Tamas Guna	.099 (310)	.066 (308)	.011 (307)	.151** (304)	.004 (293)

Note: Figures in parenthesis represent $\underline{N}$ (sample size) ** = $\underline{P}$ < .01 * = $\underline{P}$ < .05.

It was observed that Vignette one and two, i.e., 'new and improved marketing strategy', and 'gifts and bribes' were not significantly correlated with any of the *Guna*s. Vignette three ('padding up the expenses bills') and Vignette five ('inside trading') were found correlated to *Rajas Guna*. In both the cases the relationship was significant. It implies that the individuals high on *Rajas* would also tend to behave towards the *Compromise* (unethical) direction of decision making in these two situations.

While Vignette four ('nepotism') was found significantly correlated to the *Tamas Guna*. The relationship was highly significant. It also indicated that individuals high on *Tamas* characteristics would also favour nepotism (*Compromise* direction of decision making).

The interaction effect of these three *Guna*s was also observed on the ethical decision-making behaviour of Indian managers, through the use of hierarchical regression (Table 5.5).

Table 5.5

Results of Hierarchical Regression to Discover the Effect of Interaction among
*Guna*s on Ethical Decision Making in Five Given Situations

Decision Making	β *Coefficient*				
	Vignette 1	*Vignette 2*	*Vignette 3*	*Vignette 4*	*Vignette 5*
Rajas and **Tamas**	−0.0317	0.0444 *	0.0295	0.133 *	0.0197
	(0.016)	(0.006)	(0.017)	(0.043)	(0.013)
Rajas and **Sattwa**	0.0703	−0.217	−0.0879	−0.0075	−0.135
	(0.015)	(0.025)	(0.017)	(0.013)	(0.023)
Tamas and **Sattwa**	0.0901	0.0344	−0.201 *	−0.0323	−0.0102
	(0.015)	(0.005)	(0.024)	(0.024)	(0.003)

Note: * = $P < 0.05$
Figures in parenthesis represents 'R' squares change values.
Figures not in parenthesis represent 'β' values.

None of the interactions predicted decision making in the case of
situation one ('new and improved marketing strategy') and situation
five ('insider trading').

Decisions in the case of Vignette two ('gifts and bribes') could be
predicted through interaction between *Rajas* and *Tamas Guna*s. The
relationships is also shown graphically through Figure 5.5. It shows
that in case of Vignette two, an individual would score highest, i.e.,
towards the *Compromise* dimension of ethical decision making if he/
she has low *Rajas* but high *Sattwa*. At the same time, the decision
would be towards the *Values* dimension of ethical decision making,
with low scores on both *Rajas* as well as *Sattwa* variables.

Figure 5.5

Interaction Effect of *Rajas* and *Tamas* on Decision Making (Vignette 2)

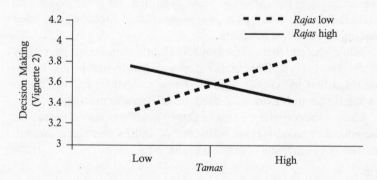

In case of the Vignette three ('padding up of the expense bills') the relationship between *Tamas* and *Sattwa* could predict the decision. It implies that in case of individuals with high scores on *Tamas* and low scores on *Sattwa*, decision making is predicted in the *Compromise* direction, whereas the decision would be towards *Value* in the case of individuals with high scores on both *Tamas* and *Sattwa*. Results are also represented graphically in Figure 5.6.

Figure 5.6

Interaction Effect of *Tamas* and *Sattwa* on Decision Making (Vignette 3)

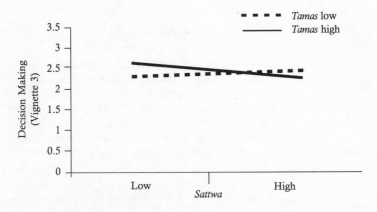

The results of the hierarchical regression also showed that the decision in the case of Vignette four ('nepotism') could be predicted by observing the interaction effects between *Rajas* and *Tamas Guna*. On the other hand, high scores on *Rajas* and low scores on *Tamas* could predict the individual decision towards the *Values* dimension of ethical decision making. The interaction is also demonstrated graphically through Figure 5.7.

The Indian viewpoint posits that attainment of *Sattwa Guna* is one of the most desirable things that one should strive for.

The strengthening of *Sattwa* hasten our approach towards purer mind, taking it closer to the *poorna* (complete) or *atman* (soul) aspect of our being. Our idiosyncrasies and biases then begin to be reduced, for *Sattwa* is the substance of purity and light itself. And thus we can move closer to *"understanding things as they are"*. The *Guna* viewpoint apparently subscribes

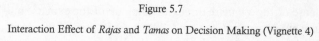

Figure 5.7

Interaction Effect of *Rajas* and *Tamas* on Decision Making (Vignette 4)

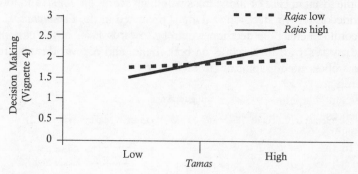

to the view that the route of the welfare of the human kind goes through spiritual well being, and for which an exalted *Sattwa* is a prerequisite. The exaltation of the *Sattwa* however, may not necessarily imply a cessation of the " worldly" human endeavours. The implication really is: progress and achievement have to be turned towards the inner world of man also. Then only the worth value of so called progress and achievement in the external world will be judged in proper perspective (Chakraborty, 1987: 79).

CHAPTER OVERVIEW

Guna is a construct of Indian origin, which is quite close to the concept of personality and considered quite relevant. *Guna* when translated, would mean characteristics of people. The ethical and spiritual philosophy in India has a rich element of virtues. Interestingly, the virtues identified in the *Gita*, though have a spiritual objective (of union with God), they are reflected in the thoughts, feelings and behaviour of the people. They are referred to as *Guna*s. The rich discussion of these *Guna*s in the *Gita*, itself and its subsequent interpretation make it an eminent object of study in the context of ethics.

*Guna*s is the preponderance of a given type of temperament in one's inner nature. The human mind and intellect function constantly, but they always come to function under the different 'climatic conditions' within our mind.

The human traits associated with ethics are discussed as *Guna*s in The *Gita*. Much in line with the ethics of virtues, *Guna*s, if literally translated, would mean inherent attributes, or character (or psychogenic substances as termed by Chakraborty, 1985). When the theory of the 'humours' of the body dominated physiology, individuals were divided into the sanguine, the bilious, the lymphatic and the nervous, according to the predominance of one over the other. *Gunas*, however, are psychic in nature. The term *Guna*, used in The *Gita*, indicates the basis of attitudes with which the mind functions. The psychological being in everyone of us comes under the influence of three different 'climatic conditions' prevalent in our minds. They are the influences under which mind and intellect live (Chinmayananda, 1992). The three *Gunas* identified by The *Gita* are *Sattwa*, *Rajas* and *Tamas*.

In the fourteenth chapter of the *Gita*, there is a very detailed description and definition of the three. Of these, *Sattwa*, being immaculate, is illuminating and flawless (14.6), *Rajas*, which is of the nature of passion (14.7), and *Tamas* signifies dullness (14.8). The three *Gunas* coexist in every individual. However, there can be predominance of either of the three. The characteristics associated with the three *Gunas* are mutually different.

Illumination is a state of knowledge and peace, where the mind is purified from all its agitations and the intellect is cleansed of passions and criminal lust. There is inward peace and happiness and the individual enjoys a greater share of subtle understanding and intellectual comprehension. The ego is dissolved and the actions are purely for the sake of actions. Desire is the hallmark of passion as the name indicates. Such a person looks for the satisfaction of all his/her desires. Desire is our mental relationship towards objects, which have not yet been acquired by us. A strong attachment binds the person to the objects acquired. These two—desire for the acquisition of things and the creation and attachment to the things so acquired—characterize a person with passion. Such a person is constantly guided by a desire for things not acquired and becomes entangled in the joys of his successes. *Rajas* is distraction or turbulence in the mind that causes us to look outward and seek fulfillment in the external world. It is the mind agitated by desire, which when frustrated creates anger. *Rajas* is disturbed thoughts and imaginings. It includes willfulness, manipulativeness and ego. It involves power seeking, stimulation and entertainment. *Rajasic* types have a nature that tries to overpower others. They manifest a propulsive and dynamic energy. They are always dissatisfied with the positions and possessions they have, and always want more. They are ambitious and industrious to climb to a higher status in life at every opportunity. *Tamas* is dullness, darkness and the inability to perceive. It is the mind clouded by ignorance and fear. *Tamas* creates laziness, sleep and inattention. It involves lack of mental activity, insensitivity and domination of the mind by external or subconscious forces. *Tamasic* people are lazy and ignorant, they lack intelligence and prefer to just sleep and eat.

The consequences of all the three *Guna*s are also different. The *Sattwa, Rajas,* and *Tamas* correspond to *sukha* (happiness), *dukha* (agony), and *moha* (attachment) respectively (Chakraborty, 1987: 78).

The behavioural manifestation of these three *Guna*s in terms of the kind of sacrifices, austerity, charity, abandonment, knowledge, duty, understanding, actions, pleasure and fortitude being practiced by *Sattwic, Rajasic* and *Tamasic* individuals, is described in detail in the *Bhagwad Gita.*

The empirical evidence in the study suggest that among all the three *Guna*s, it is the *Rajas Guna* which most closely found associated with the ethical decision-making behaviour of the individuals in situations of ethical dilemma. In two out of five situations used in the study, people significantly high on *Rajas* characteristics also took unethical decisions. Chakraborty (1987: 79) also observed that a correspondence could be seen between the attitude of the modern man towards life and some of the characteristics of *Rajas*. These include love of fame, pride, and display of power. Therefore, it can be said that the construct of *Guna* is very important in the context of ethics.

6

Political Orientation, Locus of Control and Ethics

In the previous chapter, we dealt with the Indian concept of *Guna* in relation to ethics and ethical decision making. The psychological characteristics or traits that determine his/her personal preferences and individual style of behaviour are very important to be studied in reference to ethical ideologies and differences. These psychological differences together determine personality. Personality distinguishes one individual from another and defines his or her general nature.

Dunham (1984) admits that although personality factors can change over an extended period of time, the process is slow and tends to be stable from one situation to another. He also adds that this understanding enhances our knowledge of why people react to organizational events as they do, and provides guidance to organizations in the management of their human resources. Therefore, personality factors are expected to influence the decision-making behaviour of the individual. Individuals, in general and in organizations in particular, face situations of ethical dilemma every now and then. How individual personality variables influence the decision in situations of ethical dilemma has been an interesting topic of research for quite some time. Political orientation, and locus of control are two such personality attributes, which have been found through different researches influencing the individual ethical ideology and thereby, the decision-making process in situations of ethical dilemma.

Political Orientation and Ethics

Power and politics are inherent parts of an organization. Just as organizations provide the context for political activities, individuals have the predisposition and predilection towards political activities. The most widely used construct for measuring political orientation of an individual is that of Machiavellianism.

The personality characteristics of a Machiavellian (mach) are named after Niccolo Machiavelli, who wrote on how to gain and use power in the sixteenth century. As stated by Vleeming (1979), an individual high in Machiavellianism is pragmatic, maintains emotional distance, and believes that ends can justify means. The adage 'if it works, use it', is consistent with a high mach perspective. A considerable amount of research has been directed towards relating high and low mach personalities to certain behavioural outcomes. According to Christie and Geis (1970), high machs manipulate more, win more, are per-suaded less, and persuade others more than low machs. Yet, these high mach outcomes are moderated by situational factors. Byravan and Detwiler (1994) reported that it has been found that high machs flourish: (a) when they interact face to face with others rather than indirectly; (b) when the situation has a minimum number of rules and regulations, thus allowing latitude for improvization; and (c) when emotional involvement with details irrelevant to winning distracts low machs.

Christie and Geis (1970) further add that Machivellianism describes an individual who has an immoral reputation for dealing with others to accomplish his/her own objectives and for manipulating others for his/her own purpose. According to Robinson and Shaver (1973), Machiavellianism orientation of an individual means an individual's strategy for dealing with others and the degree to which individuals feel that they can manipulate others in interpersonal situations. Colhoon (1969) felt that the modern day Machiavellian employs ag-gressive, manipulating and devious moves to achieve personal or or-ganizational objectives.

The Gemmill and Heiseler (1972) study discusses the relationship between Machiavellianism orientation and several job-related corre-lates. Their study found that the Machiavellian orientation associates positively with more job strain, less job satisfaction, and less perceived opportunity for formal control.

Siegel (1973) examined the extent to which managers, MBA students and faculty members exhibit the Machiavellianism, manipulative interpersonal behaviour and leadership using their MACH scale and theory X/Y leadership scale. The study found the following ranking of Machiavellian orientation: managers (lowest), students, faculty (highest). They found Machiavellianism related negatively to participative leadership attitudes for both students and managers.

Heisler and Gemmell (1977) found that a Machiavellianism orientation consistently relates to job satisfaction and job strain across a variety of organizational settings. They also found that Machiavellianism demonstrates a consistent directional trend related to organizational success and satisfaction with a manager's upward mobility as determined by his/her current salary.

Drory and Gluskinos (1980) also studied the relevance of Machiavellianism as a personality style with leadership and concluded that the high mach leaders gave more orders and were less involved in reducing tension in the experimental task group. They were also less directive and requested more assistance when the situation was more unfavourable, whereas the low machs' behaviour across situations remained unchanged.

The findings were further endorsed by the results of the investigation by Rayburn and Rayburn (1996), where they found intelligence to be positively associated with Machiavellianism personality. They also found Machiavellians to be less ethically oriented than non Machiavellians. Jones and Kavangh (1996), in their investigation of the effect of individual and situational factors on unethical behaviour, also concluded that individuals with a high Machiavellian personality were more likely to behave unethically than the individuals low on this construct.

Hegarty and Sims (1979) identified Machiavellianism as one of the personality variables that was a significant covariate in graduate business students' ethics studies. Their findings indicate that the individuals who appeared to have greater Machiavellian traits behaved less ethically than the other study participants.

Thus, the understanding of the Machiavellian personality trait is very important and has implications for organizations in designing their systems, particularly human resource development systems.

Depending upon the type of job and whether ethical implications in evaluating performance is considered important, it could be the criterion in deciding what degree of mach personality would fit the job. Based upon the theoretical logic, it could be said that in jobs that require bargaining skills (such as labour negotiations), or in those that offer substantial rewards for winning (as in commissioned sales), high machs may be more productive.

However, if ends cannot justify the means, if there are absolute standards of behaviour, or if the three situational factors noted by Byravan and Detwiler (1994) in the preceding paragraph are not in evidence, our ability to predict a high mach's performance will be severely curtailed.

The construct of Machiavellianism and its relationship with individual ethical ideology emerged to be an important one.

In Indian literature, Kautilya's work is often compared with Machiavelli's *The Prince* because of its sometimes ruthless approach to practical politics. Kautilya's reputation as the Machiavelli of India rests largely on the sensationalistic and intrigue-laden advice given in the *Arthashâstra*.

Kautilya (more popularly known as Chanakya), who was a Brahmin minister under Chandragupta Maurya wrote the *Arthashâstra*, which means 'the Science of Material Gain' or 'the Science of Polity'. Though it was written at the end of the fourth century BC, it appears to have been rediscovered only in 1905, after centuries of oblivion. According to Kautilya, a ruler should use any means to attain his goal and his actions required no moral sanction. The only problems discussed are of the most practical kind. Though the kings were allowed a free rein, the citizens were subject to a rigid set of rules. This double standard has been cited as an excuse for the obsolescence of the *Arthashâstra*, though the real cause of its ultimate neglect, as the Indian historian Thapar (1966) suggests, was the formation of a totally different society to which these methods no longer applied.

According to Shamasastry (1951), although often compared to Machiavelli's *The Prince* because of its sometimes ruthless approach to practical politics, Kautilya's work is far more varied—and entertaining—than usual accounts of it indicate. He mixes the harsh pragmatism for which he is famed, with compassion for the poor, for slaves, and for women. He reveals the imagination of a romancer in imagining all manner of scenarios which can hardly have been commonplace in real life. Shamasastry (ibid.) further adds that one of the most notorious features of the *Arthashâstra* is its obsession with spying on the king's subjects. Kautilya sometimes goes to amusingly absurd lengths to imagine various sorts of spies. He even cynically proposes using fake holy men for this purpose. Far from being single-mindedly aimed at preserving the monarch's power for its own sake, like Machiavelli's *The Prince*, the *Arthashâstra* requires the ruler to benefit and protect his citizens, including the peasants, whom Kautilya correctly believes to the ultimate source of the prosperity of the kingdom. He therefore advocates what is now called 'land reform'. Slaves were not as common in ancient India as in other civilizations, partly because the lower castes were forced voluntarily to take on many unsavoury tasks that would have been performed by slaves elsewhere. However, they did exist, and Kautilya's regulations governing them are among the most liberal in history. For example, upper-caste slaves were protected from demeaning labour that was reserved for the lowest castes, and the chastity of female slaves was protected (even ancient Judaism and Islam explicitly allowed a master to have sex with his slave women). It is unknown how widely observed these idealistic regulations were. Compare these laws on slavery with those in *Hammurabi's Code* and the Hebrew *Bible*. In what ways did caste affect the way slaves were to be treated? Unlike most political treatises, the *Arthashâstra* makes highly entertaining reading, partly because of the mini-narratives in which Kautilya describes how a king may retain his power or preserve his life after he has been overthrown.

The *Arthashâstra* remains the most unique piece of Indian literature. However, paucity of empirical work in this area and the absence of psychometric measures limited our exploration of the treatment of ethical issues according to the *Arthashâstra*. The study has been limited to Machiavellianism, for which previously tested sound constructs were available, however the power of the concepts for predicting ethical conduct undoubtedly holds true.

LOCUS OF CONTROL AND ETHICS

Locus of control reflects an individual's belief about his or her behaviour and the consequences of that behaviour (Rotter, 1966). According to Dunham (1984), a locus of control personality trait determines the degree to which one believes that one's action influence the outcomes one experiences in life.

Even though this personality trait can take any value on the internal-external scale, it is possible to characterize people as primarily having either an internal or external locus of control. People who believe that they are in control of their own destiny have an internal locus of control, those who believe that what happens to them is the result of fate or the behaviour of other people, are said to have external locus of control.

Locus of control is the perceived source of control over our behaviour. People with internal locus of control believe they control their own destiny. They tend to be convinced that their own skill, ability and efforts determine the bulk of their life experiences. In contrast, people with external locus of control believe that their lives are determined mainly by sources outside themselves—fate, chance, luck or powerful others.

Your life is profoundly influenced by whether you perceive control over your life as predominantly internal or external. Locus of control influences the way you view yourself and your opportunities.

Simons et al. (1987) concluded that with all the studies done in this area, research findings have shown the following characteristics to be more typical of internals.

1. Internals are more likely to work for achievements, to tolerate delays in rewards and to plan for long-term goals.
2. After experiencing success in a task, internals are likely to raise their behavioural goals. In contrast, externals are more likely to lower their goals.
3. After failing a task, internals re-evaluate future performances and lower their expectations of success. After failure, externals raise their expectations.
4. Internals are better able to resist coercion.
5. Internals are more likely to learn about their surroundings and from their past experiences.
6. Internals experience more anxiety and guilt with their failures and use more repression to forget about their disappointments.
7. Internals find solving their own bouts of depression easier. Similarly, they are less prone to learned helplessness and serious depression.
8. Internals are better at tolerating ambiguous situations.
9. Internals are less willing to take risks.
10. Internals are more willing to work on self-improvement and better themselves through remedial work.
11. Internals derive greater benefits from social support systems.
12. Internals make better mental health recovery in the long-term adjustment to physical disability.
13. Internals are more likely to prefer games based on skill, while externals prefer games based on chance or luck.

Simons et al. (ibid.) further added that the development of locus of control is associated with family style and resources, cultural stability and experiences with efforts leading to reward. Many internals have grown up with families that modelled typical internal beliefs. These families emphasized effort, education, responsibility and thinking. Parents typically gave their children rewards they had promised them.

Links have been found between locus of control and behaviour patterns in a number of different areas. People with an internal locus of control are inclined to take responsibility for their actions, are not easily influenced by the opinions of others, and tend to do better at tasks when they can work at their own pace. By comparison, people with an external locus of control tend to blame outside circumstances for their mistakes and credit their successes to luck rather than to their own efforts. They are readily influenced by the opinions of others and are more likely to pay attention to the status of the opinion-holder, while people with an internal locus of control pay more attention to the content of the opinion regardless of who holds it. Some researchers have claimed that internals tend to be more intelligent and more success-oriented than externals. In the elementary grades, children with an internal locus of control have been found to earn higher grades, although there are conflicting reports about whether there is a relationship between college grades and locus of control. There is also a relationship between a child's locus of control and his or her ability to delay gratification (i.e., to forgo an immediate pleasure or desire in order to be rewarded with a more substantial one later). In middle childhood, children with an internal locus of control are relatively successful in the delay of gratification, while children with an external locus of control are likely to make less of an effort to exert self-control in the present because they doubt their ability to influence events in the future (*Gale Encyclopaedia of Psychology,* 2001).

In contrast, externals are typically associated with lower socioeconomic status, because poor people have less control over their lives. Societies experiencing social unrest increase the expectancy of being out-of-control, so people in such societies become more external. Many—though not all—psychologists believe that internals are psychologically more healthy than externals. According to one psychologist who analyzed many locus of control studies, 'There is good reason to believe, on the basis of the research reviewed, that external control orientation and abnormal personal functioning are correlated'. However, the outlook is far from hopeless for those who have predominantly external locus of control. The locus of control orientation can be modified by psychotherapy and by life experiences.

A large number of scholars have taken up work related to the concept of internal-external control of reinforcement and numerous studies have found that internals as compared to externals perceived events as a result of their own actions more often (Hammer and Vardi, 1981); perceived more alternatives in a choice situation (Harvey, et al., 1975); and tended to seek situations in which control was possible (Julian and Katz, 1968; Kabanoff and O'Brien, 1980; Kahel, 1980).

Researchers have explored the relationship between locus of control and other factors. Kaur (1992), when reviewing the literature on locus of control, identified concepts such as leadership style, chronological age, performance and job satisfaction related to locus of control. She reported that the concept of locus of control has been found to be related to leadership. Internal leaders' preferences for a particular style to deal with their subordinates have been found to be different from external leaders' preference for a particular style (Anderson and Sceneier, 1978; Goodstadt and Hjelle, 1973; Pryer and Distefano, 1971). Similarly, subordinates' reactions to the leadership style have also been found to be related to locus of control (Abdel-Halim, 1981; Cravens and Worchel, 1977).

The relationship between chronological age has also been explored (Lao, 1976), and most studies reported that internality increases with age (Duke, et al., 1974; Knoop, 1981; Lao, 1976; Walls and Miller, 1970).

The relationship between other personality attributes and locus of control has also been explored. Several studies have demonstrated that internals perform better than externals (Andrisani and Nestel, 1976; Broedling, 1975; DuCette and Wolk, 1973; Lied and Pritchard, 1976; Majumdar et al., 1977). Spector (1982) suggested that internals would perform better by utilizing information only in complex situations, and would exert efforts to perform better only if they perceived that efforts would lead to valued rewards.

In general, internals are found to be high on job satisfaction in comparison to externals (Kulkarni, 1983; Pettersen, 1985; Singh, 1978; Vecchio, 1981). One exception is Dailey's (1978) study, that contradicts the internal locus of control and high satisfaction relationship. Dailey (ibid.) found internals to be less satisfied with their co-workers and explained these results in terms of the greater social orientation of the externals.

The literature suggests that there could be specific relationships between the construct of locus of control and other variable of organizational relevance. Following the experiences of success or failure, shifts in locus of control has been indicated (Krolick, 1979). Anderson and Sceneier (1978) reported that internals whose performance improved, tended to shift towards greater internality, whereas externals whose performance detoriated, shifted towards great externality. Furthermore, the shift in the locus of control was found to be occurring in both internals and externals, but improved externals did not shift towards internality and poorly performing internals did not shift towards externality. Andrisani and Nestel (1976) found that career success led to internality. It has been found that internals occupy higher status and position in comparison to externals (Andrisani and Nestel, 1976; Davidson and Bailey, 1978; Miller, et al., 1982).

Locus of control has a number of significant implications for organizations. Dunham (1984) reported that management techniques such as organizational behaviour modifications and goal setting are more likely to work for internal locus of control individuals. An external person on the other hand, is not likely to believe that a particular pattern of behaviour influences the outcomes received and thus, is less motivated by such a programme.

Empirical tests on the relationship between the locus of control and ethical/unethical behaviour has been quite limited and the results have been quite inconsistent. Some of the studies (Christie and Geis, 1970; Galli, et al., 1986; Russell, 1974) found a relationship between the locus of control and Machiavellianism. Hegarty and Sims (1978, 1979) reported three experiments where several individual differences, including locus of control, were used as covariates of unethical decision behaviour. Locus of control in their studies was found to be related to unethical decision behaviour in two of the three experiments, but the direction of the relationship was not specified. Stead, et al. (1990) found locus of control to be unrelated to ethical/unethical decision behaviour in five of six experimental trials. In one trial, where a significant relationship was found, externals were more unethical than internals—a finding that is consistent with theoretical logic. Jones and Kavanagh (1996) also concluded in their investigation, that externals were more likely to behave unethically than internals. The findings were consistent with prior research findings by Trevino and Youngblood (1990).

Logic suggests that internals should have higher ethical standards than externals. Ethical literature indicates that people who engage in unethical acts often justify their behaviour in one or more of the following ways: (a) the organization expects unethical behaviour; (b) everybody else behaves unethically; (c) behaving unethically is the only way one can get ahead; (d) the activity is not truly immoral or illegal; (e) the behaviour is in the best interest of the individual and/or the company; (f) the unethical actions would never be discovered; and/or (g) the company will condone the unethical behaviour if it helps the organization (Cooke, 1986; Cuilla, 1985; Gellerman, 1986). These reasons seek to rationalize unethical behaviour by placing responsibility for the behaviour on someone or something external to the individual who is exhibiting the behaviour. Thus, these rationales invoke an external locus of control explanation.

Theoretical support between locus of control and ethical beliefs is also provided by linking key research findings on locus of control to important arguments made by business ethicists. After reviewing the locus of control literature, Maddi (1976) concluded that internals tend to be more active and effective in their functioning. Some business ethicists argue that being ethical is the more effective way of behaving in business (Brown, 1987). Since internals function more effectively, and since being ethical represents more effective business behaviour, internals should have higher ethical standards than externals (McCuddy and Peery, 1996).

Thus, locus of control appears to be a very important personality attribute in general at the workplace and work ethics in particular. However, more studies are needed in the field in order to generalize the findings to enable their use at the workplace to make it more congenial and productive for everyone.

PERSONALITY, ETHICAL FRAMEWORKS AND ETHICAL DECISION MAKING

The literature provides enough evidence on the importance of these two personality dimensions in relation to the individual ethical ideology. How much these personality dimensions influence the ethical ideologies and decision making of Indian managers needs to be empirically tested. When both these personality attributes are seen to individually influence ethical ideologies and ethical decision making, it is of interest to examine whether any mutual relationship between two exists. Thus, to explore the mutual relationship between Machiavellianism and locus of control, a statistical correlation was calculated.

These two personality variables were found to be highly but negatively correlated with each other. A significant negative correlation implies that the relationship between Machiavellianism and locus of control is such that the high score on one dimension corresponds with the low scores on the other. In the present case, the items of the instrument used to measure locus of control were designed in such a way (for details see Chapter 2) that the lower values of locus of control correspond to external locus of control. This negative relationship could be understood as the greater the external locus of control (low scores on locus of control measure used in the present study), the higher would be the score on the Machiavellianism construct. It means that it is quite likely that the person who has a greater orientation towards Machiavellianism, also has the characteristics of a person with external locus of control. Gemmill and Heisler (1972) discussed the relationship between a Machiavellianism and several job-related correlates. Their study found that a Machiavellianism orientation associates positively with more job strain, less job satisfaction, and less opportunity for formal control. At the same time, externals are also found to be low on job satisfaction in comparison to internals (Kulkarni, 1983; Singh, 1978). This correspondence between external locus of control and high Machiavellianism might explain the high negative correlation between Machiavellianism and locus of control, as low scores on the locus of control measure (used in the present study) meant external locus of control.

This mutual relationship found between Machiavellianism and locus of control might help in explaining the influence of personality attributes on the choice of ethical frameworks (ideologies) and ethical decision making.

PERSONALITY VARIABLES AND INDIVIDUAL ETHICAL FRAMEWORKS

In the present context, the individual ethical ideologies (mental makeup) are studied through the use of ethical frameworks. An instrument is specially developed to apply this concept and empirically measure the ethical ideologies of Indian managers (for details see

Chapter 2). To explore the statistical relationship between ethical frameworks and different personality attributes, the correlation was calculated. The results of the correlation test on the data are given in Table 6.1.

Locus of control and Machiavellianism constructs both had strong mutual relationships (significantly correlated) with both the individual religious and individual pragmatic ethical frameworks. Similar results were also obtained in the past in other studies, where locus of control and Machiavellianism were found to be related with ethical frameworks and ethical decision-making behaviour (Hegarty and Sims, 1978).

Table 6.1
Correlation among Ethical Frameworks and Personality Variables

	Individual Religious Framework	Individual Pragmatic Framework
Locus of Control	−.318 **(303)	.280 **(304)
Machiavellianism	.166 **(298)	−.137 * (298)

Note: Figures in parenthesis represent $\underline{N}$ (sample size). ** = $\underline{P}$ < .01 * = $\underline{P}$ < .05.

Locus of Control had a highly significant negative correlation with the individual religious framework and an equally significant positive relationship with the individual pragmatic ethical framework. As mentioned earlier, in the present context low scores on locus of control corresponds to an inclination towards external locus of control. Therefore, the results implied that an individual with external locus of control is also expected to have a tendency to make use of the religious framework. On the other hand, a positive significant correlation of locus of control with pragmatic framework confirmed the reverse, i.e., internals (high scores on the locus of control measure) scored high on the pragmatic framework.

In the case of Machiavellians, high machs had a greater preference (indicated by highly significant and positive correlation) for religious framework, whereas low machs scored higher on pragmatic frameworks.

The positive significant relationship between the religious framework and high machs, requires deeper probing.

Since Machiavellianism and locus of control are correlated, it was important to identify their relationships separately with the two ethical frameworks. In order to separate their effect on ethical frameworks, a partial correlation was calculated. The results of the partial correlation analysis are given in Table A.21 (Annexure I).

The results showed that the locus of control personality attribute was a better predictor of individuals' ethical framework than Machiavellianism in both the cases, i.e., religious framework and pragmatic framework.

PERSONALITY AND ETHICAL DECISION MAKING

To understand the manifestation of these ethical frameworks in decision-making behaviour, they were presented with five situations of ethical dilemma (for details see Chapter 2). To see the relationship of coexistence of the personality attributes (Machiavellianism and locus of control) and the inclination towards taking an ethical decision, the statistical correlations were calculated. The results of the correlation analysis between personality variables and ethical decision making are reported in Table 6.2.

Table 6.2
Correlation between Ethical Decision Making and Different Personality
Variables for Different Situations

Decision Making	Vignette 1	Vignette 2	Vignette 3	Vignette 4	Vignette 5
Locus of Control	−.169 **	−.152 **	−.206 **	−.056	−.120 *
	(311)	(309)	(308)	(305)	(294)
Machiavellianism	.201**	.136 *	.212 **	.159 **	.016
	(305)	(303)	(302)	(299)	(289)

Note: Figures in parenthesis represent $\underline{N}$ (sample size) ** = $\underline{P}$ < .01 * = $\underline{P}$ < .05.

It was observed that Vignette one, two and three, i.e., 'new and improved marketing strategy', 'gifts and Bribes', and 'padding up the expenses bills' respectively, were significantly correlated with both locus of control and Machiavellianism. Whereas Vignette four ('nepotism') was found significantly correlated only with Machiavellianism. Vignette five ('inside trading') had a significant correlation with locus of control. It was observed earlier that Machiavellianism and locus of control had a high correlation. In the case of the three vignettes both were found to have significantly strong relationships. Therefore, in order to separate the effect of their coexistence in case of Vignette one, two and three, a partial correlation of Machiavellianism, and locus of control was analyzed statistically (the results are reported in

Table A.21, Annexure I). The statistical test indicated that Machiavellianism for Vignette one, and for locus of control for Vignette two, were the best predictors of ethical decision-making behaviour. In case of Vignette three, both locus of control and Machiavellianism were found to influence the decision choice.

Vignette one was about a marketing strategy, where the managers were asked whether they approved of a product advertisement using the slogan of 'new and improved' (without actually making any improvements) to increase its sales. Machiavellianism was found to be a better predictor of the decision in this case. The direction of the relationship showed that individuals (Table 6.2) scoring higher towards a *Compromise* (unethical) decision in this case would also have strong mach traits. As discussed at length at the beginning of this chapter, mach individuals follow the basic philosophy that everything is fair in business till the time it produces good profits, which explains this relationship.

In the second vignette, in which managers were asked to respond to a situation where 'gifts and bribes' were proposed to be used to obtain favours for the company, locus of control was found to be a better predictor of decision making. The direction of the relationship (Table 6.2) indicated that the chances are, that the individuals who have external locus of control (low scores on the measure) would also agree with the proposal by scoring high in the *Compromise* direction. The external locus of control characteristic is related with having more dependency on external anchors to find a solution to problems. A similar observation is also reflected in this relationship.

In the case of vignette three, both locus of control and Machiavellianism were found to predict the response together. The vignette was about 'padding up the expense bills'. The direction of the relationship predicted that managers with high external locus of control and high Machiavellianism would decide in favour, i.e., high scores towards the *Compromise* (unethical) direction of decision making.

High scores on the Machiavellianism personality attribute were found to be related with high scores towards the *Compromise* direction in the case of Vignette 4 ('nepotism'). The situation was about favouring someone in a job interview because of his/her family connection. It implies that individuals who have a strong Machiavellian personality are more likely to do such a favour. The fifth situation was about 'insider trading'. Where it was observed that the decision in favour of it, is more likely to occur in the case of individuals with higher external locus of control (low scores on locus of control measure).

Therefore, the results implied that both the personality construct of Machiavellianism and locus of control significantly influenced the choice of the cognitive ethical frameworks and also the decision-making behaviour in situations of ethical dilemmas. An individual with external locus of control is also expected to make greater use of the choices from the religious framework. On the other hand, managers with internal locus of control were observed to use more of the pragmatic framework. Individuals choosing the religious framework are basically guided by their religious conviction. They have immense faith in their spiritual leaders and religion. Most of the time, these individuals praise or blame their fate for the events that surround them, corresponding to the characteristics of those with external locus of control. The relationship drawn between *Karma*, an Indian philosophical concept, and external locus of control might also help in explaining the coexistence of external locus of control and religious conviction among Indian managers. It is possible that an individual with strong religious convictions also believes in the theory of *Karma*, where his main concern is on performing his duty and leaving the rest to God. Individuals who choose the pragmatic framework are expected to be more practical in their approach with an emphasis on long-term perspectives and justice. Similarly, individuals with internal locus of control have faith in their own choice, higher self-esteem, occupy higher status and position and are more successful and satisfied as compared to externals. In the case of Machiavellianism, high machs had a stronger preference (indicated by the highly significant correlation) for the religious framework, whereas low machs scored higher on pragmatic frameworks. The pragmatic framework in the present research has the components of justice, utilitarianism and long-term perspective (the greatest good for the greater number). The characteristics of the pragmatic framework do not match with the quality of a high Machiavellian personality, which explains the negative relationship of a pragmatic framework with a high Machiavellian score.

At the same time, a positive significant relationship of the religious framework with high Machiavellianism required deeper probing. The analysis of the items of Machiavellianism measure (for example, if there is any chance that a recommendation might backfire, be very cautious in recommending anyone; one should upset as few people as possible and so on; see Annexure III for details), showed that these items were mostly to pacify others and maintain the peace. It was quite possible for an individual to have all these characteristics and still follow religious convictions. In most of the religious ideologies, emphasis is always laid on maintaining harmony and making others happy.

In situations of ethical decision making, both the personality constructs were found to be operative. It can thus be concluded that individuals with stronger Machiavellianism traits and with external locus of control were found to take decisions towards the *Compromise* (unethical) direction.

DEMOGRAPHY AND ETHICS.

Further studies were carried out to explore whether the relationship of personality varies with age and gender. To study the gender differences, the correlation of personality variables and ethical frameworks was computed separately for men and women*.

For men, locus of control was negatively related to individuals' religious framework and was positively related with individuals' pragmatic ethical frameworks. Higher scores on locus of control would mean internal locus of control and lower scores would mean external locus of control. That means the external locus of control was positively related to individual religious ethical frameworks and negatively related to pragmatic frameworks. Similar results were also observed when the same correlation analysis was conducted for the total sample. This could be due to the fact that the majority of respondents in the samples were male, which would reflect the characteristics of the total sample.

In the case of Machiavellianism also, the same trend as that of the total sample was observed among men. However, those with the relationship was significant only in the case of the religious ethical framework, where high Machiavellianism scores also scored high on the religious ethical framework choices.

In the case of women, only the locus of control was found to be significantly related to the individual religious framework. The direction of the relationship was the same as in the case of male executives, i.e., internals scored low on religious framework choices as compared to individuals with external locus of control. No other

---

* Table A.23 and Table A.24 (Annexure I) provide the relationship between personality variables and ethical frameworks for men and women respectively.

relationship was found significant in the case of women. A word of caution is in order as the sample size of the female respondents was too small to generalize the results obtained.

A similar analysis was also conducted for three different age groups**. The relationship between Machiavellianism and ethical frameworks was an interesting one. In the case of the younger age group, both the frameworks were negatively related to Machiavellianism, though the relationship was not significant. It implies that individuals scoring high on the religious framework would scores lower on locus of control (corresponding with external locus of control) and on Machiavellian traits. Whereas in the case of the pragmatic framework, young managers would tend to score high on locus of control (corresponding with internal locus of control) and low on Machiavellianism, with high scores on this framework.

In the case of both middle and old age groups, the religious framework had a highly significant positive relationship with Machiavellianism and a significantly negative relationship with locus of control. This means that individuals belonging to middle and old age groups, who also scored high on religious framework would also tend to score high on Machiavellianism and towards external locus of control. In the case of pragmatic framework also, managers in both the categories (middle age and old age group) had a significant positive relationship with locus of control. It implies that individuals who score high on this framework are more likely to have internal locus of control. The relationship with Machiavellianism was significant only in the case of the old age group. The direction of the relationship indicated that the managers with high scores on the pragmatic framework would also tend to score lower on Machiavellianism traits. The finding was similar to the findings for the whole group.

The interaction effects of gender, age and personality variables were also studied on ethical decision making through a simple correlation.

For men, all the relationships observed* here are similar to that of the total sample. Again, the similarity of the results for male responses with that of the total sample could be explained on the basis of the

---

** Tables A.25, 26 and 27 (Annexure I) report the results of the relationship between ethical frameworks and different personality variables for young, middle and old age groups respectively.
* Table A.28 (Annexure I) depicts the relationship of personality variables with different ethical decision-making vignettes for men.

fact that the majority of the sample included in the study was that of male respondents.

In case of women[**], only two relationships were found significant. The relationships were Vignette five ('insider trading') with locus of control, and Vignette one ('new and improved marketing strategy') with Machiavellianism. Thus, in the case of Vignette one, women managers with high scores on Machiavellianism and in Vignette five, with low scores on locus of control (corresponding to external locus of control), are more likely to score in the *Compromise* direction of ethical decision making.

A similar relationships, i.e., between Vignette one with Machiavellianism, also existed for the whole sample, as well as for male respondents. Though the relationship between Vignette five and locus of control were not there for the total sample or for male respondents, the direction of the relationship was similar to the one between the other vignettes and locus of control for men. This phenomenon can be explained on the basis of the 'self selection' as well as 'structural' theories explained at the beginning of this chapter. The self-selection theory asserts that women who choose business careers have traits different from those typical of their gender. Similarly, the structural theory believes that differences between genders due to early socialization will be overridden in the work environment by perceived costs and rewards associated with occupational goals; thus, while women may enter business careers with values different from men; they will respond similarly to the same training and occupational environment and become more like men in their actions and perceptions.

The analysis of the results of the effect of the interaction between personality variables and age on ethical decision making gave the following results[*].

For young managers, all the significant relationships and the direction of the relationship was the same as that for the whole group (see Chapter 4).

In the middle age group, there were only two significant correlations, i.e., the correlation of Vignette two ('gifts and bribe') and Vignette three ('padding up the expense bills') with locus of control. In

---

[**] (Table A.29 Annexure I).
[*] The results are also reported in Table 30, 31 and 32 for young, middle and old age groups respectively.

both the cases, the direction of the relationship was the same as that for the whole group (see chapter on age and gender). It appears that for middle age group managers, locus of control could be the only personality variable, which influences the nature of decisions taken in situations of ethical dilemma.

Interestingly, for the old age group the important personality variable influencing the choice of decisions in given ethical situations was Machiavellianism. The only two significant relationships obtained for the old age group were between Machiavellianism and Vignette one ('new and improved marketing strategy') and Vignette three ('padding up of the expense bills'). It implies that people in the old age group having high scores on the Machiavellianism scale would also score higher (*Compromise*) on the ethical decision-making scale. The results here support the results reported in the chapter on age and gender, where responses of the old age group category scored higher towards the *Compromise* dimension of ethical decision making than other age group responses (for both Vignette one and Vignette three).

On the whole, it was observed that the interaction of age and gender with personality produced results on the ethical decision-making behaviour measure that were similar to the whole sample results taken together, implying that age and gender were irrelevant when discussing the influence of personality on ethical behaviour. However, these findings cannot be generalized without its confirmation on a bigger and varied population.

HOW DO LOCUS OF CONTROL AND MACHIAVELLIANISM TOGETHER AFFECT ETHICAL BEHAVIOUR

It has already been discussed that there exists a significant mutual relationship among the two personality attributes. Their independent relationship with ethical decision-making situations were studied through simple correlations. It was interesting to see the interaction of Machiavellianism and locus of control on ethical decision-making behaviour.

The personality variables were also found to interact among themselves and predict ethical decision-making behaviour in the given five situations (Table 6.3). A description of the relationships is given after the table.

Table 6.3
Results of Hierarchical Regression to Discover the Effect of Interaction among
Personality Variables on Ethical Decision Making in Five Given Situations

Decision Making	β Coefficient				
	Vignette 1	Vignette 2	Vignette 3	Vignette 4	Vignette 5
Machiavellianism	0.0087	0.143*	0.114	0.303**	0.136
& Locus of	(0.050)	(0.044)	(0.073)	(0.074)	(0.023)
Control					

Note: * = $P < 0.05$ ** = $P < 0.01$
Figures in parenthesis represents 'R' squares change values.
Figures not in parenthesis represent 'β' values.

The decision in Vignette two ('gifts and bribes') and four could be
predicted through the interaction between locus of control and
Machiavellianism. The relationships are also shown graphically
through Figure 6.1 and Figure 6.2.

The interaction effect shows that in Vignette two, an individual
with high Machiavellianism but external locus of control would score
towards a *Compromise* and an individual with low Machiavellianism
and internal locus of control would score towards the *Values* dimension of ethical decision making. In Vignette four, individual decisions
could be in the *Compromise* direction with internal locus of control
and high Machiavellianism.

Figure 6.1

Interaction Effect of Locus of Control and Machiavellianism
on Decision Making (Vignette 2)

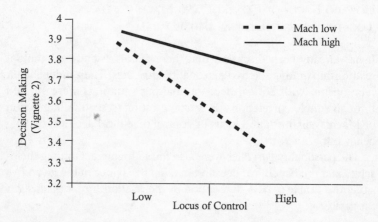

Figure 6.2

Interaction Effect of Locus of Control and Machiavellianism
on Decision Making (Vignette 4)

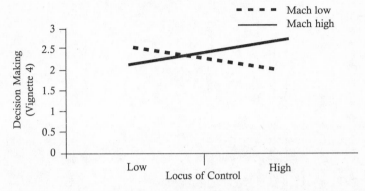

On the other hand, internal locus of control and low scores on Machiavellianism could predict the individual decision towards the *Values* dimension of ethical decision making. The results are shown graphically in Figure 6.2. Thus, it can be concluded that both Machiavellianism and locus of control are very important personality variables in the context of ethics in general and work ethics in particular. Generally, individuals with external locus of control and low Machiavellian qualities use pragmatic cognitive ethical frameworks and take more ethical decisions.

CHAPTER OVERVIEW

Personality distinguishes one individual from another and defines his or her general nature. The personality of an individual is developed over the years as a result of the influence of several factors during the process of socialization, resulting in different psychological characteristics. These differences together determine personality. The psychological characteristics or traits that determine his/her personal preferences and individual style of behaviour are very important to be studied with reference to ethical ideologies and differences (Sharma and Bhal, 2003). Therefore, personality factors are expected to influence the decision-making behaviour of the individual. Individuals, in general and organizations in particular, often face situations of ethical dilemma. Political orientation and locus of control are two such

Table 6.4
Individuals of Different Age, Gender and Personality and their Choice of Ethical Frameworks and Decision Making in Situations of Ethical Dilemma

Personality Type	Choice of Framework	Direction of Decision Making				
		Vignette 1	Vignette 2	Vignette 3	Vignette 4	Vignette 5
General						
High Mach	Religious**	Compromise**	Compromise*	Compromise**	Compromise**	
Low Mach	Pragmatic*	Value**	Value*	Value**	Value**	
Internal locus of control	Pragmatic**	Value**	Value**	Value**		Value*
External locus of control	Religious**	Compromise**	Compromise**	Compromise**		Compromise*
Men						
High Mach	Religious**	Compromise**	Compromise*	Compromise**	Compromise**	
Low Mach		Value**	Value*	Value**	Value**	
Internal locus of control	Pragmatic**	Value**	Value**			
External locus of control	Religious**	Compromise**	Compromise**			
Women						
High Mach		Compromise**				
Low Mach		Value**				
Internal locus of control						Value*
External locus of control	Religious*					Compromise*
Young						
High Mach		Compromise*		Compromise**	Compromise*	
Low Mach		Value*		Value**	Value*	
Internal locus of control	Pragmatic**					
External locus of control	Religious**					

(Table Contd.)

Personality Type	Choice of Framework	Direction of Decision Making				
		Vignette 1	Vignette 2	Vignette 3	Vignette 4	Vignette 5
Middle						
High Mach	Religious**					
Low Mach						
Internal locus of control	Pragmatic**		Value*	Value**		
External locus of control	Religious**		Compromise *	Compromise **		
Old Age Group						
High Mach	Religious*	Compromise **		Compromise **		
Low Mach	Pragmatic**	Value**		Value**		
Internal locus of control	Pragmatic**					
External locus of control	Religious*					

Note: * = P < 0.05; ** = P < 0.01.

personality attributes, which have been found to influence the individual ethical ideology, through different studies and thereby the decision-making process in situations of ethical dilemma. Machiavellianism is the most widely used construct for measuring political orientation of an individual.

How these personality variables influence the individual choice of cognitive ethical frameworks and their decision-making process in situations of ethical dilemma, was found out empirically. Direct relationships were studied through the t-test, simple correlation and one-way ANOVA. The interaction effects were studied using two-way ANOVA and hierarchical regression (see Chapter 2 for the details of the methodology followed). Some of the key results are as follows: the two personality variables, i.e., locus of control and Machiavellianism were found to significantly affect the individual's choice of frameworks and decisions in situations of ethical dilemmas. These two constructs were found to coexist. A relationship was also observed between external locus of control and high Machiavellianism. The overall results of the chapter are summarized in Table 6.4.

Observing the overall results, it can be said that both Machiavellianism and locus of control are important personality dimensions in the context of ethics. It is also observed that individuals with internal locus of control and low Machiavellianism make greater use of pragmatic ethical frameworks and also make more ethical decisions. Though both constructs are important, locus of control was found to be a more accurate predictor of the ethical decision-making behaviour of an individual.

7

LEADERSHIP AND ETHICS

The relevance and centrality of leadership in organizations has been widely emphasized and rightly so. This fact becomes more evident when it is asserted that, in most cases, the failure of new organizations right at the start is due to poor leadership (Schultz, 1982). Therefore, an organization's leaders are a major determinant of its success or failure (Katz and Khan, 1978).

The importance of leadership is well established, at the same time the complexity of leadership influence cannot be denied. According to Enderle (1987), business leadership would be relatively simple if corporations only had to produce a product or service, without being concerned about employees; if management only had to deal with concepts, structures and strategies, without worrying about human relations; if businesses just had to resolve their own problems, without being obligated to take the interests of individuals or society into consideration. However, society is now beginning to demand greater accountability in business ethics from our business leaders and public servants, to conform to an even higher standard of behaviour than we might demand and expect of ourselves.

An increasing importance is being placed on *ethical* and socially responsible attitudes towards business. Central issues of organizational effectiveness and organizational efficiency, with directors thinking in terms of goal achievement for their respective organizations, have now been augmented by an awareness of issues in business *ethics,* and a requirement for members of corporate governing bodies to behave in more socially responsible ways (Minkes, et al., 1999).

While describing a framework of the Six Facets of Ethical Leadership (SFEL), Laszlo and Nash (2001) commented that ethics is indivisible and it needs to focus on all the stakeholders of a business. The six facets are the six stakeholders, like the facets of a cut diamond. Each is an integral part of the whole. The SFEL is presented sequentially and companies can choose the ones they wish to start with. However, they have to understand that the six facets are essentially inseparable, thereby implying that the interests of all the stakeholders have to be considered in any decision making by the top leaders of an organization. The most important insight is the connection between them. Their (ibid.) framework consists of a set of high-level criteria that individual companies use to specify ethical leadership according to their own business needs. The items of the six components of the framework are given below:

Shareholders

- The company meets shareholder expectations without impairing its social, physical, or business environment.
- Annual reporting is provided to shareholders on legal and regulatory compliance, as well as on social and environmental initiatives beyond compliance.
- The company's investment strategy has negative selection criteria for activities that involve undesirable social and environmental business practices.
- The company's investment strategy has positive selection criteria for activities that involve desirable social and environmental business practices.

Employees

- The company's vision and *Values* are articulated to employees with measurable standards of business ethics, social responsibility, and environmental sustainability.
- Employees contribute to the formulation of the vision and *Values* at their level and embody them in day-to-day practices.
- Annual performance evaluations, compensation systems and career progression criteria fully integrate the vision and *Values*.
- The company is actively engaged in the lives of its employees, learning their concerns, understanding their needs, and contributing to their development.

Customers

- The company accurately represents its products and services relative to their long-term benefits and costs, including safety, social consequences, environmental toxicity, reusability and recyclability.

- The company strives to educate customers as to the social and environmental impact of its products and services from the cradle to the grave.
- Innovation and new product development shape the industry toward greater sustainability, social responsibility, and corporate citizenship.

Business Partners

- The company does not engage in business with companies that knowingly degrade or otherwise cause significant damage to shareholders, employees, customers, business partners, communities, or the environment.
- The company offers preferential status whenever possible to business partners evidencing new ethical leadership.

Local Communities

- The company complies with environmental regulations and laws.
- The company consistently seeks pollution prevention and waste minimization in its supply chain. It anticipates environmental regulations in reducing negative impacts on the environment.
- The company establishes its own environmental management systems.
- The company is actively pursuing eco-efficiency and dematerialization of its value-added to customers.
- The company is continually designing itself for environmental. sustainability, including the recycling of non-renewable resources, consuming renewable resources at a rate that allows them to regenerate, and limiting the reduction of biodiversity.

The ethics of leadership—whether they are good or bad, positive or negative—affect the ethos of the workplace and thereby, help to form the ethical choices and decisions of the workers in the workplace. Leaders help to set the tone, develop the vision, and shape the behaviour of all those involved in organizational life. According to Burns (1979), leadership is not just about directed results; it is also about offering followers a choice among real alternatives. Hence, leadership assumes competition, conflict, and debate. An essential component of leadership is power and its judicious use. 'Leadership mobilizes', said Burns (ibid.) and 'naked power coerces'. However, power need not be dictatorial or punitive to be effective. Power can also be used in a non-coercive manner to orchestrate, direct, and guide members of an organization in the pursuit of a goal or series of objectives. Leaders must engage followers, not merely direct them. Leaders must serve as models and mentors, not martinets. Hence, the use of power requires the direction and control of morality and ethics.

Next, we look at the ways in which leadership has been studied by behavioural scientists and examine the ethical/moral component in those conceptualizations. It needs to be mentioned that since most of the theories are prescriptive, they do have an element of ethics. However, since the prescriptions are often based on efficiency/effectiveness criteria, we identify the moral/ethical angle in these theories.

ETHICAL DIMENSION OF APPROACHES TO STUDY LEADERSHIP

Given the importance and pervasiveness of the phenomenon, leadership has received a fair amount of attention from researchers and practitioners alike. As a result, it has been defined, understood, and explained in various ways. One reason for the far-reaching effects of leadership is probably its multifaceted nature. Before proceeding further to explore the issue of ethical leadership, a brief introduction to the various conceptualizations indicating the many faces of the concept is briefly discussed below.

TRAIT APPROACHES

The earliest understanding of the concept focused on people or the individual leader as the focus of the study. This assumed that some people were leaders but others were not, and led to the use of personality characteristics or traits as the differentiating factor between the leaders and the non leaders. It could be anything from the strength of a particular trait (Bowden, 1926) to the presence of a number of desirable traits (Bingham, 1927).

These are the earliest approaches based on the assumption that some people were born leaders. This means that there are some personality characteristics or traits that differentiate a leader from others. If they are traits, they are relatively fixed with no scope for 'flexibility' or 'development'. In this approach, all researchers aim at identifying these traits or characteristics by evaluating and analyzing those of effective leaders, generally chosen from a vast array of fields like politics and religion. The growth and development of the traits approach was influenced by the emphasis on psychological testing from 1920 to 1950. Since most of the tests were aimed at identifying personality characteristics or intelligence, they added impetus to trait research.

Intellectual fortitude and integrity of character were identified as important traits of mature and effective leaders (Bernard, 1928; Carlson and Harrell, 1942). A stable ego and a strength of conviction too have been reported as significant predictions of effective leadership (Moore, 1932; Webb, 1915).

One of the major component of the traits of leadership is the integrity and ethical/moral orientation of the leader. In the context of charismatic leaders this assumes greater significance, as the leader's behaviour has tremendous potential to impact the way the followers and the company are guided and managed.

BEHAVIOURAL APPROACHES

Another aspect of leadership, which has generated a lot of interest and consequently a flood of research, is the behaviour of leaders. From this view point, leadership behaviour may involve directing the activities of the group (Hemphill, 1949) or making the followers work towards a common goal (Shartle, 1956). In the context of organizations, in particular, a behavioural definition of leadership which is representative of most theories, is as follows:

> ... a behavioural definition of leadership which represents most theorizations would focus on leader behaviour where the leader aims to get the job done from the members. This may be achieved, by the leader, either by identifying new work relationships, praising or criticizing the members and showing a concern for their feelings (Fiedler, 1967).

This set of theorists focus on the acts or behaviours of the leader. The question in this approach shifts to 'what leaders do'. Research has been directed at identifying leader behaviour on the job. The actions of the leaders are variously termed as 'activity patterns', 'managerial roles', or 'behaviour category'. The aim is to identify such behaviours that differentiate between effective and ineffective leaders. Given below are a few representative behavioural theories.

AUTHORITARIAN DEMOCRATIC DICHOTOMY

Lewin, Lippitt and White (1939) conducted an experimental study. Their aim was to investigate the effects of climates created by differing leadership behaviours on the attitudinal and behavioural outcomes for the members. The three leadship styles included in the study were authoritarian, democratic and laissez faire. The authoritarian leader made all decisions single-handedly and had full control over the activities of the members. Consequently, members did not have any knowledge of what they had to do in the future and were totally dependent on the leader for this. The leader decided the nature of the job and work companion for every member. Finally, the leader was personal in praising or criticizing the members. The leader did not participate in group activities. The democratic leader, at the other extreme, was open and participative. Policies were decided on the basis of group discussion and only general instructions about work were given to the members. The laissez faire style was characterized by an apathetic leadership. The leader's participation in group activities was minimal. Working material and information were given only when asked for by members.

The findings of the Lewin et al. study (ibid.) can be summarized as follows. In the authoritarian style of leadership, the members were more dependent on their leader and were more dissatisfied with the activities of the group. The interactions between the group members were marked with aggression and irritability. Although the group produced a lot of work, the quality of the output was only average. On the other hand, in the democratic leadership style, members were less dependent on the leader and more satisfied with the group activities. Their interactions were devoid of aggression or irritability. Although the quantum of work produced was only average, the output was of high quality. Members in this group also showed more 'we' feelings than 'I' feelings. The production of work was the lowest in the laissez-faire group. In this study, the two dimension of leadership behaviour form two discrete categories. Next, a formulation that treats the behaviour categories as orthogonal is discussed.

The ethical dimensions of autocratic and democratic leadership have been widely debated. The general prescription has been for a democratic style with the focus on people.

A series of studies was initiated in 1945 by the Bureau of Business Research under the leadship of C.L. Shartle. After the unsuccessful trait approach, an attempt was made to identify relevant leader behaviours. This theorization was more directly relevant to organizational settings.

The first objective of this effort was, of course, to unearth the various leader behaviours. In the first phase of the research, a questionnaire was to be developed. Beginning with 1,800 examples of leader behaviour, the identification pinpointed 150 items that were contained in the Leader Behaviour Description Questionnaire (LBDQ). The responses on these items were factor analyzed and showed that the subordinates perceived their leaders' behaviour in terms of two distinct categories (Fleishman, 1953, 1957; Halpin and Winer, 1957; Hemphill and Coons, 1957). Subsequently, these two behaviour categories were called 'consideration' and 'initiating structure'. They were characterized as follows:

> Consideration included behaviour items concerned with leader supportiveness, friendliness, consideration, consultation with subordinates, representation of subordinate interests, openness of communication with subordinates and recognition of subordinate contributions.
>
> Initiating structure included behaviour items concerned with directing subordinates, clarifying subordinate roles, planning, coordinating, problem solving, criticizing poor work and pressurizing subordinates to perform better (Yukl, 1981).

Thus, consideration parallels a 'relationship' aspect and initiating structure, the 'work' aspect.

A detailed analysis of the two dimensions revealed that they were factorially independent and distinct. This implied that the two were orthogonal dimensions and that a leader could have any combination of the two. That is, having one kind of behaviour did not rule out the possibility of having another.

Another major programme on leadership research began at the University of Michigan at about the same time the Ohio State University (OSU) studies were being conducted. The prime objective was to discover leadership behaviours that led to effective performance of the group.

Studies testing the link between effectiveness and leader behaviour provided interesting results. Effective leaders indulged more in supervisory behaviour, like planning and scheduling the work and coordinating subordinate activities. They were also more considerate, supportive and helpful. That is to say, leaders high on both the dimensions were found to be more effective (Katz and Kahn, 1952; Katz, et al., 1950; Mann and Dent, 1954).

Another series of studies were concerned with evaluating the leader behaviour towards subordinates for decision-making processes. The various analyses showed that the effectiveness of a leader was positively correlated with the subordinate participation in decision making (Coch and French, 1948; French, 1950).

Likert (1961, 1967) compiled all the data and results of the Michigan University studies. He identified system IV (the participative style) as the most effective style of leadership. It was characterized by three elements: (a) the use of supportive relations by the managers; (b) group decision making and group methods of supervision; and (c) high performance goals.

MANAGERIAL GRID

Blake and Mouton (1964) initiated their studies with the two dimensions given by the OSU studies. They popularized the concepts and made extensive use of them in management development programmes.

In their formulation, they identified a plane between two orthogonal dimensions of 'concern for task' (varying from 1 = low, to 9 = high) and 'concern for people' (varying from 1 = low, to 9 = high). They identified five cut points corresponding to five leadership styles in the plane. This gave rise to a kind of grid, which was termed the managerial grid. The five styles are as follows:

Impoverished (1, 1)—low on both the concerns. Minimal effort is expended to get work done or maintain relationships. The only concern is to maintain the organizational membership.

Country Club (1, 9)—high concern for relationships and low concern for carrying out tasks. The prime concern is to satisfy the relationships and maintain a friendly atmosphere.

Task (9, 1)—high concern for task and low concern for relationship. Efficiency of work is the prime concern with very little attention paid towards maintaining relationships.

Middle of the road (5, 5)—moderate concern both for task and for relationship. Adequate work is sought to be done by maintaining the morale of the people in the organization.

Team (9, 9)—a high concern both for task and for relationship. Tasks or jobs are done through committed people.

Blake and Mouton (ibid.) emphasize the normative use of the team (9, 9) style of leadership for effective functioning of the group. They have devised programmes that are aimed at developing the managerial style towards this style of functioning.

All the behavioural theories described above identify two strikingly clear-cut dimensions of leader behaviour—the work and the interpersonal—prescribing an effective leadership style. Thus, whether it is participative leadership (Likert, 1967), or teamwork style of management (Blake and Mouton, 1964), the emphasis is on developing both the dimensions of tasks and relationships. There is evidence, all the same, of inconsistency in the same results (Halpin and Winer, 1957; Likert, 1961). A possible explanation for the inconsistency is sought in terms of the total neglect of situations. That is to say, the role situational variables in deciding the effectiveness of a particular style. This contention has been taken care of in the next subsection on contingency situational theories.

Though management studies have recommended a high combination of focusing on tasks and people, it must be kept in mind that an excess focus on relationships is likely to lead to what is termed favouritism and unethical practices. Thus, it is important for a leader to strike a balance in his/her behaviour towards subordinates. Trevino, et al. (2003) have developed a 10-item scale to measure ethical leadership.

THE NURTURANT TASK LEADERSHIP: AN INDIAN FORMULATION

The theory at the grassroot level evaluates the impact of social environment on management practices. The formulator, Sinha (1980), proposes that 'an effective leader will be required to incorporate the relevant meta *Values* of the system while designing his action strategies for leading his group.

According to Sinha (ibid.) the normative use of the participative or democratic style of leadership is not advisable. These styles will be effective only if the needs and *Values* (for example, egalitarian) of the leaders match the *Values* inherent in these conceptualizations. Also, the needs, *Values* and goals of the leader, the follower, and the organization have to be in harmony. If these requirements are not met, the use of any style is deemed to be a failure. Socio-cultural realities are the global *Values* that are shared by all alike. Hence, an evaluation of the value system at that level will be applicable to all.

Sinha (ibid.) identified six meta *Values* of the Indian socio-cultural mien. They are: lack of commitment, showing off, preference for personalized relationships, dependence proneness, lack of team orientation, and hankering for *aram* (tendency to relax or rest without being tired).

If one were to fit the theory within a contingency framework, the meta *Values* of the society would be the situational variables. Sinha (ibid.) recommends a Nurturant task (N) leadership for the Indian social milieu. N leadership has elements of task and nurturance. Further, the N leader initiates, guides and directs his subordinates to work hard and maintains a high level of productivity, both quantitatively and qualitatively. His task orientation, however, has the mix of nurturance. He cares for his subordinates, shows affections, takes a personal interest in their well-being, and above all, is committed to their growth.

This should not be taken to mean that the N style of leadership is the best or the most effective. It is considered flexible and transitional. The universal goodness of the participative style is accepted. In this light, it is suggested that given the Indian work *Values*, subordinates are not mature enough to make the participative style successful. N works as a preparatory device. It helps the subordinates grow and respond positively to the participative style of leadership. Thus, it is recommended to shift from the N to the participative style once the subordinates are responsible and mature enough.

All the situational theories ask for an understanding of complex situational variables. Thus, if a manager has to be effective, he or she has to analyze the situation in-depth each time he or she indulges in the acts of leadership. With the hectic and fragmented pace of managerial activities, it is not possible for a manager to do so (McCall, 1977). McCall (ibid.) also criticizes the emphasis on one style being effective in a given situation. The situations are so dynamic that more than one style may be effective.

Thus far, conceptualizations have focused on the elements of individuals or the environment in understanding the concept of leadership. It could also be understood in terms of focusing on the phenomenon itself. This will lead to process oriented definitions. Thus, for some, leadership is the art of inducing compliance. The thrust here is on uni-directional, single handed exertion of influence. In this light, it is 'social control' (Allport, 1954) and 'force of morale' (Munson, 1921). It is a phenomenon characterized with 'inducing others to do what one wants them to do' (Bundel, 1930). This conceptualization does not even recognize the necessities and sensitivities of the group members. As a result, it smacks of overemphasis on the authoritarian dimension of leadership (Bass, 1980).

The emphasis thus shifts to influence, which is more general and less value laden. In this framework, leadership is the 'interpersonal influence exercised in a situation and directed through the communication process toward the attainment of a specified goal or goals' (Tannenbaum, et al., 1961). More generally, it is an 'influence process whereby leaders, actions change followers behaviour and views, the influence attempt as being legitimate and the change as being consistent' (Kochan, et al., 1975). Stressing the importance of referent power, Katz and Kahn (1978) define leadership as the influential increment over and above mechanical compliance with the routine directives of the organization.

A cognitive approach to the phenomenon would emphasize perceptual and cognitive aspects of the process. This might focus on attribution processes (Calder, 1977; Pfeffer, 1997) in leader perceptions, the subordinates' implicit theories of their leader (Bernardin and Alvares, 1975; Ilgen and Fujii, 1976), or the problem-solving skills of the leader (Lord, 1976; Newell and Simon, 1972).

More directly, process oriented formulations view leadership as an interaction process (Anderson, 1940; Pigors, 1935). This, for some theorists, means a form of an exchange wherein the group members make a contribution to the group at a cost to themselves and receive returns at a cost to the group (Gergen, 1969; Homans, 1958; March and Simon, 1958; Thibaut and Kelley, 1959).

TRANSFORMATIONAL LEADERSHIP

Burns (1978) proposed that the leadership process occurs as either transactional or transformational. Transactional leadership is based on bureaucratic authority and legitimate power in the organization. Transactional leaders emphasize task assignments, work standards, and employee compliance. These leaders rely on rewards and punishment to influence employee performance. Transformational leadership, on the other hand, is a process that motivates followers by appealing to higher ideals and moral *Values*. Transformational leaders are able to define and articulate a vision for the organization and then inspire followers to carry it out.

Transformational leadership has been related to the long-standing literature on virtue and moral character, such as the Socratic and Confucian typologies (Bass, 1999). This style is seen as originating in the personal *Values* and beliefs of leaders, not in an exchange relationship between leaders and followers (Bass, 1985; Burns, 1978). Transformational leaders are believed to operate out of deeply held personal value systems that include *Values* such as justice and integrity (Bass, 1999; Kuhnert and Lewis, 1987). Burns (1978) notes that these *Values* cannot be negotiated or exchanged between individuals, and that transformational leadership is moral if it deals with the true needs of the followers as defined by the followers. The leader is guided by *Values* such as respect for human dignity and equality of human rights. The moral leader supports and enacts comprehensive *Values* that 'express followers' more fundamental and enduring needs' (ibid.: 42).

The vision and *Values* of leadership must have their origins and resolutions in the community of followers, of whom they are a part, and whom they wish to serve. Leaders can drive, lead, orchestrate, and cajole, but they cannot force, dictate, or demand. Leaders can be the catalyst for morally sound behaviour, but they are not, by themselves, a sufficient condition. By means of their demeanor and message, leaders must be able to convince, not just tell others, that collaboration serves the conjoint interest and well-being of all involved. Leaders may offer a vision, but followers must buy into it. Leaders may organize a plan, but followers must decide to take it on. Leaders may demonstrate conviction and willpower, but followers, in the new paradigm of leadership, should not allow the leader's will to replace their own (Jackall,1988).

THE NOTION OF ETHICAL LEADERSHIP

Ethical leadership is the demonstration of normatively appropriate conduct through personal actions and interpersonal relationships, and promotion of such conduct among followers through two-way communication, reinforcement, and decision-making processes (Treviño, Brown and Pincus-Hartman, 2003).

The traits that executives most often associate with ethical leadership are honesty, trustworthiness, and integrity. First and foremost, executives believe that ethical leaders do the right thing; Second, they also believe that ethical leaders show concern for people through their actions. They treat people well—with dignity and respect. They encourage openness and treat bad news as a problem to be addressed rather than punished.

Every organization requires capable people to carry out its functions effectively and efficiently, and every manager needs the skills of leaders. The leadership abilities of a manager are very important skills, which must be learned and practised in order to achieve organizational objectives consistently. Bassett (1977) wrote that leadership is best thought of as the manager's way of handling specific aspects of his role, establishing performance criteria, assigning responsibility and maintaining a relationship with his people. Biswas (1994), while studying leadership styles and its effect on organizational culture, defined leadership as 'the interpersonal influence exercised in situations and directed through communication process towards the attainment of a specific goal or a series of goals'. This influence is exercised through a pattern of behaviour followed by leaders, and known as their leadership style.

Sims and Brinkman (2002) argue that leaders shape and reinforce an ethical or unethical organizational climate by what they pay attention to, how they react to crises, how they behave, how they allocate rewards, and how they hire and fire individuals while discussing unethical behaviour in organizations, as a result of (interacting) disputable leadership and ethical climate.

While discussing the influence of leaders on followers, Gini (1996) commented that the principle of the 'witness of another', or what we now refer to as 'patterning' 'role modelling', or 'mentoring', is predicated in a four-step process, three of which are: (*a*) as communal creatures, we learn to conduct ourselves primarily through the actions of significant others; (*b*) when the behaviour of others is repeated often enough and proves to be peer-group positive, we emulate these actions; (*c*) if and when our actions are in turn reinforced by others, they become acquired characteristics, or behavioural habits. The fourth and final step in the process must include reflection, evaluation, choice, and conscious intent on the part of the actor, because ethics is always 'an inside-out proposition', involving free will.

While exploring the influence of group context on the ethical predisposition of group members, Schminke and Wells (1999) concluded that groups exert a powerful influence on individuals' ethical frameworks, and that the patterns of these influences differ depending on the type of ethical framework involved. Individuals' *ethical* utilitarianism was affected by both leadership style and group cohesiveness. Ethical formalism was most affected by the leadership style in the group.

In a study conducted by Jose and Thibodeaux (1999), the managers perceived implicit forms of institutionalizing ethics (for example, leadership, corporate culture, top management support) to be more effective than the explicit forms of institutionalizing ethics (for example, ethics ombudspeople, ethics committees, ethics newsletters).

Petrick and Quinn (2001) propound holding contemporary business leaders accountable for enhancing the intangible strategic asset of integrity capacity in organizations. After deframing integrity capacity and framing it as part of a strategic resource model of sustainable global competitive advantage, the stakeholder costs of integrity capacity neglect are delineated. To address this neglect issue, the authors focus on the cultivation of judgement integrity to handle behavioural, moral and hypothesized economic complexities as key dimensions of integrity capacity.

Gullillen and Gonzatez (2001), in their paper on ethical dimensions of managerial leadership in Total Quality Management (TQM), suggested that committed managers may lead the process of quality, by exclusively using their formal authority; those who are leaders generate a kind of influence that goes further than that. Only by considering the ethical dimension of leadership, together with technical and psychoemotive ones, it is possible to explain more accurately interpersonal influences beyond the scope of power.

In his paper 'How Virtue Fits Within Business *Ethics*', Whetstone (2001) proposes that managers add an attention to virtues and vices of human character as a full complement to moral reasoning according to a deontological focus on obligations to act and a teleological focus on consequences (a balanced tripartite approach). He further suggests that an interactive tripartite approach is superior for meeting the complex requirements of an applied ethic. To illustrate how deficiencies of a 'strong' virtue ethics formulation can be overcome by a balanced tripartite approach, he compares normative leadership paradigms (each based on a combination of virtue, deontology, or consequentialist perspectives) and the dangers inherent in each, and emerges with a preferred paradigm—servant leadership, grounded in a tripartite ethics.

ORGANIZATIONAL CULTURE AND LEADERSHIP

Singh (1990) in his paper on organizational culture and leadership fit, commented that a fit between leadership and organizational culture is essential for the overall organizational performance and career success of managers. A manager has two-fold responsibilities in this regard. First, he/she should adapt to the existing organizational culture. Second, he/she should also go beyond it if it is a construct for organizational effectiveness. Thus, a leader's role in relation to organizational culture is paradoxical. He/she lives with organizational culture and yet is sometimes expected to transcend it. A judicious mix of these two is conducive to organizational effectiveness. Singh (ibid.) further adds that although leaders at the organizational apex play a pivotal role in creating and sustaining an organizational culture, senior and middle-level managers are expected to shape their behaviour in accordance with prevalent organizational *Values*, norms, beliefs and traditions. Dimensions of leadership behaviour will vary from one organizational culture to another.

Schein (1985) notes that top managers attempt to communicate their organizational *Values* to employees to shape behaviour and lead the firm. The ethical orientation of the manager, in terms of traits and behaviours, is a key factor in promoting ethical behaviour in an organization (Carlson and Perrewe, 1995; Posner and Schmidt, 1992), and to creating an ethical organizational culture (Trevino, 1986; Trevino, 1990).

Selznik (1957) argued that the real task of leadership is to create a social structure of shared *Values*. After this structure has been established, the organization attempts to maintain the underlying *Values* as the environmental context changes.

The relationship between leadership and *Values* has long been studied in management literature (Barnard, 1938, Selznick, 1957). More recent literature on organizational culture has observed the guiding and directing purposes of *Values* in the functioning of organizations (Enz, 1988; Sathe, 1983; Schein, 1985).

Laszlo and Nash (2001) also suggested a five-step process to ethical leadership development. This process focuses on the timing and levels of organization involved. The sequence can vary depending on a company's starting point, but in general takes the following order:

1. Discovery: inquiry and dialogue on what ethical leadership means for each company are initially held on two levels—middle-level management, and senior leadership. An internal assessment of the sustainability of current business activities identifies areas that forward both shareholder value and social responsibility. New distinctions in business ethics are introduced.

2. Strategy: provides a framework and the tools for developing a corporate intention that integrates ethical leadership into business objectives. People rethink and redesign the activities that deliver value to customers, within the context of sustainability, profit and growth.

3. Action: requires incubation projects and business-altering 'pilots' that demonstrate the company's strategic intention and make it possible to accomplish the key objectives of SFEL with speed and efficiency. It integrates the specific breakthroughs generated from combining ethical inquiry and profitability targets into the current fiscal year's priorities.

4. Change Competency: develops cultural and organizational capabilities for change. A structure of support is put in place so that people are aligned on the company's purpose. In their day-to-day work, they perpetuate value-added practices for sustainability consistent with increased shareholder value.

5. Recognition: is in the form of a 'Certificate of Ethical Leadership', awarded by the Club of Budapest and backed by its world-renowned members. It is provided to companies interested in a high-profile recognition for their declared commitment to the New Ethics. It requires companies to take a stand for ethical leadership by declaring their intention to the market-place, and it requires measurable or observable achievements over a twelve-month period.

INDIVIDUAL AND ETHICAL LEADERSHIP

Being an ethical person is the substantive basis of ethical leadership. However, in order to develop a reputation for ethical leadership, the leader's challenge is conveying that substance to others. Being viewed as an ethical person means that people think of you as having certain traits, engaging in certain kinds of behaviours, and making decisions based upon ethical principles. Traits are stable personal characteristics, meaning that individuals behave in fairly predictable ways across time and situations, and observers come to describe the individual in those terms.

Personal morality is associated with ethical leadership. 'You can not be an ethical leader if your personal morality is in question. ... To be a leader... what you do privately reflects on that organization. Secondly, to be a leader you have a greater standard, a greater responsibility than the average person would have to live up to' (Trevino, et al., 2000).

To summarize, the 'moral person' pillar of ethical leadership represents the substance of ethical leadership. It is an important prerequisite to developing a reputation for ethical leadership because leaders become associated with their traits, behaviours, and decisions, as long as others know about them. With the moral person pillar in place, you should have a reputation for being an ethical person. You can think of this as the ethical part of the term 'ethical leadership'. Having a reputation for being a moral person tells employees what you are likely to do—a good start, but it does not necessarily tell them what they should do. That requires moral managing—taking the ethics message to the rest of the organization. To develop a reputation for ethical leadership with employees, leaders must make ethics and *Values* a salient aspect of their leadership agenda, so that the message reaches more distant employees. To do this, they must be moral managers as well as moral persons. If people do not hear about ethics and *Values* from the top, it is not clear to employees that ethics and *Values* are important.

Tom Peters and Bob Waterman (1982) asserted that the real role of leadership is to manage the *Values* of an organization. All leadership is value-laden, and all leadership, whether good or bad, is moral leadership at the descriptive, if not the normative level. To put it more accurately, all leadership is ideologically driven or motivated by a certain religious perspective, which upon analysis and judgment may or may not prove to be morally acceptable in the colloquial sense. All leaders have an agenda, a series of beliefs, proposals, *Values*, ideas, and issues that they wish to 'put on the table'. In fact, as Burns (1979) has suggested, leadership only asserts itself, and followers only become evident, when there is something at stake—ideas to be clarified, issues to be determined, *Values* to be adjudicated.

How do we judge the ethics of a leader? Clearly, we cannot expect every decision and action of a leader to be perfect. As Gardner (1990) has pointed out, particular consequences are never a reliable assessment of leadership. The quality and worth of leadership can only be measured in terms of what a leader intends, *Values*, believes in, or stands for—in other words, character. In *Character: America's Search for Leadership*, Sheehy (1990) argues, that character is the most crucial and most elusive element of leadership. The root of the word 'character' comes from the Greek word for engraving. As applied to human beings, it refers to the enduring marks or etched-in factors in our personality, which include our inborn talents as well as the learned and acquired traits imposed upon us by life and experience. These engravings define us, set us apart, and motivate behaviour.

With regard to leadership, says Sheehy (ibid.), character is fundamental and prophetic. The 'issues [of leadership] are today and will change in time. Character is what was yesterday and will be tomorrow'. Character establishes both our day-to-day demeanour and our destiny. Therefore, it is not only useful but essential to examine the character of those who desire to lead us.

Hood (2003) analyzed the relationship between CEO *Values*, leadership style and ethical practices in organizations. There were four categories of *Values* based on Rokeach's (1973) typology, including personal, social, competency-based and morality-based *Values* that were included in the study. The results indicated that all four types of *Values* were positively and significantly related to transformational leadership, with transactional leadership positively related to morality-based and personal *Values*, and laissez-faire leadership negatively related to competency-based *Values*. When the size of company and *Values* are controlled, transformational leadership explains a significant amount of change in the formal statement of *ethics*, and transactional leadership explains a significant amount of change in diversity training.

There are individual differences in adopting a specific style of leadership. It is interesting to note that there are as many leadership styles as there are authors writing about leadership.

McBer and Company (1980) identified six managerial styles, viz., coercive, authoritative, affiliatives, democratic, pace setting and coaching. Individuals adopting the coercive style dictate the rules, control their subordinates and motivate them by threats and discipline. The individuals who adopt the authoritative style remain firm and fair in giving directions to subordinates. Persuasion and performance feedbacks are used for motivation. The affiliative leader tries to create harmony and build strong emotional bonds, gives people freedom to innovate, and positive feedback. Individuals who follow the democratic style allow their subordinates to participate in the decision-making and problem-solving process. The pace style necessitates managers to be working for themselves. The main concern of managers who follow the coaching style is the development of their subordinates by providing more opportunities for professional development.

Analyzing the various approaches to leadership style, Biswas (1994) grouped all the leadership styles into two broad categories: (a) the negative style or the negative approach to leadership; and (b) the positive style or the positive approach to leadership. The negative approach to leadership included autocratic, bureaucratic, laissez-faire and manipulative styles. The positive approach to leadership included expressive leadership, the conserving benevolent style and the participative style of leadership. The four types of leadership styles proposed by Singh (1990) were paternalistic leadership, nurtrant-task and participative leadership, pioneering and innovative leadership, egalitarian and entrepreneurial leadership.

Hitt (1990) conceptualized leadership as conduct fundamentally anchored in ethical attitudes and choices about ways to use one's power and influence over others. Recent findings (Girodo, 1998) indicate that transformational leaders following a developmental view concerning interpersonal ethics. Thus, although *Values* are the foundation upon which the transformational leader operates, transformational leader behaviours go beyond a *Values* basis. The transformational leader is said to exhibit inspirational leadership that includes individual consideration, intellectual stimulation, and charisma (Bass, 1985; Bass and Avolio, 1990). Thus, the transformational leader will take actions that enhance the well-being of the organization and its members, regardless of his or her foundational *Values*.

The ethical nature of transformational leadership has been fiercely debated. This debate is demonstrated in the range of descriptors that have been used to label transformational leaders, including narcissistic, manipulative, and self-centred, but also ethical, just and effective. In a sample of 1,354 managers a moderate to strong positive relationship was found between perceived integrity and the demonstration of transformational leadership behaviours. A similar relationship was found between perceived integrity and developmental exchange leadership. Perceived integrity was also found to correlate positively with leader and organizational effectiveness measures (Parry and Proctor-Thomson, 2002).

The quality of our ethical choices cannot be measured solely in terms of achievements. Ultimately and ethically, intention, commitment and concerted effort are as important as outcome: What/why did leader/followers try to do? How did they try to do it?

The brief review of literature highlights the importance of ethical leadership in an organization and the significance of individual differences towards cultivating and adopting the ethical culture in an organization. However, a new dimension to the issue of ethical leadership is to be treated as the outcome variable, i.e., leadership style as the outcome of the individual's ethical ideology. The relationship between the individual ethical ideology and its influence on the leadership style is an unexplored one. The present research tries to explore this new field and set a few indicators to guide future research in this direction. The findings might have implications for the development of the HR systems of organizations.

ETHICAL FRAMEWORKS DECISION MAKING AND LEADERSHIP STYLE

As already discussed in the previous section of this chapter, leadership has been an important area of concern for philosophers and writers. Though the studies related to leadership and its relationship with different individual and organizational variables are unaccountable, the field of individual ethical ideology and its influence on leadership styles seem to be unexplored. The present research is the beginning of work in this direction. The influence of individual ethical frameworks is studied on leadership style.

A correlation has been found between the ethical frameworks and the leadership styles. The details of the leadership style used in this study (Chapter 2) and the ethical frameworks (Chapter 3) have already been previously discussed. The results of the correlation test are given in Table 7.1.

Table 7.1
Correlation between Individual Ethical Frameworks and Leadership Style

	Religious Framework	Pragmatic Framework
Nurturant task	0.146*	−0.0360
Participative	−0.0568	0.2916**
Authoritative	0.1899**	−0.0012

Note: $N = 300$ * $P < 0.05$ ** $P < 0.01$.

It is evident from Table 7.1, that all the three leadership styles included in the study had significant correlations with one or the other individual ethical framework. Interestingly, the nurturant task leadership style had a positive and significant relationship with the religious ethical framework. In the present context, a nurturant task leader is one who is nurturant to those subordinates who work hard and sincerely. Hence, the positive significant relationship between nurturant task leadership and the religious ethical framework implies that individuals having a nurturant task leadership style would also make more frequent use of the religious framework of ethics. This could be due to the fact that people who have a high religious conviction are also expected to trust others.

In the case of participative leadership, a highly significant and positive relationship was found to exist with the pragmatic ethical framework. In the present context, a participative leader is characterized by three features: (a) he/she believes that all group members have resources which are important and can be utilized by facilitating frank discussions and joint decisions; (b) he/she creates a condition in which group members maintain an ego-supportive (rather than an ego-deflative) relationship; and (c) he/she sets high performance standards. The present positive relationship between pragmatic ethical framework and participative leadership style is in accordance to the logical expectation. The acknowledgment of the potential of others and the creation of an work environment where they can make positive contributions based on this factor are qualities of a pragmatic team manager.

Another interesting relationship which is positive and highly significant was between the authoritative leadership style and the religious ethical framework. This relationship requires deeper probing. It appears that individuals with high religious convictions believe in the idea of one supreme power, an ideology that is manifested in their practising authoritative style of leadership. However, seeing the limitation of the study, these results can be taken only as indicators. The generalization of the results require extensive research on a significantly larger sample.

The overall conclusion of the results of the relationship between leadership styles and individual ethical frameworks could be that individuals who are inclined to follow the religious framework use more of nurturant task and authoritative leadership styles, and that participative leadership is followed by those who use the pragmatic framework of ethical decision making more frequently.

The relationship between ethical decision-making behaviour and leadership styles is also explored under the present study. The results are depicted in Table A. 34 (Annexure I). The relationship was found to be significant only in one out of all the cases, i.e., Vignette 3 ('padding up the expense bill') and nurturant task leadership. In this situation, people who scored high on the nurturant task style of leadership made ethical decisions (scored low on the scale meaning decisions in the *Value* direction or ethical decision). The individuals who were inclined towards the nurturant task leadership style were those who believed in the welfare and development of their subordinates in a positive way. Therefore, such people would never appreciate ignorance of such activities such as inflating expense bills by any of their subordinates. According to them the relaxation of the rules would only set a wrong precedence.

It needs to be mentioned here that though only one relationship was statistically significant, the directions of other relationships indicate that participative leaders make more *Values* response (in four out of five situations). However, authoritarian leaders make more *Compromise* responses (in all five situations). We would like to add a caveat that these results are only indicative and need to be tested in subsequent studies.

CHAPTER OVERVIEW

An organization's leaders are a major determinant of its success or failure. Therefore, the relevance and centrality of leadership in organizations has been widely emphasized and rightly so. Though the importance of leadership is well-established, at the same time, the complexity of leadership influence cannot be denied. The task of the leaders in organizations has never been more demanding than it is at present. In addition to the internal stakeholders, they are also accountable to the public on the issues of social responsibility of the organization. An increasing importance has been placed on ethical and socially responsible attitudes towards business. Central issues of organizational effectiveness and organizational efficiency, with directors thinking in terms of goal achievement for their respective organizations, have now been augmented by an awareness of issues in business ethics, and a requirement for members of the corporate governing bodies to behave in more socially responsible ways (Minkes, et al., 1999). The ethics of leadership—whether they are good or bad, positive or negative—affect the ethos of the workplace and thereby help to form the ethical choices and decisions of the workers at the workplace. Leaders help to set the tone, develop the vision, and shape the behaviour of all those involved in organizational life.

Behavioural scientists have proposed several approaches to study leadership. The earliest of them all is the trait approach. The approach used personality characteristics or traits as the differentiating factor between the leaders and the nonleaders. Integrity and ethical/moral orientation of the leader were considered to be one of the major components of the traits of an effective leader. Behavioural approaches suggested that leadership behaviour may involve directing the activities of the group (Hemphill, 1949), or making the followers work towards a common goal. According to the nurturant task leadership, an effective leader will be required to incorporate the relevant meta *Values* of the system while designing his action strategies for leading his group.

Burns (1978) proposed that the leadership process is either transactional or transformational. Transactional leadership is based on bureaucratic authority and legitimate power in the organization. Transactional leaders emphasize task assignments, work standards, and employee compliance. Ethical leadership is the demonstration of normatively appropriate conduct through personal actions and interpersonal relationships, and promotion of such conduct among followers through two-way communication, reinforcement, and decision-making processes (Treviño, Brown and Pincus-Hartman, 2003).

Singh (1990) in his paper on organizational culture and leadership fit commented that a fit between leadership and organizational culture is essential for the overall organizational performance and career success of managers. A manager has two-fold responsibilities in this regard. First, he/she should adapt to the organizational existing culture. Second, he/she should also go beyond it if it is a construct for organizational effectiveness. Being an ethical person is the substantive basis of ethical leadership.

The relationship between leadership styles and individual ethical frameworks was studied through a small empirical study that indicated individuals who were more inclined to follow the religious framework made greater use of nurturant tasks. The authoritative and participative leadership styles were followed by those who use the pragmatic framework of ethical decision making more frequently.

It was also observed that more ethical decisions would be taken by individuals who practiced the participative style of decision making. These individuals were found to be using the pragmatic style of leadership.

8

Role of the Organizational Context in Ethical Conduct

Individuals develop a network of ethical norms and principles through the process of socialization (Kohlberg, 1981), which constitutes their ethical philosophy and affects their decision making in situations involving an ethical component. There is little doubt that individual attributes relate to moral reasoning and ethical conduct, but it has been argued by researchers that they may not be the only factors involved (Bommer, et al., 1987; Trevino, 1986). This approach asserts that the situational aspects such as the organization's reward system, peer influence, the influence of superiors and organizational norms (Trevino and Youngblood, 1990), philosophy of the top management (Arlow and Ulrich, 1980), managerial behaviour (Nielsen, 1988), the firm's reinforcement system (Hegarty and Sims, 1979), the nature of the issues involved (Bhal, 2000) and job dimensions (Trevino, 1986), have a demonstrable effect on the ethical decision-making behaviour of the individuals. The environment in which the organization exists has shown to be an important determinant of ethical behaviour.

Organizational Culture and Ethics

Corporate culture is a construct with multiple facets. In describing corporate culture, for example, Homans (1950) stressed the norms that evoke in work groups, Goffman (1959) wrote of the observed behavioural irregularities in people's interactions, Van Maanen (1976) focused on the rules for getting along in an organization, and Ouchi (1981) emphasized on the philosophy that influences organizational policy.

To date, no single, universally accepted definition exists; however, the term organizational culture generally is accepted as referring to the shared meanings, beliefs, and understanding held by a particular group or organization about its problems, practices, and goals (Reichers and Schneider, 1990).

According to Schein (1985: 9), the essence of culture is the basic assumptions and beliefs that are 'invented, discovered, or developed' by all members of a group as it copes with its problems of 'external adoption and internal integration' and which are 'taught to new members as a correct way to perceive, think and feel in relation to those problems'.

Morgan (1986) contends that the organizational culture evolves from the social practices of the members of the organization and are, therefore, socially created realities that exist in the heads and minds of the organizational members, as well as in the formal rules, policies, and procedure of organizational structures. According to Morgan (ibid.), culture is an ongoing process of reality construction, providing a pattern of understanding that helps members of organizations to interpret events and to give meaning to their working worlds. Thus, culture is an evolutionary and dynamic process that incorporates changing *Values*, beliefs, and underlying assumptions regarding: the nature of relationship between the organization and the environment, the nature of reality and truth, the nature of human nature, the nature of human activity, and the nature of human relationship.

The above are core and fundamental assumptions about core and global realities that result in *cultural predispositions* that subsequently derive the more 'superficial' cultural manifestations, such as overt behaviour, norms and espoused *Values*.

Schein (1985) believes that organizational cultures are initially created by founders of organizations and are subsequently maintained by the founders' chosen leaders. Founders form organizations based on personal beliefs about how to interact with the environment and about the natures of reality, people, activities, and relationships. They make presumptions about what should and should not be, what works or what does not, and what constitutes appropriate or inappropriate organizational activity. Founders' goals, assumptions, and visions of reality come to be shared by others in their organizations, particularly the leaders.

Over time, shared realities evolve into consensually validated organizational culture that becomes the 'correct' way of solving organizational problems related to survival and adaptation to the external environment, and to integration of the internal processes required to ensure survival and adaptation.

Thus, organizational culture becomes the normative *glue* that structures the milieu and makes it possible for people to derive meaning from their work, to work comfortably with others, and to focus on key organizational tasks (Morgan, 1986).

It is believed that 'dissimilar cultures socialize their young differently according to what is acceptable behaviour' (Lysonski and Gaidis, 1991:142) and it frequently seems to be taken for granted that ethical practices vary substantially from culture to culture. International business and marketing textbooks... often cite the impact of culture on beliefs and behaviour' (Abratt, et al., 1992:30). Prasad and Rao (1982) state that there are ethical norms which are shared by virtually all cultures, but that adherence to these norms varies widely from group to group.

Bartels (1967) was one of the first to note the importance of the role of culture in ethical decision making, identifying cultural factors such as *Values* and customs, religion, law, respect for individuality, national identity and loyalty (or patriotism), and right of property as influencing ethics. In their general theory of marketing ethics, Hunt and Vitell (1986, 1992) incorporated cultural norms as one of the constructs that affect one's perceptions in ethical situations.

The influence of cultural and group norms/*Values* on individual behaviour was also noted by Ferrell and Gresham (1985) in their contingency framework for understanding ethical decision making within a business context.

There are many others who argue that ethical behaviour stems from an ethical corporate culture (Fisse and Braithwite, 1983; Murphy, 1989; Reidenbach and Robin, 1991; Sims, 1992). Organizations often produce a corporate mentality, which encourages people to behave in ways that are not necessarily consistent with individual or societal norms. The more ethical the culture of an organization, the more ethical will be an individual's decision-making behaviour (Ford and Richardson, 1994; Sinclair, 1993).

However, individuals do not operate in a vacuum. Individuals are influenced by organizations and their common goals and beliefs. Corporations construct cultures that can exercise good or bad influences depending on their goals, policies, structures and strategies (Brown, 1987). Sims (1992) recognizes that organizational culture has

significant influence on establishing ethical behaviour in an organization, and enumerates normative recommendations for creating a culture that supports individual ethical behaviour.

There are many cross-cultural studies establishing the influence of
culture on behaviour, for example, Jackson and Artola (1997) conducted a cross-cultural empirical study to examine the ethical beliefs
and behaviours among French, US, Israeli and German managers.
Comparisons were made between what managers say they believe,
and what they do, between managers and their peers' attitudes and
behaviours, and between perceived top management attitudes and the
existence of company policy. In the latter, significant differences were
found by national ownership of the company, rather than the country
in which it is situated. Significant differences were also found, for
both individual managers by nationality, and for companies by nationality of parents, in the area of 'organizational loyalty', indicating
the influence of culture on a manager's behaviour.

Honeycutt et al. (1995) carried out a cross-cultural comparison of
automotive salespeople in the US and Taiwan, to examine business
ethics and job-related constructs (job satisfaction, customer orientation, ethics and ethical training). The relationships of these variables
to sales person's performance were also investigated. Customer orientation in both countries was influenced by ethics training. The researchers suggested that managers should evaluate current ethics training
programmes to ensure that correct ethical behaviour is taught and
rewarded.

On the contrary, Abratt et al. (1992), Izraeli (1988), Lee (1981),
Lysonski and Gaidis (1991), and Tsalikis and Nwachukwu (1988), all
found little variation in ethical beliefs from culture to culture. These
studies involved respondents from a number of different countries,
including: the US, New Zealand, Denmark, Greece, Israel, Australia
and South Africa.

The perception of the organizational culture by its employees constitutes the organizational climate. Organizational climate is reflected
in the way an organization works and is developed by the organizational processes.

Pareek (1989) observes that the organizational climate is created
by the interaction of an organization's 'structures, systems, cultures,
leader behaviour and psychological needs' (p.161). From a review of
studies by Likert (1967), Litwin and Stringer (1968), and others, Pareek
(1989) identified the following twelve dimensions of organizational

climate: *orientation:* members' principal concern (control, excellence, and so on); *interpersonal relationship:* such as cliques or dependency; *supervision:* supervisors' influence on employee motivation; *problem management:* how the organization views and solves problems; *management of mistakes:* leaders' attitudes towards subordinates' errors; *conflict management:* processes used to resolve conflicts; *communication:* prevalent styles and characteristics of communication; *decision making:* how decisions are made and by whom; how the decision-making process affects relationship; *trust:* who trusts whom for what; *management of rewards:* what behaviours are reinforced; *risk taking:* the organization's way of handling risky situations; and *innovation and change:* who is responsible for instigating change, by what methods, and to what effect.

Victor and Cullen (1987, 1988) have addressed the issue of managing ethics in organizations through the concept of 'ethical climate'. An *ethical climate* refers to the stable, psychologically meaningful perception members of organizations hold concerning ethical procedures and policies existing in their organizations and organizational sub units. Ethical climate is important because it is believed that varying dimensions of ethical climate may be associated with very different types of ethical behaviour (Cullen, et al., 1989; Wimbush and Shepard, 1994).

Chen et al., (1997), while investigating the issue of reinforcing ethical decision making through corporate culture, in terms of how Total Quality (TQ) techniques can facilitate the development of a cooperative culture that promotes and encourage ethical behaviour throughout an organization, emphasized that if an individual is 'involved' in an ethical misconduct, this is a reflection on the inadequacy of the institution as well. According to them, TQ techniques provide a cohesive framework and can create a corporate culture that promotes and encourages ethical behaviour.

A study by Wimbush, et al. (1997) supported the relationship between ethical climate and behaviour. However, the findings also emphasized the importance of examining climate at the appropriate level. Since ethical climate is not always found at the level where they are believed to exist, managers should identify where climates are within their organizations. Knowing the climate of various sub-groups may enable managers to take appropriate measures to curb unethical or counterproductive behaviour, which may stem from the climate.

Deshpande (1996) conducted a study to examine the ethical climate and the link between success and ethical behaviour of managers of large non-profit organizations. They investigated the influence of different dimensions of ethical climate on perceived ethical practices of successful managers. Those who believed that their organization had a 'caring' climate perceived a strong positive link between success and ethical behaviour. Those who believed that their organization had an 'instrumental' climate perceived a strong negative link between success and ethical behaviour.

Sims and Keon (1997) studied ethical work climate as a factor in the development of person-organization fit. The relationship between an individual's stage of moral development (Kohlberg, 1969) stages of moral development, and his or her perceived ethical work environment was examined using a sample of working students. The results indicated that a match between individual preferences and their present position proved most satisfying. Subjects expressing a match between their preference for an ethical work climate and their present ethical work climate indicated that they were less likely to leave their positions.

A retrospection of the above literature review on the topic suggested that the organizational culture and climate are important variables, which might influence the individual ethical decision making. The contention that organizational culture influences ethical decision making is not disputable, however, the extent to which it influences and the ways in which it influences ethical decision making is a topic for debate and investigation. In the Indian context, public and private organizations have provided examples of cultural divides. Thus, they provide good examples of cultural/contextual variations.

ETHICAL CULTURE IN PUBLIC AND PRIVATE SECTOR ORGANIZATIONS

A major factor that distinguishes the public and the private sector is the nature of the market, which has been studied by ethicists as an important variable. Typically, researchers have focused on the issues of 'planned economy' vs 'free markets'. The debate has largely focused on the societal or public welfare as an outcome. Lodge (1990), for example, has identified 'individualistic' and 'communitarian' ideologies, wherein the former includes elements of government control and the latter places emphasis on free markets. Lodge (ibid.) argues in favour of more communitarian mechanisms for the US, especially in the light of Japan emerging as an economic power. One of the prime defenses in favour of unregulated free markets is based on the utilitarian argument that such markets produce greater benefits as compared to any other system. Adam Smith (1723–1790), the originator of this argument, stresses on the selfish motive of the people and rests his tenets on this basic human nature. In one of his most famous quotes, he asserts that, 'It is not from the benevolence of the butcher, the baker and the brewer that we expect our dinner but from their regard for their own self-interest'. (Smith, 1776:14). He further adds that when individuals or organizations are left free, the invisible hand of the market results in 'public welfare'. As he states, 'By pursuing his own interest he frequently promotes that of society more effectively than when he really intends to promote it' (ibid.: 423). Thus, the nature of the market in which the business is done seems to be a strong predictor of ethical activity. Though Adam Smith (ibid.) and others (for example, Hosmer, 1987) believe that by focusing on their individual selfish interests businesses would act morally under the control of the market, there are many who feel that the market and the competitiveness itself may lead to unethical practices (Chakraborty, 1991; Lunati, 1996; Mckenna, 1996).

Public and private sector organizations provide a good case study to test for this assertion (Bhal and Sharma, 2000a). In India, public and private sector organizations present a contrast not only in terms of their internal dynamics but also in terms of the environment (market) in which they exist. Public enterprise in India confines itself to central/state government industrial and commercial enterprise, organized as an autonomous corporation or a company. The public sector in India has emerged not as a result of nationalization of private industries but by taking over the responsibilities of industries of national importance by the state. Many public sector organizations are engaged in heavy investment and high-risk sectors, as well as the promotion of public welfare by entering in areas where a countervailing force is needed to check the exploitation of consumers through price and quality manoeuvres by private entrepreneurs. For this reason, the goals and ethos of the public sector are qualitatively different from those of the private sector.

In India, the twin primary objectives of public enterprises are the augmentation of production and the mobilization of resources for further economic development. The public sector has thus become an essential feature and dynamic instrument for achieving socialism. The socialistic pattern of society has been accepted as a national goal which promises an equitable standard of living for the vast majority in order to whole heartedly serve the cause of economic progress.

Public and private sector organizations differ from one another on various aspects, such as their objectives, leadership, accountability, structure and functions.

Prakash (1987:272) stated, that unlike private enterprise, public enterprises are required to fulfill a host of objectives, including political, economic, and social objectives, which are often conflicting in nature. Therefore, the very objective for the existence of private and public sector enterprises differ from each other. Other structural and functional differences also exist between public sector and private sector enterprises. These differences also amount to differences in the culture and climate of the two types of organizations (Bhal, 1998) and hence, its influence on the ethical ideology of the organization as well as the individuals working in them.

Sapru and Matta (1987) observed that in private sector undertakings, the management is accountable to the shareholders who are satisfied if they get a decent dividend and bonus shares at regular intervals. In the case of public sector enterprises, the position is, however, quite different. Since they are financed by public money and are established for the benefit of the public at large, accountability of management is all-pervasive and continuous. They (ibid.) were of the opinion that most public enterprises suffer from lack of suitable leadership.

Chatterjee (1979) observed that employees in public sector companies, particularly the top ones, suffer from low levels of motivation, commitment and loyalty. It is common to hear a senior manager of a public sector company criticize his own organization. Given the opportunity in the public sector, executives, particularly at the middle level, prefer to shift to the private sector. Chatterjee (ibid.) also added that the research reveals that by and large people in the public sector do not take pride in their jobs. Sinha (1973) found that executives in the private sector were more satisfied than their counterparts in the public sector.

In the Indian context, employment, especially in the public sector, often implies a life-long career with a single organization. Mobility of personnel is severely limited, except at the very top. Appointments are generally made at the lowest level of officers, supervisors and workers. Higher posts within the three groups are, in most organizations, filled entirely by promotion from within.

The environment in which public enterprises operate is very complicated. Several studies (for example, Maheshwari and Maheshwari, 1985) reveal that the lack of concomitants, such as role and goal confusion and lack of commitment, are the major inhibitors to higher performance of the enterprise. Contrary to expectations, there is no appreciable sense of belongingness amongst public enterprise employees, as found in their counterparts in the private corporate sector.

Maheshwari (1985), while writing his observations about the existing realities in public sector organizations, observed that the appropriate systems for managing large and complex public sector organizations were still lacking. Planning systems were weak, either nonexistent or mechanistic and rudimentary. While long-range planning somehow could be related to national planning, operational planning needed considerable improvement. He further adds that utilization of competence is less than satisfactory and personnel policies and practices fail to convert this competence into managerial effectiveness. Moreover, unplanned and sudden changes at the top, and also delay in filling key positions often cause serious damage to the managerial morale.

A comparison of public and private sector large-scale manufacturing organizations reveals that rigidity of rules is higher in the public sector than in private sector. Organizations in the public sector follow the recruitment and promotion criteria rigidly, whereas in the private sector the discretionary power of the person in authority intervenes. It was also found that the formality in decision making and communications were observed more frequently in organizations belonging to the public sector. The degree of overall bureaucratization was also slightly higher in the public sector (Kaur, 1987).

The process of decision making in the public sector is slightly different from the private sector. The stakes in the results of the private sector are for a limited number, due to ownership differences, whereas in the public sector these stakes are for the nation and its people. A manager in the private sector can take decisions at will. His decisions are generally not questioned by any outside agency. Sometimes, the shareholders in the company's annual general meeting might question the decisions of the management but such happenings are also very rare. In the public sector, however, there are agencies which scrutinize the decisions taken by management from time to time. Further, the decisions in the private sector are taken mostly on economic considerations, with the sole objective of maximizing profits. Decision making in the public sector is not so simple. It is absolutely essential that this process in the public sector is a structured one, i.e., a decision where all alternatives and their pros and cons have been considered and recorded in a logical manner. The decision taken and the reasons for taking such a decision should be clearly mentioned. Arriving at and obtaining administrative approval by justifying the proposals in writing is absolutely necessary in all public sector undertakings. This also results in differences in the *Values* of public and private sector organizations (Bhal, 1998).

Chatterjee (1979) observed that in public sector organizations, over-centralization at the top level results in overworking the senior executives, who do not have ample opportunities for taking initiatives. The public sector depends heavily on bureaucracy. Every small decision is taken at the top level. There is a tendency to direct the decision levels upwards. In such conditions, even the moderate participation of employees at various levels is practically non-existent.

From the above review, it could be concluded that public and private sector organizations differ from one another on various aspects. These differences contribute to differences in the work culture and climate of the two types of organizations, which may influence the ethical ideology of both the organization, as well as the individuals working for these organizations. Most of the work relating to markets and ethics has focused on societal good, with little or no focus on the individual managers within the organization. This book attempts to focus on individuals in public and private sector organizations. Specifically, it aims to compare the nature of decision making (ethical or unethical) by the managers in public and private sector organizations to test for the above- mentioned assertion. The rest of the chapter reports some empirical evidence regarding comparisons of individual responses obtained from public and private sector organizations included in the study. This portion of the chapter is divided into two sections. In the first section, the differences in the ethical decision-making behaviour of the respondents from public and private sector organizations is reported. The second section contains the observation about the differences spotted between public and private sector organizations towards ethical behaviour of their managers through two case studies. This portion also gives details of the methodology adopted during the case studies. The results from the quantitative as well as the qualitative study are also compared to draw the congruence of or the absence of the results and the reasons for the same.

METHODOLOGY

The study was carried out in 10 organizations located in and around Delhi, of which five organizations chosen were from the public sector (government owned) and five were privately managed. A brief description of the organizations follows.

Public Sector Organizations

Public Sector Organization (Pub. Org.)-1: Pub.Org.-1 was established in 1965 to provide engineering and related technical services for the petroleum industry. *Public Sector Organization (Pub. Org.)-2*: Pub. Org.-2 is a large commercial bank in India. *Public Sector Organization (Pub. Org.)-3*. Pub. Org.-3 operates in the sphere of development of water and power resources. *Public Sector Organization (Pub. Org.)-4*: Pub. Org.-4 is a part of the heavy electrical equipment industry in India. *Public Sector Organization (Pub. Org)-5*: Pub. Org.-5 is into power generation.

Private Sector Organizations

Private Organization (Pvt Org.)-1: has specialized in water and waste water treatment for over three decades. *Private Organization (Pvt Org.)-2* manufactures and markets automotive and industrial lubes. *Private Organization (Pvt Org.)-3* is a software organization having its operations all over the world. The products of the company are software, services, and document processing systems. *Private Organization (Pvt Org.)-4* is a cigarette company in India. *Private Organization (Pvt Org.)-5* was incorporated in 1962 and went public in 1973. The company manufactures branded generic pharmaceuticals, bulk activities and intermediates.

PARTICIPANTS

Altogether, there were 319 executives from 10 different organizations who constituted the sample for the study. Care was taken to include participants from different divisions of the organizations, like production, accounts, sales and personnel, as well as from the lower, middle and higher managerial levels. Organization and gender-wise split of the sample can be seen in the Table A.1 (Annexure I). Thus, 190 managers from the public sector and 129 managers from the private sector constituted the sample for the study.

QUESTIONNAIRE

The questionnaire used in the study was scenario- based. Ethical decision making was assessed through five situations, wherein the respondents could either make a *Values* (strongly disagree and disagree) response, or a *Compromise* (strongly agree and agree) response. These two dimensions formed two poles of a *continuum* with *neutral* as the mid point. *Compromise* was defined as the response of an individual to a situation of ethical dilemma, where a decision is taken based upon the need of the situation, rather than what is commonly considered morally correct in the society and would be considered unethical. A *Values* decision was defined as the response to a situation of ethical dilemma, which is socially considered morally correct. Thus, the unethical responses were termed as *Compromise* decisions and the ethical ones were termed as *Values* decisions. The five situations included in the questionnaire were (see Annexure I for the situations):

- New and improved marketing strategy
- Gifts and bribes
- Padding up the expense bills
- Nepotism
- Insider trading

At the end of the each vignette, a decision was taken and the respondents were asked to give their responses on a five-point scale as to what extent they agreed or disagreed with the decision. On the continuum, a higher score referred to a *Compromise* and a lower score to the *Values* dimension of ethical decision making.

RESULTS

With the objective of assessing the nature of decision making in the public and private sector organizations, the responses of the managers in five given situations were analyzed. The responses ranged from 5 = strongly agree (*Compromise*) to 1 = strongly disagree (*Values*). Prior to testing for the significance of the differences, the frequency of the responses are reported to give an indication of the trend.

The first situation concerned 'new and improved marketing strategy'. The situation involved using unethical means for the benefit of the company. The responses of the managers from the two types of organizations are reported in Table 8.1.

It is interesting to note that the responses of the managers from the private sector were more unethical than those from the public sector managers.

Table 8.1
Frequency of Responses: 'New and Improved Marketing Strategy' (Situation 1)

	Response Categories	Private Sector		Public Sector	
		Frequency	Percentages	Frequency	Percentages
Values {	1	45	35.2	65	34
	2	40	31.2	71	37.2
Neutral	3	9	7.0	9	4.7
	4	24	18.8	24	12.6
Compromise {	5	7	5.5	17	8.9
	Total	125	97.7	186	97.4

Note. 1 & 2 = Strongly Disagree & Agree (*Values*); 4 & 5 = Agree & Strongly Agree (*Compromise*)

Situation 2 was concerned with gifts and bribes. Table 8.2 reports the responses from our sample managers. For this situation, there were fewer *Value* responses from the public sector managers than the private sector managers and higher *Compromise* responses from the public sector managers. Gifts and bribes have benefits for the individual as opposed to the first situation.

Table 8.2
Frequency of Responses: 'Gifts and Bribes' (Situation 2)

	Response Categories	Private Sector Org.		Public Sector Org.	
		Frequency	Percentages	Frequency	Percentages
Values {	1	8	6.3	6	3.1
	2	20	15.6	24	12.6
Neutral	3	13	10.2	5	2.6
	4	61	47.7	103	53.9
Compromise {	5	23	18.0	46	24.1
	Total	125	97.7	184	96.3

Situation 3 concerns the practice of inflating the expense bills by the employees. A look at Table 8.3 reveals that there are fewer *Values* responses from the public sector managers than from the private sector managers. Public sector employees made more *Compromise* responses in this situation. This situation again benefits the individual.

Table 8.3
Frequency of Responses: 'Padding up the Expense Bills' (Situation 3)

	Response Categories	Private Sector Org.		Public Sector Org.	
		Frequency	Percentages	Frequency	Percentages
Values {	1	42	32.8	24	12.6
	2	42	32.8	62	32.5
Neutral	3	13	10.2	37	19.4
Compromise {	4	25	19.5	47	24.6
	5	3	2.3	13	6.8
	Total	125	97.7	181	95.8

Situation 4 concerns nepotism, wherein favours are given to one's relatives and friends. The frequency is given in Table 8.4. For this situation, though the *Values* responses were fairly similar for both, i.e., public and private sector managers, there were more *neutral* responses from the private sector managers and relatively more *Compromise* responses from the public sector managers. For this situation in particular, public sector employees were expected to give more *Compromise* responses, however, the percentage of managers giving a *Values* response, was more or less the same for both.

Table 8.4
Frequency of Responses: 'Nepotism' (Situation 4)

	Response Categories	Private Sector Org.		Public Sector Org.	
		Frequency	Percentages	Frequency	Percentages
Values {	1	48	37.5	51	26.7
	2	32	25	67	35.1
Neutral	3	25	19.5	20	10.5
Compromise {	4	15	11.7	32	16.8
	5	4	3.1	11	5.8
	Total	124	96.9	181	94.8

Finally, Situation 5 dealt with insider trading. The frequency of the responses are given in Table 8.5. The maximum number of private sector managers gave a *neutral* response, though more public sector managers gave a *Values* as well as *Compromise* response, as compared to the private sector managers.

Table 8.5
Frequency of Responses: 'Insider Trading' (Situation 5)

Response Categories		Private Sector Org.		Private Sector Org.	
		Frequency	*Percentages*	*Frequency*	*Percentages*
Values	{ 1	19	14.8	22	11.5
	2	15	11.7	41	21.5
Neutral	3	37	28.9	27	14.1
Compromise	{ 4	36	28.1	64	36.1
	5	12	9.4	16	8.4
	Total	119	93	175	91.6

To test the significance of the difference between the public and private sector organizations regarding ethical decision making, t-tests for responses on each of the five scenarios were conducted. Table 8.6 reports the results of the t-test.

Table 8.6
T-test: Difference in Ethical Decision Making in
Public and Private Sector Organizations

Situation	Type of Organization	*N*	Mean	Mean Difference	t
1	Public Sector	186	2.2312	−0.0328	−0.22
	Private Sector	125	2.2640		
2	Public Sector	184	3.8641	0.2961	2.31*
	Private Sector	125	3.5680		
3	Public Sector	183	2.7978	0.5578	4.08**
	Private Sector	125	2.2400		
4	Public Sector	181	2.3646	0.2114	1.50
	Private Sector	124	2.1532		
5	Public Sector	175	3.0914	0.0326	0.22
	Private Sector	119	3.0588		

Note: * $P < 0.05$ ** $P < 0.01$.

The study showed some interesting results. It can be seen that the managers of the public and private sector organizations differ significantly in two out of five situations.

Situation 2 was about 'gifts and bribes'. It was observed that in this situation, public sector employees scored higher towards *Compromise,* i.e., unethical decisions, they felt no inhibition in receiving or giving gifts and bribes. In Situation 3, which was related to 'padding up the expense bills' the public sector employees scored significantly higher on *Compromise* responses. The other situations with no significant differences observed were 'new and improved marketing strategy' (situation 1); 'nepotism' (Situation 2) and 'insider trading' (Situation 5). It was interesting to note that whether the difference between public and private sector respondents were significant or not, in four out of five situations, the public sector respondents scored higher, i.e., towards the *Compromise* dimension of ethical decision making. It was also observed that all four situations were concerned with individual benefits.

The only situation which was concerned with benefits for the organization was Situation 1 ('new and improved marketing strategy'). In this situation, though the difference was not significant, the respondents from the private sector organizations scored higher towards the *Compromise* dimension of ethical decision making. The case studies of a public and private sector organization also supported these results.

ETHICS IN PUBLIC AND PRIVATE SECTOR ORGANIZATIONS: CASE STUDIES

Brigley (1995:222) suggested that the major advantage of a case study lies in its naturalistic interpretation of social action. The most appropriate metaphor for case-study research has been found in the hologram (Lincoln and Guba, 1985). The smallest fragment of a holographic plate contains all the visual 'information' needed to construct the whole image. Laser light, like a significant case study, processes exceptional coherence and ability to illuminate different features of the same phenomenon.

For the purpose of validation of these quantitative perceptual results, it was decided to collect some qualitative data from at least two organizations. The qualitative data could also help in highlighting the manifestation of the organizational ethical decision-making culture on individuals working in these organizations. Keeping the above two objectives in mind, two case studies were carried out.

METHODOLOGY

There were two organizations that were selected for the purpose of case study—one from public sector and the other from the private sector. The following steps were taken to gather qualitative data from the two selected organizations:

1. Some real-life incidents from the past in the organizations were identified by interviewing the top management. These incidents related to three functions, viz., finance, marketing and people management. These were the incidents or cases where organizations had taken a decision.
2. Vignettes were then prepared, based on the cases developed. Respondents were asked what decision the organization would have taken in such a situation and why. There were 20 respondents from Pvt Org.-3, and 18 respondents from Pub. Org.-6, who were included in the sample.
3. A content analysis of the responses yielded the nature of decision making and reasons for making that decision as perceived by the individuals.
4. People's perception of the decision taken was matched with the actual decisions taken to check for the validity of the perceptions.

The case studies included observations of real-life practices, analysis of some records and interviews with key people. Since the objective was to study the ethical components of culture, the symbols, language and heroes of the organization were analyzed keeping in mind the ethical component. Further, certain real-life decisions taken in the organization were analyzed; care was taken to choose such situations that involved ethical dilemmas. For this purpose, five senior executives each from these two organizations were interviewed (with the assumption that their opinion reflected the overall philosophy of the organization). The schedule used for data collection was unstructured. During the interview, the respondents were asked to recall any real incidence within the company where some important decision was taken in areas of that related to marketing, finance or human resource management. Care was taken not to mention that the interest of the researcher was in the matters related to ethical decision making, to avoid any kind of social desirability bias.

OBSERVATIONS

PVT ORG.-3

Background

The company has specialized in water and waste-water treatment for over three decades. It is a pioneer in the field in India, and one of the few in the world with a complete range of water and waste-water technologies, product and services. The company was formed as a subsidy to a UK Company in 1964. It has its business spread all over India, as well as the international market, including Russia, Southeast Asia, Japan, Africa, Egypt, the Middle East, the US and the UK, in addition to neighbouring countries like Bangladesh, Nepal, Mauritius and Sri Lanka.

In India, the company has built a widespread infrastructure of sales offices and production facilities, service companies, dealers, agents and stockists. Globally, the company is represented by an extensive network of overseas offices, agents and stockists.

Incident 1

Mr Lele was an ambitious, well-qualified intelligent engineer who joined this company in 1970 as an engineer trainee. At that time, the company had a turnover of about one billion. Mr Lele's hard work, sincerity and honesty was duly rewarded. In a short period of 12 years, he was appointed general manager (GM) of the company.

At this point of time, the turnover of the company was around three billion. The company had already realized Mr Lele's potential and creditability and he was indirectly selected among a few others to be groomed for future leadership in the company. Mr Lele was also quite certain that he would be selected for the post of deputy managing director (the highest post in the company). Prior to his being appointed GM, Mr Lele's qualities of working in a team were not noticed. There were a few adjustment problems that related to him and his colleagues in the past but these were ignored. However, once he became GM, it became quite clear to the management that Mr Lele had lot of problems working in a team, whereas as an individual worker he was excellent. He did not want to open up with others, specially the subordinates, nor did he want to groom his subordinates in the field. Due to his superior intelligence and expertize, he had a lot of ego problems in discussing issues with his colleagues and subordinates. A series of complaints from both sides started mounting. The management had no choice but to take some suitable action, keeping in mind the company's interests. Therefore, a decision to change Mr Lele's portfolio was taken. He was given only a designing job and the execution was taken away from him. In a way, he was sidelined.

During the same time, Mr Gupta a very close friend of Mr. Lele, as well as his junior, was appointed deputy managing director. Mr Lele found it very hard to adjust to these developments. Since the company had respected Mr Lele's hard and sincere work and did not want to lose him, he was appointed as a vice-president in the company. Mr Lele, however, failed to adjust to the new circumstances of his position and decided to resign and take voluntary retirement. He, however, continued to be associated with the company as a consultant on a part-time assignment basis.

Incident 2

A young man called Sudhir who joined the company was soon identified to have a lot of potential. In the first few months, he performed very well. Since his job also involved handling some export assignments, he frequently travelled. However, the company's internal audit department soon noticed some discrepancies in his expense sheet. The matter was reported to the top management.

Before taking action, the management required evidence in support of the internal audit's report. Therefore, a person was deployed by the company to make inquiries from the hotels where he stayed during his tour. The internal audit report was quickly confirmed. The management then took prompt action and confronted Sudhir with the evidence it had gathered. Sudhir was asked to submit his resignation immediately.

Our interviews with the company's top management revealed that they often faced such situations. Similar action was always taken, irrespective of the performance of the individual involved in the case. In several such incidents, it was found that the guilty person was also handling some important and critical assignment. In those cases, the management waited for the assignment to be complete before disclosing the matter and firing the employee.

Incident 3

In another incidents, an industrial customer wanted to buy a de-mineralizing (DM) plant for water treatment for his company. As the tube well in his factory was not yet installed, the customer took water from the neighbour's factory and had it tested. The customer made the report of the water available to the company. In addition to this company (our focus), there was another company in competition for the order. The competitor was ready to supply the DM plant to the customer. However, Pvt Org.-3 realized, based on the water sample report, that the DM plant was not the solution to the client's water problem, and communicated this finding to the client. The company also advised the client that he should immediately install a tube well in his factory, so that the water sample that was to be treated would be from the same source. The company, based on its experience, also warned the client to expect an even worse analysis report from the water in his factory. The company also supported all its recommendations with other reports from the same area.

The customer followed the company's advice and had the tube well installed and the water analyzed. The company's apprehensions were found to be correct. The customer appreciated the company's approach and finally bought a much more expensive plant from the company for his factory.

It was quite possible that the client would not have agreed to the company's advice and purchased the DM plant from the other company. However, the company was not willing to *Compromise* for the customer's interests.

The company also admits that due to tough competition in the market, they often have to oblige some middlemen for orders to be finalized but they never *Compromise* with the quality of the product required, or the services rendered.

Like most of the other companies in today's economic scenario. Pvt Org.-3 is also facing a resource crunch. Thus, there are several austerity measures taken by the company, to reduce expenditure where possible. Stay during tours is recommended in smaller hotels, telephone bills are checked more carefully, etc. The fact that needs to be highlighted here, is that the initiative to follow these measures is first taken by the top management, so that others down the line follow easily and without question.

Other Incidents

Apart from these austerity measures, the company decided to integrate its operations and cut down costs wherever possible. Therefore, it combined two of its factories. The company had two chemical factories situated around 1 km apart. While one of them had a fully automated plant and very few workers (around 50) to operate the factory, the other had a manual plant that employed around a 100 people. A team studied the functioning of the two factories, and reported that though the two factories produced different chemicals, many of their operations were common to both. The report also said that a lot of the infrastructure could have been the same for both the factories. The result of the cost-benefit analysis showed that if the manually operated plant was replaced with the automated plant, and if both the plants from the two factories were combined, than the company could receive returns on the additional investment within a period of 18 months only. It was also emphasized that this change would substantially reduce the manufacturing cost of the product, which would be of better quality and thereby become more competitive. However, this whole exercise also involved the removal of 40 per cent of its employees. The company decided to go ahead with restructuring exercise. The workers who were removed were given voluntary retirement benefits after mutual discussion and agreement between the two parties.

People's Perception

Based upon the incidences reported above, three vignettes were developed to be included in the questionnaire. After each vignette the respondents were asked to decide as to what their organization would do in such a situation and why. The questionnaire was given to 20 managers in the same organization.

The responses were pooled together, the frequency of responses were calculated and the explanations (reasons) were categorized (based upon the content analysis of the responses).

Vignette 1a

Mr Vittal has been working in your company for the last 25 years. He is a very sincere and honest man, as well as an excellent worker. The company has rewarded his contribution through promotions and other benefits. Mr Gupta who is relatively junior to Mr Vittal but equally efficient, sincere and honest, is also Mr Vittal's competitor for the post of vice president. Mr Vittal, who otherwise works well independently, fails to work effectively together in a team.

Question: Who do you think would be promoted in this situation—Mr Vittal, or Mr Gupta—why?

Table 8.7
Response Categories and Frequency for Vignette 1a

Response Categories	Reasons	Frequency
Mr Vittal. = 0	–	–
Mr Gupta. = 20	• For a high managerial post such as vice president, the quality of a team player is very important.	8
	• To promote a person to such a high level with better managerial skills and leadership qualities is in the interest of the company.	11
	• To promote teamwork and teamworkers has always been the company's policy.	1

Table 8.7 reports the responses to Vignette 1a. All the managers perceived that the company would promote an individual to the vice president's post only when he/she possessed effective managerial skills and leadership qualities. Followed by another response, which stated

that for a person to work at such a high post teamwork was an important quality to have and it had been the company's policy to promote people possessing teamwork skills. The responses to the vignette matched with the actual incidence that occurred in the company.

Sudhir was a young employee who joined the company and was soon identified to have good future potential. In the initial months, he performed well. His job also involved handling export assignments, thus it included frequent travelling and staying in hotels. After some time, the internal audit noticed some discrepancies in his expense sheet. The matter was reported to the top management. When the case was investigated, the management found enough evidence against Sudhir.

Question: What do you think the company would do? Why?

Table 8.8
Response Categories and Frequency for Vignette 2a

Response Categories	Reasons	Frequency
Sudhir would be given a chance to improve. = 1	● The person involved is a good resource to the company, therefore he should be give a chance to improve with proper guidance.	1
Sudhir would be asked to resign. = 19	● Otherwise it would send a wrong message to the other workers.	5
	● Dishonesty in any form is not tolerated in the company.	5
	● If ignored it can lead to the perpetration of greater fraud in the company by the same person as well as by others.	1
	● The company has a strong code of ethics and does not tolerate any kind of irregularity.	8

Table 8.8 depicts the responses to Vignette 2a. A majority of the respondents were clear that any kind of dishonesty is intolerable in their organization. A significant portion of the respondents, while giving their responses expressed their own opinion that any such incidence if ignored may lead to greater fraud being perpetrated in the company by the same person, as well as by others. The guilty individual should be given a chance to improve himself, was the opinion expressed by one of the respondents. In general, the responses to the vignette situation matched with the response of the company in an actual situation cited earlier.

You are the marketing manager in your company. Recently the competition in the market for your product has increased. There is a lot of pressure from the top to achieve targets. You are also trying hard with your team to increase the sales. One of your team members has obtained a large order for the industrial plant, after a great deal of effort. When you study the case in-depth you find the order that has been placed does not serve the customer's requirement. In such a situation, if you go back to the customer and try to rectify the mistake, it is quite possible that you might lose the order.

Question: What would the company do? Why?

Table 8.9 reports the responses to Vignette 3a. The general response to the vignette was that the organization would never cheat the customer. This practice in the long run would turn out to be a disadvantage to the company and an advantage to the competitor. The responses to the vignette also matched with the reaction of the organization to the actual situation cited in the previous section of the case study.

Table 8.9
Response Categories and Frequency for Vignette 3a

Response Categories	Reasons	Frequency
The company would execute the order. =1	● The order would be implemented but only after rectifying the mistake, so that the confidence of the client in the company is further strengthened.	1
Company would clarify the mistake with the customer. =19	● In this competitive world, it is very important for the company to keep its integrity without any *Compromise*.	3
	● Customers are very important for the company. Any such action can result in losing credibility with the client and also giving the competitor an opportunity to take advantage and damage the company's image in the market.	12
	● It is a short-term gain and may result in losing the confidence of the customer forever.	2
	● Rectifying the mistake might gain customer confidence in obtaining future order.	2

The analysis of the quantitative data obtained about the ethical framework of the organization through respondents' individual perceptions about the ethical ideology of the organization revealed two important frameworks to be followed by the organization, i.e., long-term perspective and justice. From the above discussion of the organization's reaction to the real-life situations of ethical dilemma and the responses of the managers to the similar cases later on, also indicated the usage of these frameworks. Hence, the qualitative data obtained supports the results obtained from the quantitative data.

PUB. ORG. 6

Background

Pub. Org.-6 is one of the jewels of the public sector with over 24,000 professionals working for it. It has almost one-fifth of the total power generating capacity of the country in all sectors put together. It is also one of the few public sector companies which is highly profitable. However, the problem that is faces is that it cannot store the power generated. Therefore, it has to supply power despite overdue payments. In addition, the organization is too large to bother about this issue, as there is a huge amount of capital flow and finance generation from various other sources.

General Observations

There is an overall feeling in the organization that the salary structures in the organization are satisfactory. The senior officials also feel that though there is a promotion policy, it is not very transparent. Until a certain level, the promotion is time-bound and on a seniority basis but after that there is stagnation.

Promotions at the higher level are quite manipulative. Lately, a new trend has been observed, that the people at senior levels are inducted from other organizations. The new practice is not really a welcome one as it takes away promotion chances of the senior people within the company.

The organization has its operations spread all over the country. Therefore, transfers of employees occur on a daily basis. However, the company's transfer policy is also not very clear. The policy mentions that transfers are carried out on the basis of requirement. This clause is frequently manipulated. Quite often, there is a case in the company where the supervisors are found to use transfers as punishment or reward to their subordinates or even due to personal reasons.

Being a public sector organization it is fairly bureaucratic. There are many rules and regulations which can be manipulated to suit individual requirements. Many officers reported that the personal appraisal system of the company is also not very transparent. Everything is bounded by rules. There is not enough flexibility. Thus, even while following the rules, you can sometimes get away with wrongdoing also.

There is a general feeling among senior company officials who have seen the organization grow over the years, that as the organization is growing in size there is also a shift in the *Value* system of the new people joining the organization. The feeling of belongingness, which was prevalent earlier, is now missing.

Incident 1

There was a very senior officer who was on very good terms with the chairman of the company. However, due to a misunderstanding, the equation between the two was disturbed. As a result the chairman transferred that officer to some other station and asked him to leave immediately. However, the officer was unable to go because his wife was working and his children were in school. Finally, the officer resigned from the company.

Such cases occur frequently in the company. Often, transfers are used to give benefits to friends and family by sending them to choice postings, and sometimes they are used as punishments.

Incident 2

A branch manager of one of the power plants and his immediate subordinate officer were on good terms with each other. When the branch head was due for transfer, the officer under him kept some of the office belongings with the Head, for his personal use, to oblige him. Soon, it was the officer's turn to be transfered, so he also tried to take some of the office equipment with him but he was caught. He immediately apologized to the head of the project. However, when he reached his new posting, the project head was already aware of this incident and decided not to keep the employee at his branch. The officer was thus transferred again to another area.

Incident 3

In another case, an employee of the company used to drink alcohol even during the day. Due to this habit, he was transferred many times to different project sites. At one of the project sites, he became violent while drunk and tried to beat another employee. The officer who cited this case was the officer-in-charge of the project that time, and had suspended this person. The officer further added that it was also possible to terminate such a person but they had to consider the repercussion to his family. The same officer reported that in another such cases, where the employee was found to possess a false schedule-caste certificate, his services were terminated immediately.

It was discovered that the people in the support departments had less accountability and more advantages. Corruption was thus rampant in the purchase and supply department. The officers admitted that like any other public sector organization, in this one also, people in some departments used malpractices to make extra money. Such things were considered part of the system and ignored, unless large amounts of money were involved.

In an another case at one of the plants, the officer-in-charge of the finance was caught involved in a financial scam amounting to millions of rupees. He was able to manipulate the rules because they were not fool proof. He was suspended from duty and a case was filed against him.

As far as marketing in the organization is concerned, it is responsible for the power supply to the areas falling in its territory. This supply of power is on a payment basis. However, almost all the buyer states and other areas have outstanding payments more than are permitted.

People's Perception

Based upon the incidences reported above, three vignettes were developed to be included in the questionnaire. After each vignette a decision was taken. The questionnaire with these vignettes was given to 20 managers of the same organization. The respondents were asked to give their responses on a five-point scale expressing the chances of the decision being taken in their organization at the end of each vignette. The respondents were also asked to give reasons for their replies. Out of 20, 18 completed questionnaires were returned.

The responses were pooled together, the frequency of responses were calculated and the explanations (reasons) were categorized (based upon the content analysis of the responses).

Vignette 1b

Mr Krishnan and Mr Bhandari were colleagues. Mr Krishnan was a very hard-working and principled man. Other employees in the organization had a great deal of respect for him as a very sincere worker. At the same time, though Mr Bhandari also had a good reputation, he had a casual attitude towards work. Soon a promotion committee was to be set up. Both Krishnan and Bhandari were the candidates chosen for promotion. Bhandari was confident of the appointment because he was related to the general manager, who also happened to be a politically well-connected man.

Question: Who would be promoted in your organization? Why?

Table 8.10 reports the responses to vignette 1b. Vignette one was about nepotism and political interference in the promotion procedures. The majority appeared to agree that such practices existed in the organization. At the same time, some of the respondents expressed their own feelings while giving responses like 'more importance should be given to the job-related qualities of a person rather than then his/her connections'.

Table 8.10
Response Categories and Frequency for Vignette 1b

Response Categories	Reasons	Frequency
Mr Bhandari. = 12	● Political interference is the general practice these days especially in public sector organizations.	12
Any body. = 4	● Anything is possible. It depends upon the character and morality of the GM.	4
Mr Krishnan. = 2	● More importance should be given to the job-related qualities of the person rather than his/her connections.	2

The second response highlights the importance of individual integrity. In general, the responses matched with the response of the organization to a similar real-life situation.

Vignette 2b

Mr Divaker has recently joined the purchase department of your organization. Immediately after joining the post, Divaker was given the assignment of inviting tenders for a very large order of furniture for the recently renovated office. Divaker was directed by his supervisor to issue the tender form to only one company, which he specified. When Divaker questioned his supervisor as to how they would receive three quotations by issuing the tender form only to one company, his supervisor told him that it is the problem of the company who will file the tender. Divaker was also assured of some benefits occurring from the whole deal.

Question: What is the possibility of such thing happening in your company? Why?

Table 8.11
Response Categories and Frequency for Vignette 2b

Response Categories	Reasons	Frequency
Quite possible. = 9	● It is quite possible because people join such posts to earn extra money.	4
	● It is possible but depends upon the situation and the individual involved in the situation.	5
Possibility is very low. = 9	● The purchase committees and the procedures are not so easy to manipulate.	4
	● Rules and procedures do not allow such things to take place.	5

The responses to Vignette 2b are reported in Table 8.11. The responses to Vignette 2b had a variety of answers as most of the manager were not directly involved with the purchase department and did not know about the existing practices there. Therefore, their responses were based upon their own assumptions. At the same time, the single message conveyed by almost all the respondents, was that the rules and procedures as such do not allow such irregularities but depending upon the individual's manipulative skills, it was quite possible. It was a typical example of a bureaucratic set up in the public sector organization.

Vignette 3b

Mr Suresh is well-settled in his job as well as in his family. He has two children who attend a very good school in the town and his wife works with a private firm. Though Suresh's job is transferable, he enjoys a very good relationship with the project head so he is not unduly concerned. Suddenly, the old project head was transferred and a new officer joined in his place. Suresh tried hard to adjust to working with the new project head but found it very difficult. One day, on the issue of assigning shift duties to different officers, Suresh had an argument with his boss. Then, Suresh wanted some free time as his children had exams, but his request was refused. Suresh decided arbitrarily to take the rest of the day off. At that time, since there was also a shortage of staff, his boss became annoyed and transferred Suresh from the project. Suresh was asked to leave the station overnight and report at the new site.

Question: What is the possibility of such an incident occurring in your company? Why?

Table 8.12
Response Categories and Frequency for Vignette 3b

Response Categories	Reasons	Frequency
Very high possibility. = 13	● Once the boss is offended he can use his powers to transfer you.	6
	● Transfers are generally carried out as a punishment or reward to the subordinates.	5
	● Transfer is possible in such circumstances but might not be that urgent.	2
Neutral. = 3	● It is possible to transfer the subordinate but it depends upon the individual.	3
Very low possibility. =2	● One cannot be inconsiderate enough not to take into account others' problems.	2

Table 8.12 indicates the responses to Vignette 3b. The third vignette was about the transfer of an employee for disobeying his seniors. A majority of the respondents agreed with the possibility of such a thing happening in their organization. Once again, the individual character of the senior manager was observed to play an important role in the given situation. Respondents expressed their feelings through the second response.

It was observed that the responses to the three vignettes discussed above matched with the reaction of the organization in the real-life situation cited in the section reporting the actual incidents that occurred, implying the manifestation of the organizational ethical decision-making culture on individuals working in these organizations.

As as far as the match between the qualitative and quantitative data for this particular organization is concerned, the results were not very positive. The quantitative data revealed long-term perspective and justice as two important frameworks practiced by both the organizations. However, the content analysis of the responses of the organization to the real-life situations of ethical dilemmas and the subsequent responses of the managers to similar situations did not support the quantitative data findings. The reasons could be attributed to the assumption of the bureaucratic nature of the organization, where a plethora of rules exist. Following these rules would definitely lead to the ideal situation of justice and long-term perspective. It might also be possible that the quantitative data expresses the perception of the respondents about the rules and regulations meant for the employees, rather than what follows in actual practice. It was also observed that the organization seemed to be inclined to be bound by the rules, indicating a predominant ethical framework. However, this framework was not included in the study and the questionnaire was a structured one. It was found to be one of the limitations of the structured questionnaire.

The decision-making behaviour of the managers in situations of ethical dilemma from the public sector managers indicated more *Compromise* responses (Bhal and Sharma, 2000b, 2002; Sharma and Bhal, 2001). This is ironical because these organizations follow rigid procedures with multiple checks and balances as opposed to private organizations. It implies that for ethical behaviour to occur, rules are not sufficient. The impersonal work environment, which is a characteristic feature of a bureaucratic organization, too makes the individual less responsible for his or her own act. As Jones (1991:376) points out, 'intuitively people care more about other people who are close to them'.

De-linking individuals from work in a certain sense also detaches an individual's sense of responsibility towards the organization. Future studies may not only identify the common practices/systems used in ethical organizations but also look at the underlying dynamics of these practices to provide more useful insights into developing ethical organizations. Thus, it is important to develop appropriate systems and processes, which bureaucratic organizations do very well, and also develop culture, *Values* and norms that support ethical conduct.

As mentioned earlier, the external environment for the two types of organizations was also different. While the private sector has been operating in fairly competitive environments, most of the public sector organizations have operated in a protected environment away from market pressures and demands. Though many would argue against Adam Smith's (1976) contention that the invisible hand of the market allows the ultimate good to emerge as a by-product of selfishness, seems to be true. This by no means implies that the market mechanisms would result in greater ethical behaviour by the firm. All it means is that removing the organization from the market does not lead to ethical or moral behaviour, instead it leads to unethical behaviour at a different level, an assertion that may be tested in subsequent studies.

CHAPTER OVERVIEW

In this chapter, the public and the private sector organizations were compared and differences in the ethical decision-making behaviour were observed in case of two situations ('gifts and bribes' and 'padding up of expense bills'). In both these situations the difference was positively significant and individuals working in public sector organizations were found to score high, i.e., towards *Compromise*. The unethical activities of the public sector managers centred around the giving/taking of bribes and padding up the expense bills. For the purpose of validation of the quantitative data obtained from the survey research, two case studies, one for the public sector organization and the other for the private sector organization, were carried out. Unstructured interviews were also held with the top management of the companies. Care was taken to ensure representation of all the major departments. These managers were asked to report actual incidents where the company had to take some important decisions. Among these incidents, a few that dealt with ethical decision making were selected for the purpose of this study. Based upon the incidents reported by the top managers, questionnaires (for both organizations) were developed. In the questionnaire, three situations of ethical dilemma were given. These situations were similar to the situations reported by the managers. The questionnaire was given to 20 respondents from each of the two organizations. These responses were categorized and analyzed. The responses were matched with the responses obtained from the questionnaire-based research results. There appeared to be a complete match between the quantitative and qualitative data in the private sector organization. However, similar results were not obtained in the case of the public sector organization.

Sekhar (1998) uses the utilitarian approach and appealing to conscience as two possible ways of explaining this kind unethical behaviour, and concluded that it is usually economic logic which is at the heart of such activities.

Maheshwari (1985) observes that the organization structures in the public sector were flabby with too many levels and provided ample scope for diluting accountability. Control systems were petty-minded and inappropriate for the size of these organizations. Controls were not output oriented, and detailed controls tended to be ineffective. The results of our study do provide support to the market-oriented systems as possible controls for unethical behaviour. This nature of control also has implications for the principal-agent relationship as propounded in the Agency theory, which is centred around studying the relationship between two parties where one (principal) delegates work to another party (agent) (Jensen and Meckling, 1976). This relationship in a public sector organization takes a new dimension as the principal is diffused and has no financial stake in the performance of the organization. However, when both the principal and the agent work for the same rewards, chances of self-serving unethical behaviour are few (Eisenhardt, 1989; Jensen and Meckling, 1976). Lack of clear-cut ownership (principal) may mean a diffused sense of responsibility and accountability on the part of employees. Fama (1980) highlighted the role of capital and labour markets as information mechanisms that are used to control the self-serving behaviour of the executives in an organization.

Thus the nature and level of unethical activity varies between public and private sector organizations owing to the differences in the nature of ownership. This difference has implications for the design of control systems in these two types of organizations.

In public sector organizations, individuals are likely to work towards their own ends. In the absence of a clear owner with the objective of value maximization and profit earning, these attempts are likely to be noticed. Hence, in these kind of organizations, individual control systems needs to be built in. Conscious efforts need to be made to develop a culture and system, which reinforce appropriate *Values*. Both primary as well as secondary ways may to be used to signal the importance of ethicality and *Values* (Schien, 1985). Primary means include criteria for promotion and selection mechanisms. Through these systems, the organizations can reward and reinforce appropriate *Values*. Secondary means are the design of structures, systems, and procedures to check for any deviations from the desired ones. Although public sector organizations have these systems, the implementation of and adherence to these systems may be lacking.

In private sector organizations, though the individual activity within the organizations may be controlled, there is a likelihood of the use of unethical practices by the organization to pursue its own interests. Thus, it is likely that the organizations use resources like the environment, people, and the society unethically. This requires the control of the corporate level, and either be external (from outside the organization), or internal (from within the organization). The external control group includes pressure groups (for example, NGOs, consumer interest groups) and the government. The government has been a primary mechanism of external control. Even in the US, where traditionally the government's role has been predominantly that of protection against anti-competitive activity, there are attempts to safeguard the interest of other stakeholders like the consumer, employees, and the society through acts like the Environment Protection Act (EPA) and Occupational Safety and Health Protection Act (OSHA). Thus, the government in India too has to play a proactive role in safeguarding these interests. Further, there are internal mechanisms of control too that organizations employ. They are numerous and vary from the use of corporate social audits, to the employment of a professional code of ethics, to the creation of a corporate social responsibility.

The focus of nature of control against unethical activities in public and private sector organizations may be different owing to the differences in the genesis and manifestation of these activities in both types of organizations.

9

AN INTEGRATED VIEW

The issue of business ethics was never as important as it is today. The globalization of the market place and the revolution in information technology are the two important paradigm shifts of modern times, which offer both tremendous opportunities on one hand and threats on the other, for the business community in general and for managers in these organizations in particular. The tremendous competition resulting from opening up of the economy and the universal access to information and technology demands greater credibility both on the part of the organization, as well as the individual managers to be successful in achieving a competitive edge over others in the market-place. In this context, the issue of ethics in an organization is very relevant. It ranges from day-to-day ethical behaviour of the each employee to organizational compliance with the rules and regulations, as well as expected corporate social responsibility. The focus of the present book has been on the individual managers in business organizations.

There are two important approaches that are generally followed in dealing with the issue of ethics—normative and descriptive. Descriptive ethics explains how things are, whereas the normative or prescriptive theory tells us how things ought to be. The word 'normative' refers to guidelines or norms and is often used interchangeably with the word 'prescriptive'. Normative ethics involves arriving at moral standards that regulate right and wrong conduct. In a sense, it is a search for an ideal litmus test of proper behaviour. Thus, it is an attempt to understand what people should do or whether their current moral behaviour is reasonable. The category of descriptive ethics involves describing how people behave and/or what sort of moral standards they claim to follow. It is not designed to provide guidance to people in making moral decisions, nor is it designed to evaluate the reasonableness of moral norms. Nevertheless, actual work in moral philosophy cannot proceed very far without the knowledge gained from descriptive ethics. It is very important to understand what people claim as their moral norms. Also, how do people actually behave when it comes to moral problems? It provides insight into how individuals perceive ethical situations, and how they act in those situations. Identifying normative moral standards is one thing but how it is used by people is yet another. The understanding gained through following a descriptive enquiry gives us the answers to these questions. This understanding can help us in evolving the person-organization fit through designing of systems and processes most appropriately suited for that particular organization. The investigation approach followed in the book is descriptive in addition to the normative conceptualization.

With a focus on the individual following the descriptive approach, efforts have been made to find out answers to the following questions for the managerial sample:

- What do managers do, i.e., what kind of managerial decisions are made in situations of ethical dilemmas?
- What do the managers believe in, i.e., what are the cognitive frameworks and logics used in making ethical decisions?
- Why do they do it, i.e., what are the different personality types and what are the contexts (situations) that prompt or prevent ethical conduct?

The general understanding of the concept of ethics in the book has been taken as the system of standards for moral judgment. Individual ethical ideology is a result of the cognitive frameworks developed and nurtured during the process of socialization. An individual's moral standards are first absorbed as a child from family, friends, and various societal influences, such as the church, school, television, magazines, music and associations. Later, as the person grows up, experience, learning, and intellectual development may lead the mature person to revise these standards. Some will be discarded and new ones will be adopted to replace them. Group, organizational, and cultural ethics all exist. Each of these attempts to define acceptable behaviours. Together, they influence the personal set of *Values* one adopts to define one's own code of ethics and this code of ethics can exert a major influence on his/her behaviour in organizations. Ethical behaviour at the workplace is the result of interaction between individual ethical ideology and the situational factors.

The theories in ethics occupy an important role in explaining the concept. Ethical theories mainly concern themselves with identifying the basis for judging the ethical content of an act. The earliest understanding of ethical theories in western literature is divided into two fundamental types, teleological and deontological (Murphy and Laczniak, 1981). The two types entail different conclusions about what ought to be done. Teleological theories emphasize the importance of consequences of the actions or practices. According to the teleologists, the consequences of an action or practice determine its moral worth. The most widely studied teleological theory is Utilitarianism, especially in the context of business and public policy. According to utilitarianism, an action or practice is right if it leads to the greatest possible balance of good consequences, or to the least possible balance of bad consequences, for all the people involved.

Deontologism (derived from the Greek word for 'duty') emphasizes that the concept of duty is independent of the concept of good, and the actions are not justified by their consequences. Besides a favourable outcome, there are other factors as well which determine the rightness of the action—for example, the fairness of distribution, a personal promise, a debt to another person, or contractual relationships like parent-child, business affiliations and contracts, and friendship, which are non-consequential but also enrich the moral life.

Teleological and deontological theories are pragmatic theories of the here and now which are rooted in the logic of the present world. These theories do provide a good basis for ethical decision making. However, there are other mechanisms that govern ethical ideology. One such obvious source of morality might be thought to lie in religion. After all, if a God exists, who better than God himself to decide what is right and what is wrong? If God is omniscient, then surely he must be the best authority on matters of ethics. Therefore religious conviction is taken as a separate concept in explaining ethical ideology. Based on our understanding, reading and observation, we realized that though religion and religious prescriptions have been used in normative ethics (Protestant ethics in the west and the *Gita's* philosophy in India), they have not been included in the realm of empirical descriptive ethics. Hence, we began by looking at whether and how people use religious prescriptions in their ethical decision-making processes, and what resulted is a scale of ethical frameworks. We found that people conceptualize two types of ethical frameworks, one which is rooted in worldly logic and prescriptions (we called that pragmatic framework) and the other which uses religious prescription without necessarily taking recourse to logic (we called that religious framework). In case of both—the managers as well as the organizations—two dominating ethical frameworks emerged as a result of factor analysis, which were named Pragmatic framework and Religious framework. It was observed that the respondents had a simpler conceptualization of ethical frameworks, dividing them into two categories. The sub-categories that were identified at the beginning of the scale development process did not emerged as separate categories. The components of the pragmatic framework included utilitarianism, long-term perspective and justice. The religious framework however comprised items of religious conviction. It implies that though pragmatism dominates at the workplace, the religious conviction of the managers too, is important and expected to directly or indirectly influence their behaviour in situations of ethical dilemma at the workplace. This is an important insight into the cognitive processes of managers. The role and relevance of religion and spiritualism would be more meaningful in the context of our results.

A scale for ethical decision making was also identified for the study. The two dimensions of ethical decision-making behaviour identified and used in the scale were *Compromise* and *Values*. These two dimensions formed two poles of a continuum. Here *Compromise* was defined as the response of an individual to a situation of ethical dilemma, where the decision is taken based upon the need of the situation, rather than adhering to the rigid principles irrespective of what is considered morally correct in the society. *Values* was defined as the response to a situation of ethical dilemma, which is socially considered morally correct. The scale consisted of five situations of ethical dilemma that were often faced by managers in work situations. The five situations included in the questionnaire were: (*a*) 'New and improved marketing strategy'; (*b*) 'Gifts and bribes'; (*c*) 'Padding up the expense bills'; (*d*) 'Nepotism'; and (*e*) 'Insider trading'. It was observed that the situational factors played very important roles in influencing the process of decision making in situations of ethical dilemma. It implies that different individuals in similar situations and the same person in different situations would make different decisions. In two out of five situations, decision were taken towards the *Compromise* direction and in the other two it was taken in the *Values* direction of ethical decision making.

These are two points that can be concluded from the content analysis of the five vignettes used in the scale, along with the pattern of response in each case, i.e., people at the workplace generally take unethical decisions or use wrong means where:

- The end result is favourable and does not cause any harm to the other stakeholders.
- Second, when the consequences of the decision are not harmful though not good either, to the majority of the stakeholders.

This scale of ethical decision making was able to generate some information as to what decisions people make in different situations of ethical dilemmas. However, as mentioned earlier, it is not the end result alone but the cognitive process and the reasoning used by the individual in such situations which is equally important.

After developing some understanding of the decisions people take in different situations and their ideology behind these decisions it became important also to understand in this context, what the individual factors are that differentiate one individual from another regarding their ethical behaviour. Therefore, a few individual factors, such as age, gender and personality were included to be studied in details.

Age and gender are two very important individual variables in the context of ethical behaviour at the workplace. The issue of age and experience is crucial to an employee, as well as to the organization he/she works with. Age and experience are considered from the date of appointment to promotion and then retirement. There is a vast body of literature based on the research findings which try to analyze the relationship between age and experience and individual behaviour in the organization. There were significant differences in ethical decision making in given situations and also the choice of ethical framework among the three age groups considered for the present work, i.e., young, middle age and old. Among all the three pairs, i.e., young-old, middle-young and middle-old, the respondents of the younger age group categories scored higher in their choice for pragmatic framework than their older age group counterparts, who had higher scores on the religious frameworks.

There has been a long tradition of empirical research into the differences between men and women. Some of the common points emerging from the review are that women have been found more concerned, sensitive and critical of ethical issues (Beltramini, et al., 1984; Chonko and Hunt, 1985; Ferrell and Skinner, 1988; Jones and Gautschi, 1988; Whipple and Swords, 1992); they have been found to be more ethical in their decisions than their male counterparts (Betz, et al., 1989; Glover, et al., 1997; Ruegger and King, 1992). Significant differences in the ethical *Values*, decision process, moral reasoning and ethical judgment have been observed between men and women (Harris,1990; Freeman and Giebink, 1979); situational differences have been observed between male and female ethical decision choices (Dawson, 1997). Men and women have also been found to differ in the use of ethical frameworks (Schminke, 1997). The empirical results showed that there was a significant difference between men and women in the choice of both the ethical frameworks. Women managers were found to use more of the pragmatic ethical framework, while the religious framework was more frequently used by male managers. In case of situations of ethical dilemma, women were found to make more ethical decisions than their male counterparts.

A construct of Indian origin, which is quite close to the concept of personality and considered relevant was *Guna*. *Guna*, when translated would mean the characteristics of people. *Guna*s are the preponderance of a given type of temperament in one's inner nature. In essence, *Guna*s can be taken as personality attributes of individuals, which are deep rooted. There are three types of *Guna*s, called: unactivity (*Sattwa*), activity (*Rajas*) and inactivity (*Tamas*). These three in different proportions, influence the mental and the intellectual calibre of every individual and provide the distinct flavour in each personality. The consequences of all the three *Guna*s are also different. Thus, *Sattwa*, *Rajas*, and *Tamas* correspond to *sukha* (happiness), *duhkha* (agony), and *moha* (attachment) respectively (Chakraborty, 1987: 78). The behavioural manifestation of these three *Guna*s in terms of the kind of sacrifices, austerity, charity, abandonment, knowledge, duty, understanding, actions, pleasure and fortitude, which are practiced by *Sattwic, Rajasic* and *Tamasic* individuals, is described in detail in the *Gita*. The empirical evidence in the study suggests that among all the three *Guna*s, it is the *Rajas Guna* which most closely found to be associated with the ethical decision-making behaviour of the individuals in situations of ethical dilemma. In two out of five situations used in the study, people with significantly greater *Rajas* characteristics also took unethical decisions. Chakraborty (1987: 79) also observed that a correspondence could be seen between the attitude of the modern man towards life and some of the characteristics of *Rajas*. These include love of fame, pride, and display of power. Therefore, it can be said that the construct of *Guna* is very important in context of ethics.

The psychological characteristics or traits that determine individual beliefs, personal preferences and individual behaviour are very important to be studied with reference to ethical ideologies and differences. Over the years, as a result of the influence of several factors during the process of socialization, these different psychological characteristics of the individuals are developed. These psychological differences together determine personality. Therefore, the personality factors are expected to influence the decision-making behaviour of the individual. Political orientation, and locus of control are two such personality attributes, which have been found through different studies to influence the individual ethical ideology and thereby the decision-making process in situations of ethical dilemma. The most widely used construct for measuring political orientation of an individual is that of Machiavellianism. The empirical findings indicated that both Machiavellianism and locus of control were important personality dimensions in the context of ethics. It is also observed that individuals with internal locus of control and low Machiavellianism make greater use of pragmatic ethical frameworks and also made more ethical decisions. Though both Machiavellianism and locus of control were important personality dimensions in the context of ethics, locus of control was found to be a better predictor of the ethical decision-making behaviour of an individual.

With increasing importance being placed on ethical and socially responsible attitudes towards business, the relevance and centrality of ethical leadership in organizations gain more prominence and rightly so. The importance of leadership is well-established, at the same time the complexity of leadership influence cannot be denied. The ethics of leadership—whether they are good or bad, positive or negative—affect the ethos of the workplace and thereby help to form the ethical choices and decisions of the workers at the workplace. Leaders help to set the tone, develop the vision, and shape the behaviour of all those involved in organizational life.

If we look at the individual factors relating to managerial ethics, the *Rajas Guna* appears to be the apex or the most deeply-rooted personality factor, which probably includes Machiavellianism, external locus of control and authoritative style of leadership, and all these are likely to lead to making *Compromise* decisions. Our proposed model is given in Figure 9.1.

Figure 9.1

Integrated View of Personality Predictors of Managerial Ethics

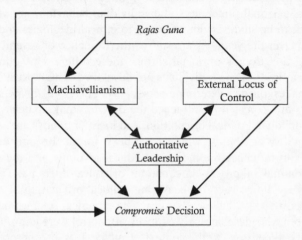

Individual managers do not perform in isolation. The environmental context is equally important. The organizational environment in which the individuals function has tremendous influence on individual behaviour. Organizations reflect the individuals that belong to them and individuals reflect the organizations they belong to, even though organizations cannot grow in the same way because they lack the inner biological drive of an individual (Argyris, 1997). However, they still mutually influence and affect each other. Thus, organizations are capable of expressing the morality that their individual members bring to the organization and in turn shape that individual morality as well. Together, this goes to make up the ethical climate of the organization and it is generally in accordance with this climate that individuals act. In the Indian context, public and private organizations have provided examples of cultural divides. Thus, they provide good example of cultural/contextual variations. There were differences observed in the nature of ethical decisions made in the two organizations and the ethical ideologies followed. It was interesting to note that in private sector organizations, the unethical activity focused on the organization's self-interest, overlooking the interests of some other stakeholders, however, in public sector organizations, the unethical activity leaned more towards the personal interests of the managers instead of the organizations. Thus, the nature of unethical activity in the two types of organizations is different owing primarily to the nature of ownership. These differences could also be due to different mechanisms used for the institutionalization of ethics in these organizations. The focus of the nature of control against unethical activities in public and private sector organizations may also be different owing to the differences in the genesis and manifestation of these activities in both types of organizations.

What Do the Results Mean?

For the Researchers

As mentioned earlier, the present study is an exploratory and descriptive study in India in the area of managerial ethics. Therefore, the results obtained in the study can be used as indicators by researchers to pursue further research in the area.

The two constructs developed in the study, i.e., ethical decision making and ethical frameworks need to be further tested on different samples, especially across cultures for further standardization of the instrument.

Among the individual variables, both demographic and personality variables of age, gender, locus of control and Machiavellianism were found to significantly affect the ethical decision and the choice of ethical framework made by individuals. Future researchers in the area can explore more individual-specific variables and their relationship with ethical decision making and individual ethical ideologies.

The influence of organizational culture (related to ethical decision making) seems to be impacting individual ethical frameworks and the choice of decisions made in situations of ethical dilemma. Therefore, this area needs further probing to obtain more specific indicators. We treated culture as individuals' perceptions; other approaches using symbols etc., to study culture, may also be identified.

The area of ethics is abstract and more subjective in nature. The case studies included in Chapter 8 indicated the importance of qualitative data in this regard. Future studies can endeavour to incorporate a greater proportion of qualitative data in their analysis.

For the Managers and Organizations

It has been recognized that individual decision making in general and specifically in situations of ethical dilemmas, results in consequences (favourable/unfavourable) for both the manager and the organization. Our results also revealed that when there are differences in the individual and organizational code of conduct (both in terms of ethical decisions as well as the use of frameworks) managers are less satisfied and are likely to perform poorly, an issue that organizations need to consider at different levels and in different forms.

The ideal situation demands a 'person-organization fit', i.e., there should be a match between what the organization expects from the individuals and what individuals expect from the organization. The understanding of how ethics operate at the workplace, especially the individual behaviour and the correlates help the managers as well as the organizations create an optimum situation. The present research might have the following implications for organizations:

At the macro level

The organization can assess the present situation in terms of the prevailing ethical culture and the required one (including all the relevant aspects). This assessment could be at individual level as well as the organizational level. This assessment could be at the individual level as well as the organizational level. It could be made by encouraging free communication and making feedback and feed forward mechanisms unbiased and operational at all levels. Based upon the assessment and identified gaps between the existing and the required situation, systems could be developed to remove this gap. The understanding of the phenomenon of ethics at the workplace and as to how it operates can help in developing sound systems, which are acceptable and feasible in the long term. Once these systems are developed, their institutionalization in a smooth way is equally important. There can be many ways for the institutionalization of organizational ethics, for example, implementing a code of ethics, organizing ethical training programmes at various levels, forming ethics committees, conducting ethics audits and constituting judiciary boards. Depending upon the specific requirements, organizations can choose one or more of the above-mentioned ways of institutionalizing ethics.

At the micro level

Once the organization correctly understands the specific requirements of manpower as far as ethics is concerned, then it would help in many

HRM and HRD activities: recruiting the right kind of people (match between the ethical ideologies of the individual and the organization); suitable job design and job delegation to match the individual profiles; and the understanding of human behaviour in general, specifically to ethical ideology, can help the organization in the development of attractive career development plans for its employees and their retention. The aforementioned issues can also be reflected in the performance appraisal systems of the organization by making them specific, easy and transparent.

In the same way, individual managers can learn more about their own self, their subordinates and their colleagues. This understanding of individual behaviour in situations of ethical dilemma can help managers in adjusting more smoothly to the work atmosphere and hence enabling a better work performance.

A WORD OF CAUTION

Social science.research deals with human beings and therefore the issue of social desirability of the responses obtained has always been very important. This issue becomes more prominent and complex, particularly when dealing with sensitive topics such as morality and ethics. In the research that forms the basis of this book, we have tried to solve this complex problem of social desirability of responses by being very rigorous in our methodology of developing the two measures on one hand and by carefully handling the collection of data on the other. While developing the measure for ethical decision-making situations, the final issues that were considered for inclusion in the study were that of ethical dilemmas. This fact was established through validity and reliability measures. The variety of the responses for all the five situations also confirms that the situations were generically different from each other and *Compromise* responses were also made in many situations. During the collection of data, the disclosure of identity of the respondent was optional. Care was also taken that the top management were not asked for critical incidents specifically related to ethical issues. Though sincere efforts were made to reduce the tendency of the respondents to reply in socially desirable ways, this could not be fully eliminated. Therefore, social desirability is the limitation faced by all social science research and the present study was no exception in this regard.

During the research, it was also observed that the issue of ethics is quite context-specific and should be dealt more with the qualitative methods of information collection. Though in the present research qualitative data (in the form of case studies) is also used, it can be collected more extensively in future research.

Methodological issues not withstanding, the need and relevance for studying descriptive ethics, or ethics in practice cannot be emphasized more. Not only does it provide insights into what people feel, think, believe and do; it also provides input into normative ethical standards and their redefinitions within the context of a particular space and time.

ANNEXURE I

Table A.1
Profiles of the Respondents of Pilot Study

	Men	Women
Age		
Up to 35 yrs	69	4
36 yrs and above	18	1
Experience		
1–5 yrs	52	4
6 yrs and above	34	2
Type of Organization		
Public Sector	18	3
Private Sector	68	3

Note: ($N = 92$)

Table A.2
Factor Loading Obtained and Scale Characteristics—*Guna* (Personality Variable)

Item No.	Items	Factor Loading		
		Factor I	*Factor II*	*Factor III*
(11)	Patience	**0.71748**	0.03449	−0.14951
(13)	Self-Control	**0.57374**	−0.17943	0.20767
(14)	Serenity	**0.67219**	−0.22986	−0.06987
(18)	Altruism	**0.66562**	0.06130	0.04102
(23)	Goodness	**0.71893**	0.01394	0.16189
(15)	Strife	0.02121	**0.62949**	0.18662
(30)	Confusion	−0.06241	**0.74091**	0.26903
(32)	Inertness	−0.06143	**0.83511**	0.04444
(34)	Unsteadiness	−0.30813	**0.64101**	−0.01930
(8)	Love of Fame	0.05368	0.31756	**0.59572**
(26)	Jealousy	−0.26946	−0.00741	**0.71990**
(27)	Pride	0.09952	−0.09545	**0.67910**
(28)	Anger	−0.09354	−0.19473	**0.55559**
(29)	Brutality	−0.08027	0.02196	**0.56254**
	Mean	18.4268	9.7416	15.0114
	Eigen Value	7.55693	3.15334	2.65311
	Percentage Variance			
	Explained	25.2	10.5	8.8
	Standard Deviation (SD)	3.0308	2.6135	3.1966
	Reliability	.7083	.7074	.7167

Table A.3
Factor Loading Obtained and Scale Characteristics—Machiavellianism

Items		Factor Loading
(40)	If there is any chance that a recommendation might backfire be very cautious in recommending anyone.	0.57045
(15)	It is wise to flatter important people.	0.62405
(46)	It is better to *Compromise* with existing evil than to go out on a limb in attacking them.	0.52776
(47)	The best way to handle people is to tell them what they want to hear.	0.55141
(52)	One should upset as few people as possible.	0.57585
(54)	Just about any thing can be justified after it is done.	0.52238
(55)	Never tell anyone the real reason you did something unless it is useful.	0.51614
	Mean	22.5281
	Percentage Variance Explained	17.7
	Standard Deviation (SD)	4.9729
	Eigen Value	3.53157
	Reliability	0.6855

Note: $\underline{N} = 89$

Table A.4
Factor Loading Obtained and Scale Characteristics—Leadership Style

		Factor Loading		
Item No.	Items	Factor I	Factor II	Factor III
(60)	I let my subordinates solve the problem jointly.	**0.55611**	0.30018	−0.09323
(62)	I mix freely with my subordinates.	**0.70638**	0.01830	−0.09046
(64)	I treat my subordinates as equals.	**0.67510**	−0.05211	−0.03921
(73)	I allow free and frank discussions whenever a situation arises.	**0.65637**	0.20202	0.05845
(83)	I am informal with my subordinates.	**0.60605**	0.10495	0.15213
(57)	I take personal interest in the promotion of those who work hard.	0.01965	**0.60975**	−0.23481
(59)	I gladly guide and direct those subordinates who work hard.	0.10561	**0.72393**	−0.11921
(69)	I openly favour those who work hard.	−0.06762	**0.51229**	0.18137
(70)	I appreciate those subordinates who want to perform better.	0.04806	**0.77614**	−0.12474
(61)	I behave as if power and prestige are necessary for getting compliance for my subordinates.	−0.22459	0.08796	**0.59743**
(77)	I make it clear to my subordinates that personal loyalty is an important virtue.	0.15556	−0.01812	**0.66858**

(79)	I do not tolerate any interference from my subordinates.	−0.09611 −0.13047	**0.58504**
(80)	I believe that if I am not always alert, there are many people who may pull me down.	0.10006 , −0.12310	**0.69843**
	Mean	9.75 6.4270	11.45
	Eigen Value	5.52 3.04	2.24
	Percentage Variance Explained	19 10.5	7.7
	Standard Deviation	2.7844 2.120	3.322
	Reliability	.6969 .6272	.6372

Table A.5
Organization Type and Gender-wise Cross Tabulation of the Respondents

	Gender		
Type of Organization	*Men*	*Women*	*Total*
Public Sector	170	21	191
Private Sector	124	4	128
Total	**294**	**25**	**319**

Table A.6
Age Group-wise Gender Cross Tabulation

	Gender		
Age Group	*Men*	*Women*	*Total*
Young	104	15	119
Middle	74	7	81
Old	116	3	119
Total	**294**	**25**	**319**

Note: Young—upto 35 years, Middle—36 to 45 years, Old—46 years and above.

Table A.7
A Summary of Studies Examining Internal Consistency and
Test-Retest Reliability of the Adult Nowicki Strickland
Internal-External (ANSIE) Control Scale

Study	*Sample*	*Results*
Chandler (1976)	70 white college students	$r = .65$ Test-Retest (7 weeks)
Chandlers & Patterson (1976)	390 white college students	Factor Analysis First Factor = 29%
Nowicki & Duke (1974)	154 college students	Odd-Even correlation = .74 $r = .83$ Test-Retest (6 weeks)
Roueche & Mink (1976)	845 college students	$r = .65$ Test-Retest (over 1 yr)

Table A.8

Factor Loading Obtained and Scale Characteristics—Satisfaction Measure

Items	Factor I	Factor II
(63) The chances of advancement in your job.	**.7392**	.1505
(64) The feeling of worthwhile accomplishment you get from doing your job.	**.5658**	.4001
(65) The amount of challenge in your job.	**.6722**	.0616
(67) The amount of personal growth and development you get in doing your job.	**.7765**	.0252
(61) The respect you receive from the people you work with.	.1757	**.7014**
(62) The amount of job security you have.	−.4520	**.7329**
(66) The friendliness of the people you work with.	.1882	**.6667**
Mean	14.878	12.080
Percentage Variance Explained	35.2	17.0
Standard Deviation (SD)	2.6640	1.8629
Eigen Value	2.4613	1.894
Reliability	.6748	.5307

Note: $\underline{N}$ = 219; Factor I = Intrinsic Factor Factor II = Extrinsic Factor.

Table A.9

Scale Characteristics of the Variables Included in the Study

Scale	Mean	St. Deviation	Alpha	No. of Items
Guna				
• Sattwa	18.4268	3.0308	0.7083	5
• Tamas	9.7416	2.6135	0.7074	4
• Rajas	15.0114	3.1966	0.7167	5
Locus of Control	14.3519	2.9610	0.6105	20
Machiavellianism	22.5912	4.9729	0.6855	7
Leadership Style				
• Participative	9.75	2.7844	0.6969	5
• Nurturant Task	6.427	2.1207	0.6272	4
• Authoritative	11.45	3.3220	0.6372	4
Job Satisfaction				
• Intrinsic	14.878	2.6640	0.6748	4
• Extrinsic	12.080	1.8629	0.5307	3

Table A.10

Differences among Different Ethical Decision-Making Vignettes

	Vignette 1	Vignette 2	Vignette 3	Vignette 4	Vignette 5
Mean	2.2305	3.7435	2.5714	2.2787	3.0782
Vignette 1	–				
Vignette 2	−17.26** (308)	–			

Vignette 3	-3.59**	13.51**	–		
	(308)	(308)			
Vignette 4	-.47	16.57**	3.51**	–	
	(305)	(305)	(305)		
Vignette 5	-8.72**	8.0**	-5.27**	-8.71**	
	(294)	(294)	(294)	(294)	–

Note: ** P < .001, Figures in parenthesis represent no. of pairs, Figures not in parenthesis are t *Values*.

Table A.11
Factors Obtained for Individual Ethical Frameworks

| | | Column 1 | | Column 2 | | Column 3 | |
| | | Total Sample | | Private Sector | | Public Sector | |
Item No.	Items	F I	F II	F I	F II	F I	F II
(82)	Immediate goals are not the only concern; one must also keep in mind the future.	**0.56**	-0.16	**0.67**	-0.10	**0.52**	-0.11
(95)	What would be the best outcome in the long run?	**0.54**	-0.03	**0.60**	0.08		
(99)	People must be treated fairly.	**0.59**	-0.10	**0.72**	-0.14	**0.56**	0.04
(100)	Consequences of the decision should affect the majority in a positive way.	**0.59**	0.05	**0.50**	0.14	**0.54**	0.07
(105)	Long-term goals are more important than short-term goals.	**0.57**	-0.00	**0.63**	0.24	**0.52**	-0.03
(107)	It is important that discriminatory practices be avoided.	**0.57**	-0.14	**0.58**	0.01	**0.56**	0.07
(111)	It is not fair to treat people as a means to an end.	**0.52**	-0.05			**0.58**	0.14
(114)	Some things in life are definitely right or wrong; there is a natural justice, which must be followed.	**0.52**	0.13	**0.64**	0.17		
(80)	It should not have a bad affect on my next life (*janma*).	-0.02	**0.56**	-0.10	**0.64**		
(90)	It should help in improving my next life (*janma*).	-0.17	**0.75**	-0.26	**0.66**	-0.20	**0.75**
(94)	Every action in judged in terms of its impact on the next life.	-0.28	**0.67**	-0.37	**0.57**	-0.30	**0.67**
(98)	What is right thing to do according to my religious beliefs?	0.14	**0.68**	-0.00	**0.69**	0.12	**0.68**

Contd.

Contd.

Item No.	Items	Column 1 Total Sample		Column 2 Private Sector		Column 3 Public Sector	
		F I	*F II*	*F I*	*F II*	*F I*	*F II*
(101)	It is in line with the advice from a religious person or source.	0.06	**0.68**	−0.28	**0.68**	0.16	**0.64**
(102)	Whatever is happening with me now, is the result of my actions in my previous life.	−0.03	**0.80**	−0.18	**0.75**	−0.07	**0.82**
(108)	My religious faith must permit such an action.	0.10	**0.56**	−0.06	**0.62**	0.12	**0.55**
(116)	I consider my next life too while making decisions.	−0.07	**0.77**	−0.13	**0.72**	−0.12	**0.79**
	Percentage Variance Explained	13.7	11.7	16.0	13.4	13.75	11.4
	Eigen Value	5.36	4.54	6.23	5.22	5.36	4.44

Table A.12

Factors Obtained for Organizational Ethical Frameworks

S. No.	Items	Factor I	Factor II
(124)	Ultimately one should ask whether one's actions are consistent with one's own goals and do what is good for oneself.	**0.51**	−0.40
(126)	It is important that justice is seen to be done.	**0.55**	−0.12
(130)	Having an eye on the future is important.	**0.63**	−0.24
(132)	What would be the best outcome in the long run?	**0.63**	−0.29
(136)	People must be treated fairly.	**0.55**	0.07
(141)	Long-term goals are more important than the short-term goals.	**0.53**	−0.31
(146)	We cannot just look at selfish interests most of the time.	**0.52**	0.05
(135)	What is the right thing to do according to my religious beliefs?	0.08	**0.53**
(138)	It is in line with the advice from a religious person or source.	0.25	**0.57**
(144)	My religious faith must permit such an action.	0.12	**0.60**
	Eigen Value	5.19	2.75
	Percentage Variance Explained	15.3	8.1
	Reliability Alpha	.77	.72
	Mean	28.44	7.31
	Standard Deviation	4.58	3.16

Table A.13
Correlation of Individual Ethical Frameworks
and Ethical Decision Making

Decision Making	Philosophical Framework	Pragmatic Framework
Vignette 1	0.1139 *	0.1419 *
Vignette 2	0.0481	0.0249
Vignette 3	0.1534 **	−0.788
Vignette 4	−0.0234	−0.1958 **
Vignette 5	0.0234	0.0031

Note: N = 300   * P < 0.05   ** P < 0.01.

Table A.14
Step-wise Regression Analysis: Ethical Framework as a Predictor of
Individual Decision Making (Vignette 1)

		Philosophical Framework	Pragmatic Framework
Vignette 1	Beta Coefficient	−0.142	0.113
	t	−0.2473*	1.987*

Note: N = 300   * P < 0.05.

Table A.15
Step-wise Regression Results: Nature of Decision Making (Vignette 1) as a
Function of Individual and Organizational Ethical Frameworks

Variables	Beta Coefficient	t	Significance
Organizational Pragmatic Ethical Framework	−.350	−3.034	.003
Individual Philosophical Ethical Framework	.062	1.051	.294
Individual Pragmatic Ethical Framework	−.104	−1.059	.112
Organizational Philosophical Ethical Framework	.041	.702	.48

Table A.16
Step-wise Regression Results: Nature of Decision Making (Vignette 3)
as a Function of Individual and Organizational Ethical Frameworks

Variables	Beta Coefficient	t	Significance
Individual Philosophical Ethical Framework	.146	1.997	.047
Individual Pragmatic Ethical Framework	−.086	−1.455	.147
Organizational Philosophical Ethical Framework	−.023	−.316	.752
Organizational Pragmatic Ethical Framework	.020	−.337	.736

Table A.17
Step-wise Regression Results: Nature of Decision Making (Vignette 5) as a
Function of Individual and Organizational Ethical Frameworks

Variables	Beta Coefficient	t	Significance
Individual Pragmatic Ethical Framework	−.436	−3.635	.000
Individual Philosophical Ethical Framework	−.032	−.550	.583
Organizational Philosophical Ethical Framework	−.105	−.249	.803
Organizational Pragmatic Ethical Framework	−.005	−.079	.937

Table A.18
T-test: Mean Difference between Genders for Ethical Decision Making

Vignette	Gender	N	Mean	Standard Deviation	T
1	Men	286	2.2832	1.311	2.34
	Women	25	1.8000	.957	*
2	Men	284	3.7465	1.109	.12
	Women	25	3.7200	.936	
3	Men	283	2.5689	1.217	−.12
	Women	25	2.6000	1.118	
4	Men	280	2.3107	1.218	1.55
	Women	25	1.9200	1.038	
5	Men	270	3.1000	1.274	1.03
	Women	24	2.8333	1.274	

Note: * = P < .05.

Table A.19
Mean Comparison of Ethical Frameworks for Age Groups (Young, Middle and Old)

	(I) Age Group	Means	N	(J) Age Group	Mean Difference (I- J)
Individual Religious Ethical Framework	Young	2.2808	116	Middle	−.1925
				Old	−.4103**
	Middle	2.4733	72	Young	.1925
				Old	−.2178
	Old	2.6911	115	Young	.4103*
				Middle	.2178
Individual Pragmatic Ethical Framework	Young	4.0259	116	Middle	.08238
				Old	.1835*
	Middle	3.9435	73	Young	−.08238
				Old	.1012
	Old	3.9367	115	Young	−.1835*
				Middle	−.1012

Note: ** = P < .01,   * = P < .05

Table A.20
Mean Comparison of Ethical Decision Making for Age Groups
(Young, Middle and Old)

Decision Making ↓	(I) Age Group	Means	N	(J) Age Group	Mean Difference (I- J)
	Young	2.3248	117	Middle	.4274
				Old	−.0718
Vignette 1	Middle	1.8974	78	Young	−.4274
				Old	−.4991*
	Old	2.3966	116	Young	.0718
				Middle	.4991*
	Young	2.4483	116	Middle	.1149
				Old	−.4114*
Vignette 3	Middle	2.3333	78	Young	−.1149
				Old	−.5263*
	Old	2.8596	114	Young	.4114*
				Middle	.5263
	Young	3.2130	108	Middle	.5643*
				Old	−.0192
Vignette 5	Middle	2.6486	74	Young	−.5643*
				Old	−.5835
	Old	3.2321	112	Young	.0192
				Middle	.5835*

Note: * = P < .05.

Table A.21
Partial Correlation of Machiavellianism and Locus of Control
with Ethical Frameworks

Controlling for Machiavellianism Locus of Control		Controlling for Locus of Control Machiavellianism	
Religious Framework	−.2924 **	Religious Framework	.0824
Pragmatic Framework	.2497 **	Pragmatic Framework	−.0644

Note: N = 295   ** = P < .01.

Table A.22
Partial Correlation of Machiavellianism and Locus of
Control with Ethical Decision Making

Vignette	Controlling for Machiavellianism	Controlling for Locus of Control
	Locus of Control	Machiavellianism
1 (305)	−.1019	.1648**
2 (303)	−.1155*	.0940
3 (303)	−.1497**	.1576**

Note: Figures in parenthesis represent N (sample size).

Table A.23
Correlation between Ethical Frameworks and Personality Variables for Men

	Individual Religious Framework	Individual Pragmatic Framework
Locus of Control	−.3117**	.2716**
	(276)	(277)
Machiavellianism	.1715**	−.1348*
	(271)	(271)

Note: Figures in parenthesis represent N (sample size) ** = P < .01 * = P < .05.

Table A.24
Correlation between Ethical Frameworks and Personality Variables for Women

	Individual Religious Framework	Individual Pragmatic Framework
Locus of Control	−.3983*	.3532
Machiavellianism	.0509	−.1349

Note: N = 25 * P < .01.

Table A.25
Correlation between Ethical Frameworks and Personality
Variables for the Young Age Group

	Individual Religious Framework	Individual Pragmatic Framework
Locus of Control	−.2382**	.1838*
Machiavellianism	−.0083	−.1421

Note: N = 116 * P < .05 ** P < .01.

Table A.26
Correlation between Ethical Frameworks and
Personality Variables for the Middle Age Group

	Individual Religious Framework	Individual Pragmatic Framework
Locus of Control	−.4933**	.3479**
Machiavellianism	.3158**	.1105

Note: N = 72 ** = P < .01.

Table A.27
Correlation between Ethical Frameworks and Personality
Variables for the Old Age Group

	Individual Religious Framework	Individual Pragmatic Framework
Locus of Control	−.2236*	.2758**
Machiavellianism	.1964*	−.2436**

Note: N = 115 * = P < .05 ** = P < .01.

Table A.28
Correlation between Ethical Decision Making and Personality Variables for Men

Decision Making →	Vignette 1	Vignette 2	Vignette 3	Vignette 4	Vignette 5
Locus of Control	−.161**	−.155**	−.203	−.059	−.090
	(286)	(284)	(283)	(280)	(270)
Machiavellianism	.177**	.145*	.226**	.161**	.019
	(280)	(278)	(277)	(274)	(265)

Note: Figures in parenthesis represent $\underline{N}$ (sample size). ** = $\underline{P}$ < .01 * = $\underline{P}$ < .05.

Table A.29
Correlation between Ethical Decision Making and Personality Variables for Women

Decision Making →	Vignette 1	Vignette 2	Vignette 3	Vignette 4	Vignette 5
Locus of Control	−.199	−.116	−.277	.083	−.440*
Machiavellianism	.576**	.013	.022	.118	−.040

Note: Figures in parenthesis represent $\underline{N}$ (sample size) ** = $\underline{P}$ < .01 * = $\underline{P}$ < .05.

Table A.30
Correlation between Ethical Decision Making and Personality Variables for the Young Age Group

Decision Making →	Vignette 1	Vignette 2	Vignette 3	Vignette 4	Vignette 5
Locus of Control	−.114	−.020	−.041	−.060	−.116
	(117)	(116)	(116)	(115)	(108)
Machiavellianism	.194*	.151	.284**	.266*	.054
	(114)	(113)	(113)	(112)	(106)

Note: Figures in parenthesis represent $\underline{N}$ (sample size) ** = $\underline{P}$ < .01 * = $\underline{P}$ < .05.

Table A.31
Correlation between Ethical Decision Making and Personality Variables for the Middle Age Group

Decision Making →	Vignette 1	Vignette 2	Vignette 3	Vignette 4	Vignette 5
Locus of Control	−.215 (78)	−.224* (78)	−.314** (78)	−.116 (77)	−.078 (74)
Machiavellianism	.199 (77)	.184 (77)	.049 (77)	.001 (76)	−.196 (73)

Note: Figures in parenthesis represent $\underline{N}$ (sample size) ** = $\underline{P}$ < .01 * = $\underline{P}$ < .05.

Table A.32
Correlation between Ethical Decision Making and Personality
Variables for the Old Age Group

Decision Making	Vignette 1	Vignette 2	Vignette 3	Vignette 4	Vignette 5
Locus of Control	−154	−.146	−.168	.024	−.096
	(116)	(115)	(114)	(113)	(112)
Machiavellianism	.197*	.057	.268**	.141	.087
	(114)	(113)	(112)	(111)	(110)

Note: Figures in parenthesis represent $\underline{N}$ (sample size). ** = $\underline{P}$ < .01 * = $\underline{P}$ < .05.

Table A.33
Correlation between Leadership Styles and Personality Variables

	Sattwa Guna	Rajas Guna	Tamas Guna	Locus of Control	Machiavellianism
Participative	−.045	0.14	.039	.116*	−.066
Nurturant Task	.031	-.066	.044	−.151**	.051
Authoritative	.088	-.013	.116*	−.293**	.210**

Table A.34
Correlation between Leadership Styles and Ethical Decision Making

	Vignette 1	Vignette 2	Vignette 3	Vignette 4	Vignette 5
Participative	−.056	−.071	−.020	−.034	.029
Nurturant Task	.040	.082	−.144*	−.089	.058
Authoritative	.089	.073	−.015	−.016	.029

ANNEXURE II

Code No._____

Dear Respondent,

Please fill the following questionnaire following the instructions given before each section. Be as honest with yourself as you can and resist the natural tendency to respond as you would 'like to think things are'. This instrument is not a 'test.' There are no right or wrong answers. Your responses will not be shown to any one. Complete anonymity will be maintained. You may not write your name in the questionnaire.

Poonam Sharma
Research Scholar
IIT, Delhi.

1. Type of organization   Public Sector ....

                            Private Sector ....

2. Present position held   ....

3. Tenure in the present position ....

4. Sex   Male ....   Female ....

5. Age ....

A) Please indicate as to what extent do you possess the following characteristics by selecting one of the five given responses against each item:

S.No.	Key		Very High	High	Average	Low	Very Low
6.	T	Forgetfulness					
7.	T	Ignorance					
9	R	Love of fame					
10.	R	Passion					
11.	R	Power					
12.	S	Patience					
13.	S	Poise					

Contd.

Contd.

S.No.	Key		Very High	High	Average	Low	Very Low
14.	S	Self-control					
15.	S	Serenity (clean & calm)					
16.	R	Strife (conflict, struggle, dispute)					
17.	R	Unrest					
18.	R	Inactive					
19.	S	Altruism					
20.	S	Compassion					
21.	S	Contentment (satisfaction)					
22.	S	Detachment (unaffected by success)					
23.	S	Discrimination (known what is right and what is wrong)					
24.	S	Goodness (kindness, excellence)					
25.	T	Greed					
26.	R	Impatience					
27.	R	Jealousy					
28.	R	Pride					
29.	T	Anger					
30.	T	Brutality					
31.	T	Confusion					
32.	T	Indolent (habitually lazy)					
33.	T	Inertness (sluggish, slow)					
34.	T	Resistant					
35.	T	Unsteadiness (unbalanced not firm)					
36.	R	Desire					

B) Choose one of the five alternatives given against each statement. Indicate your response against each statement by writing one of the corresponding numbers which represent your response correctly.

Strong disagreement	1
Some agreement	2
Indifferent or unable to decide	3
Some agreement	4
Strong agreement	5

37. _____ A white lie is often a good thing.

38. _____ There is no point in keeping a promise if it is to your advantage to break it.

39. _____ Every time one problem is avoided, another arises.

40. _____ Anyone who completely trusts anyone else is asking for trouble.

41. _____ If there is any chance that a recommendation might back-fire, be very cautious in recommending anyone.

42. _____ It is a very good policy to act as if you are doing the things you do because you have no other choice.

43. _____ It is foolish to take a very big risk unless you are willing to go the limits.

44. _____ The best way to settle an argument is for people to forget their differences of opinion as to what is right and wrong and to *Compromise* on the facts.

45. _____ Humility not only is of service but is actually harmful.

46. _____ It is wise to flatter important people.

47. _____ It is better to *Compromise* with existing evil than to go out on a limb in attacking them.

48. _____ The best way to handle people is to tell them what they want to hear.

49. _____ It is easier to take advantage of someone you love than someone you fear.

50. _____ It is safer to be feared than to be loved.

51. _____ Friends should be chosen with an eye towards what they might be able to do for you.

52. _____ If a friend asks for advice, it is smart to think about what will happen if your advice backfires.

53. _____ One should upset as few people as possible.

54. _____ It is good working policy to stay on good terms with everyone.

55. _____ Just about anything can be justified after it is done.

56. _____ Never tell anyone the real reason you did something un-less it is useful to do so.

C) The items below ask for your opinion about how you deal with your im-mediate subordinates. Each item is followed by five alternatives. Please tick the alternative which comes closest to your frank opinion about yourself. There is no right or wrong answer. The scale is meant to find out the different ways superiors act, feel, or prefer. Indicate your response by writing the corresponding number in front of each statement.

Always	1
Usually	2
Sometimes	3
Rarely	4
Never	5

Key

57. P   _____ I often consult my subordinates.

58. NT   _____ I take personal interest in the promotion of those who work hard.

59. F   _____ I keep important information to myself.

60. NT   _____ I gladely guide and direct those subordinates who work hard.

61. P   _____ I let my subordinates solve the problem jointly.

62. F   _____ I behave as if power and prestige are necessary for getting compliance for my subordinates.

63. P   _____ I mix freely with my subordinates.

64. NT   _____ I encourage my subordinates to assume greater responsibility on the job as they become more experienced.

65. P   _____ I treat my subordinates as equals.

66. P   _____ I go by the joint decisions of my group.

67. F   _____ I think that not all the employees are capable of being an executive.

68. F   _____ I am always confident of being right in making decisions.

69. NT   _____ I am kind only to those subordinates who work sincerely.

70. NT   _____ I openly favour those who work hard.

71. NT   _____ I appreciate those subordinates who want to perform better.

72. P   _____ I feel concerned about the feelings of my subordinates.

73.   F   _____ I keep an eye on what my subordinates do.

74.   P   _____ I allow free and frank discussions whenever a situation arises.

75.   NT   _____ I am very affectionate to hardworking subordinates.

76.   P   _____ I often take tea with my subordinates.

77.   NT   _____ I go out of the way to help those subordinates who maintain a high standard of performance.

78.   F   _____ I make it clear to my subordinates that personal loyalty is an important virtue.

79.   NT   _____ I openly praise those subordinates who are punctual.

80.   F   _____ I do not tolerate any interference from my subordinates.

81.   F   _____ I believe that if I am not always alert, there are many people who may pull me down.

82.   F   _____ I demand my subordinates to do what I want them to do.

83.   NT   _____ I feel good when I find my subordinates eager to learn.

84.   P   _____ I am informal with my subordinates.

85.   F   _____ I have strong likes and dislikes for my subordinates.

ANNEXURE III

Code No._____

Dear Respondent,

Please fill the following questionnaire following the instructions given before each section. Be as honest with yourself as you can and resist the natural tendency to respond as you would 'Like to think things are'. This instrument is not a 'test'. There are no right or wrong answers. Your responses will not be shown to any one. Complete anonymity will be maintained. You may not write your name in the questionnaire.

Poonam Sharma
Research Scholar
IIT, Delhi.

1. Type of organization   Public Sector ....

                                      Indian Private ....

                                      Multinational ....

2. Present position held ....

3. Tenure in the present position ....

4. Sex   Male ....   Female ....

5. Age ....

A) Please indicate as to what extent do you possess the following characteristics by selecting one of the five responses given against each item:

S.No.	Key		Very High	High	Average	Low	Very Low
6.	R	Love of fame					
7.	S	Patience					
8.	S	Self-control					
9.	S	Serenity (clean & calm)					

10.	S	Strife (conflict, struggle, dispute)
11.	S	Altruism (devotion to others or humanity
12.	S	Goodness (kindness, excellence)
13.	R	Jealousy
14.	T	Inertness (sluggish, slow)
15.	T	Unsteadiness (unbalanced not firm)
16.	R	Pride
17.	T	Anger
18.	T	Brutality
19.	T	Confusion

B) Give your response against each statement by writing either yes or no:

Response   *Items*
yes/no

_____ 20. Do you believe that most problems will solve themselves if you just don't fool with them?

_____ 21. Are some people just born lucky?

_____ 22. Are you most often blamed for things that just aren't your fault?

_____ 23. Do you feel that most of the time it doesn't pay to try hard because things never turn out right any way?

_____ 24. Do you feel that if the things start out well in the morning, it's going to be a good day no matter what you do?

_____ 25. Do you feel that wishing can make good things happen?

_____ 26. Most of the time, do you find it hard to change a friend's opinion (mind)?

_____ 27. Did you feel that it was nearly impossible to change your parents' mind about anything?

_____ 28. Do you feel that one of the best way to handle most problems is just not to think about them?

_____ 29. Do you feel that you have lot of choice in deciding who your friends are?

_____ 30. Do you believe that whether or not people like you depends on how you act?

_____ 31. Did your parents usually help you if you asked them to?

_____ 32. Have you felt that when people are angry with you it was usually for no reason at all?

_____ 33. Most of the time, do you feel that you can change what might happen tomorrow by what you do today?

_____ 34. Do you believe that when bad things are going to happen, they are just going to happen no matter what you try to do to stop them?

_____ 35. Do you think people can get their own way if they just keep trying?

_____ 36. Do you feel that when good things happen they happen because of hard work?

_____ 37. Do you feel that when someone doesn't like you there's little you can do about it?

_____ 38. Most of the time, do you feel that you have little to say about what your family decides to do?

_____ 39. Do you think that its better to be smarter than to be lucky?

C) The items below ask for your opinion about how you deal with your immediate subordinates. Each item has five alternatives i.e., Always, Usually, Sometimes, Rarely, and Never. Please select the alternative which comes closest to your frank opinion about yourself. There is no right or wrong answer. The scale is meant to find out the different ways superiors act, feel, or prefer.

Indicate your response by writing the corresponding number against each statement:

Always	1
Usually	2
Sometimes	3
Rarely	4
Never	5

Response   *Items*

_____ 40. I take personal interest in the promotion of those who work hard.

_____ 41. I gladly guide and direct those subordinates who work hard.

_____ 42. I let my subordinates solve the problem jointly.

_____ 43. I behave as if power and prestige are necessary for getting compliance for my subordinates.

_____ 44. I mix freely with my subordinates.

_____ 45. I treat my subordinates as equals.

_____ 46. I openly favour those who work hard.

_____ 47. I appreciate those subordinates who want to perform better.

_____ 48. I allow free and frank discussions whenever a situation arises.

_____ 49. I make it clear to my subordinates that personal loyalty is an important virtue.

_____ 50. I don't tolerate any interference from my subordinates.

_____ 51. I believe that if I am not always alert, there are many people who may pull me down.

_____ 52. I am informal with my subordinates.

_____ 53. I treat my subordinates as equals.

_____ 54. I am kind only to those subordinates who work sincerely.

D) Chose one of the five alternatives given against each statement. Indicate your response by writing one of the corresponding numbers which represent your response correctly against each statement:

Strong disagreement	1
Some disagreement	2
Indifferent or unable to decide	3
Some agreement	4
Strong agreement	5

_____ 55. If there is any chance that a recommendation might back-fire be very cautious in recommending anyone.

_____ 56. It is wise to flatter important people.

_____ 57. It is better to *Compromise* with existing evil than to go out on a limb in attacking them.

_____ 58. The best way to handle people is to tell them what they want to hear.

_____ 59. One should upset as few people as possible.

_____ 60. Just about anything can be justified after it is done.

_____ 61. Never tell anyone the real reason you did something unless it is useful to do so.

E) Please indicate how satisfied you are on a 5-point scale with each of the following aspects of your job. Read each item carefully and select the number of your choices in the space provided to the right of the item.

Very satisfied	5
Satisfied	4
Neutral	3
Dissatisfied	2
Very dissatisfied	1

_____ 62. The respect you receive from the people you work with.

_____ 63. The amount of job security you have.

_____ 64. The chances of advancement you have.

————————— 65. The feeling of worthwhile accomplishment you get from doing your job.

————————— 66. The amount of challenge in your job.

————————— 67. The friendliness of the people you work with.

————————— 68. The amount of personal growth and development you get in doing your job.

F) The following are some of the situations that individuals and organizations may face in their day-to-day transactions. Read each situation very carefully and on the scale given at the end of each scenario write your response. You have to decide whether you or your organization would also make the same decision or do otherwise. Response (a) is for yourself and response (b) is for your organization.

Scenario I

You are the head of the marketing department in your company. Due to the stiff competition in the detergent market (one of your company's prime products), you are looking for an idea to increase the sale of this product. The advertising people come up with a suggestion of falsely putting 'new and improved' on the product packaging and advertising, knowing that the statement is not true but it will increase the sales.

69.a) I would Strongly Agree.............. Agree............... Neutral...............
Disagree............... Strongly Disagree............... to this plan.

70.b) My company would Strongly Approve............... Approve...............
Neutral............... Disapprove............... Strongly Disapprove...............
this plan.

Scenario II

Your product has a good potential for sale in the institutions. But in institutional sales due to the high cost of your product the whole procedure of selling and then collecting the payment is quite long and time consuming. To deal with the problem a proposal is made for appointing a sub agent to handle market development and necessary gift giving and money transfers.

71.a) I would Strongly Agree............... Agree............... Neutral...............
Disagree............... Strongly Disagree............... with the decision.

72.b) It is Highly Possible............... Possible............... Fifty-fifty...............
Impossible............... Highly Impossible............... in my company.

Scenario III

One of the marketing executives in your company is showing very good results. In fact, he is the only one to meet the given monthly sales targets. His working also involves travelling. But the company comes to know that he has been padding his travelling expenses bills. But you do not fire him despite his dishonesty.

73.a) I would Strongly Agree............... Agree................ Neutral...............
Disagree............... Strongly Disagree............... with the decision.

74.b) Chances of such things being ignored in my company are: Very High .... High................ Fifty-fifty............... Low............... Very Low...............

Scenario IV

You are on the board of the selection committee for the post of manager, works. Instead of selecting a more experienced long-term employee, you favoured your first cousin who also appeared for the interview and is well-qualified for the post.

75.a) I would Strongly Agree............... Agree................ Neutral...............
Disagree............... Strongly Disagree............... with the decision.

76.b) Such things are Highly possible............... Possible............... Fifty-fifty............... Impossible............... Highly Impossible............... in my company.

Scenario V

A corporate learned that his company intended to announce a stock split and increase the dividend. On the basis of this information, he bought additional shares and sold them at a profit following the announcement.

77.a) I would Strongly Agree............... Agree................ Neutral...............
Disagree............... Strongly Disagree............... with the decision.

78.b) Such things are Highly Possible............... Possible............... Fifty-fifty............... Impossible............... Highly Impossible............... in my company.

G) When making a decision on each of the cases just presented, what factors did you generally take into consideration and what in your opinion are the factors that are considered by your organization? Review the following

statements and select one of the five responses given below for each statement.
Write the corresponding number of the selected response against each
statement in column A and B. Column A is applicable to you and column B
to your organization. Some statements that are not relevant in the
organizational context have been marked 0 and are not to be evaluated for the
organization.

Very often	5
Often	4
Sometimes	3
Rarely	2
Never	1

S.No.	Key	Items	a	b
79.		Do something that is best either for the individual or for the organization.		120.
80.		It is a waste of energy worrying about the effect that an action might have; one should just get on to what one has to do.		121.
81.		It should not have bad affect on my next *janma*.		122.
82.		Results of the duties that we perform do not fall in our jurisdiction.		123.
83.		Immediate goals are not the only concern; one must also keep in mind the future.		124.
84.		In today's business world one must look after one's self and one's interest. It may be an individual or an organization.		125.
85.		That an unethical action is okay if it is directed at an individual or organization, who/which also acts unethically.		126.
86.		What effect the action might have on my/ organization's personal reputation and future.		127.
87.		That ultimately one should ask whether actions are consistent with organizational goals and do what is good for the organization.		128.
88.		What would be the reaction I would get from my family and friends/peers if the details of this action were revealed?		129.
89.		That it is important that justice is seen to be done.		130.
90.		That sacrifices are often needed in order to secure the benefit of the larger number.		131.

S.No.	Key	Items	a	b	
91.		It should help in improving my next *janma*.			132.
92.		That many actions described as unethical are in reality common business practices.			133.
93.		Having an eye on the future is important.			134.
94.		Whether the outcome of the decision produces the greatest net value to all the parties.			135.
95.		Every action is judged in terms of its impact on the next life.			136.
96.		What would be the most efficient and effective outcome in the long run?			138.
97.		Would I/organization lose face if my/organization's involvement in this decision were publicized?			139.
98.		What would be the most equitable decision?			140.
99.		What is the right thing to do according to my religious beliefs?			141.
100.		That people must be treated fairly.			142.
101.		That as long as the consequences of my/organization's decision affects the majority in a positive way.			143.
102.		What advice is available from a religious or philosophical source?			144.
103.		Whatever is happening with me, are the results of my actions in my previous life.			145.
104.		That one cannot be expected to be responsible for everyone and everything.			146.
105.		I/organization would sacrifice personal gains if it results in the benefit of a large number of people.			147.
106.		Long-term goals are more important than the short-term goals.			148.
107.		Self-interest is not as important as the interest of the collective.			149.
108.		It is important that discriminatory practices be avoided.			150.
109.		My religious faith would not permit such an action.			151.

S.No.	Key	Items	a	b
110.		I would feel embarrassed if people found out what I had decided to do.		152.
111.		One can only progress, as a part of the society therefore larger benefits of others should dominate individual interest.		153.
112.		Not to treat people as a means to an end.		
113.		How would I feel if someone did that to me?		154.
114.		That as long as no one gets hurt an action is okay, if it serves the purpose of the majority.		155.
115.		Somethings in life are definitely right or wrong, regardless of the consequences of the decision.		156.
116.		Only thing that is in our hand is to keep performing our duties without worrying about the results.		157.
117.		I consider the impact of the action on not only in this life but also the next one.		158.
118.		I would do something that my spiritual advisor does or recommends.		159.

BIBLIOGRAPHY

Abdel–Halim, A.A. 1981. 'Personality and task moderators of subordinate responses to perceived leader behaviour', *Human Relations*, 34: 73–88.

Abratt, R., D. Nel, and **N.S. Higgs.** 1992. 'An Examination of the Ethical Beliefs of Managers using Selected Scenarios in Cross Cultural Environment', *Journal of Business Ethics*, 11: 29–35.

Adams, J.S. 1963. 'Toward an Understanding of Inequality', *Journal of Abnormal and Social Psychology*, 67: 422–436.

Akaah, I.P. 1989. 'Differences in Research Ethics Judgement Between Male and Female Marketing Professional', *Journal of Business Ethics*, 8: 375–381.

Allport, F.H. 1954. 'The Structuring of Events: Outline of General Theory with Applications to Psychology', *Psychological Review*, 61: 281–303.

Anderson, C.R. and **C.E. Sceneier.** 1978. 'Locus Of Control, Leader Behaviour And Leader Performance among Management Students', *Academy of Management Journal*, 21: 690–698.

Anderson, H.H. 1940. 'An Examination of the Concept of Dominance and Integeration in Relation to Dominance and Ascendance', *Psychological Review*, 47: 21–37.

Andrisani, P.J. and **G. Nestel.** 1976. 'Internal-External Control as Contributors to and Outcome of Work Experience', *Journal of Applied Psychology*, 61: 156–165.

Argyris, C. 1997 '*Integrating the Individual and the Organization*. New Brunswick: Transaction Publishers.

Arlow, P. and **T.A. Ulrich.** 1980. 'Social Responsibility and Business Studies: An Empirical Comparison of Clark's Study', *Akron Business and Economic Review*, 11: 17–23.

Arlow, P. 1991. 'Characteristics in College Students' Evaluations of Business Ethics and Corporate Responsibility', *Journal of Business Ethics*, 10: 63–69.

Arthur, H.B. 1984. 'Making Business Ethics Useful', *Strategic Management Journal*, 5: 319–313.

Aurobindo, S. 1977. *The Message of the Gita*. Sri Aurobindo Ashram, Pondicherry, India.

Auster, E. 1993. 'Demystifying the Glass Ceiling: Organizational and Interpersonal Dynamics of Gender Bias, *Business in ContemporaryWorld*, 3: 47–68.

Barnard, C.I. 1938. *The functions of the executive*. Cambridge, MA: Harvard University Press.

Barnett J.H. and **M.J. Karson.** 1989. 'Managers, *Values*, and Executive Decisions: An Exploration of the Role of Gender, Career Stage, Organizational Level, Function, and the Importance of Ethics, Relationships, and Results in Managerial Decision Making', *Journal of Business Ethics*, 8: 747–771.

Bartels, R. 1967. 'A Model for Ethics in Marketing', *Journal of Marketing*, 20–26.

Bartol, K.M. 1978. 'The Sex Structuring of Organizations: A Search for Possible Causes, *Academy of Management Review*, 3: 805–815.

Bass, B.M. 1960. *Leadership, Psychology and Organizational Behavior.* New York: Harper.

_____ 1975. *Exercise Supervise,* Scotsville, NY: Transnational Programs.

_____ 1980. 'Team Productivity and Individual Member Competence', *Small Group Behavior,* 11: 431–504.

_____ 1981. *Stogdill's Handbook of Leadership.* New York: Free Press.

_____ 1985. *Leadership and Performance Beyond Expectation,* New York: Free Press.

_____ 1999. 'Ethics, Character, and Transformational Leadership Behavior', *Leadership Quarterly,* 10(2): 181–217.

Bass, B.M. and **B.J. Avolio.** 1990. *Transformational Leadership Development: Manual for the Multifactor Leadership Questionnaire.* CA: Consulting Psychologists Press, Palo Alto.

_____ 1995. *Multifactor Leadership Questionnaire,* CA: Mind Garden, Palo Alto.

Bass, B.M. and **E.C. Ryterband.** 1979. *Organizational Psychology (2nd ed).* Boston, MA: Allyn & Bacon.

Bassett, G.A. 1977. *Management Style in Transition Bombay.* Taraporevala Publishing Industries Pvt. Ltd, India.

Baumhart, R.C. 1961. 'How Ethical are Businessman?' *Harvard Business Review,* 39(4): 6–8.

Bellizi, J.A. and **R.E. Hite.** 1989. 'Supervising Unethical Sales Force Behavior', *Journal of Marketing,* 53(2): 36–47.

Beltramini, R.F., R. Peterson, and **G. Kozmetsky.** 1984. 'Concerns of College Students Regarding Business Ethics', *Journal of Business Ethics,* 3: 195–200.

Bernard, J. 1928. 'Political Leadership among North American Indians', *American Journal of Sociology,* 34: 296–315.

Bernard, L.L. 1926. *An Introduction to Social Psychology.* New York: Holt, Rinehart, Winston.

Bernardin, H.J. and **K.M. Alvares.** 1975. 'The Effect of Organizational Levels on the Perceptions of Role Conflict Resolution Strategies', *Organizational Behaviour and Human Performance,* 14: 1–9.

Betz, M., L. O'Connel, and **J.M. Shepard.** 1989. 'Gender Differences in Proclivity for Unethical Behaviour', *Journal of Business Ethics,* 8: 321–342.

Bhal, K.T. 1998. Making Sense of Organizational Culture and Values. New Delhi: HPS.

_____ 2000. 'Ethical Decision-Making and the Use of Frameworks: Effect of Situation and Gender', *International Journal of Business Studies,* 8: 83–105.

_____ 2000a. 'Ethics in Public and Private Sector Organizations in India'. Paper presented in a seminar second Asia Academy of Management Conference, Singapore (December 15–17, 2000).

_____ 2000b. 'Ethical Decision Making and the Use of Frameworks: A Comparison of Public and Private Sector Organizations'. In a Global Conference on Flexible Systems Management at IIT, Delhi, India (December, 2000).

_____ 2001a. 'Ethical Decision-Making by Indian Managers: Identification of the Constructs, their Measurement and Validation', *Management and Labour Studies,* 26: 145–163.

_____ 2001b. 'Ethical Decision-Making by Indian Managers in Public and Private Sector Organizations', *Psychological Studies,* 46(3): 222–232.

_____ 2001c. 'Multiplicity of Ethical Frameworks for Ethical Decision-Making: Variations across Gender and Age Group', *Global Journal of Flexible Systems Management,* 2: 1–10.

Bhal, K.T. and **P. Sharma.** 2002. 'Managerial Ethical Behavior: Result of a Comparative Study', *Vikalpa,* 26(4): 51–58.

Bingham, W.C. 1927. 'Leadership', in H. C. Metcalf (ed.), *The Psychological foundation of Management.* New York: Shaw.

Biswas, R.K. 1994. 'Leadership Styles, its Effect on Organizational Culture', *Personnel Today.* October–December 7–11.

Blake, R.R. and **J.S. Mouton.** 1964. *The Managerial Grid.* Houston, TX: Gulf Publishing Company.

Boldizar, J.P., K.L. Wilson and **D.K. Deemer.** 1989. 'Gender, Life Experiences, a Moral Judgement Development: A Process Oriented Approach', *Journal of Personality and Social Psychology,* 57: 229–238.

Bommer, M., C. Gratto, J. Grravander, and **M. Tuttle.** 1987. 'A Behavioural Model of Ethical Decision Making', *Journal of Business Ethics,* 6: 265–280.

Borkowski, S.C. and **Y.J. Ugras.** 1992. 'The Ethical Attitudes of Students as a Function of Age, Sex and Experience', *Journal of Business Ethics,* 11: 63–69.

Bowden, A.O. 1926. 'A Study of Personality of Student Leaders in the United States', *Journal of Abnormal and Social Psychology,* 21: 149–160.

Brady, F.N. 1990. *Ethical Managing.* New York: Macmillan.

Brady, F.N. and **G.E. Wheeler.** 1996. 'An Empirical Study of Ethical Predispositions', *Journal of Business Ethics,* 15: 927–940.

Brenner, S.N. and **E.A. Molander.** 1977. 'Is the Ethics of Business Changing?', *Harvard Business Review,* 55(1): 57–71.

Brigley, S. 1995. 'Business Ethics in Context: Researching with Case Studies', *Journal of Business Ethics,* 14: 219–226.

Broedling, L.A. 1975. 'Relationship of Internal-External Control to Work Motivation and Performance in an Expectancy Model', *Journal of Applied Psychology,* 60: 65–70.

Broverman, I.S., D. Vogel, F. Broverman, P. Clarkson, and **R. Krantz.** 1972. 'Sex-role Types: A Current Appraisal', *Journal of Social Issues,* 12: 58–78.

Brown, A. 1987. 'Is Ethics Good Business', *Personnel Administrator,* February, 67–74.

Bruce, J.A. and **D.A. Waldman.** 1990. 'An Examination of Age and Cognitive Test Performance Across Job Complexity and Occupational Types', *Journal of Applied Psychology,* 75(1): 43–50.

Buchholz, R.A. 1989. *Fundamental Concepts and Problems in Business Ethics.* Englewood Cliffs, New Jersey: Prentice Hall Inc.

Bundel, C.M. 1930. 'Is Leadership Losing its Importance?', *Infantry Journal,* 36: 339–349.

Burns, J.M. 1978. *Leadership.* New York: Harper & Row.

Burns James MacGregor. 1979. *Leadership.* New York: Harper Torchbooks.

Byravan, F.R. and **J. Detwiler.** 1994. 'Revised New Personality Inventory Profiles of Machiavellian and Non-Machiavellian People' *Psychological Reports,* October, 937–38.

Calder, B.J. 1977. 'An Attribution Theory of Leadership', in B.M. Staw and G.R. Salancik (eds.), *New Directions in Organizational Behaviour.* Chicago, IL: St. Clair.

Callan, V.J. 1992. 'Predicting Ethical *Values* and Training Needs in Ethics', *Journal of Business Ethics,* 11: 761–769.

Carlson, D.S. and **P.L. Perrewe.** 1995. 'Institutionalization of Organizational Ethics through Transformational Leadership', *Journal of Business Ethics,* 14: 829–838.

Carlson, H.B. and **W. Harrell.** 1942. 'An Analysis of Life's "Ablest Congressmab" Poll', *Journal of Social Psychology,* 15: 153–158.

Carroll, A.B. 1978. 'Linking Business Ethics to Behaviour in Organizations', *Advanced Management Journal,* 43(3): 4–11.

Cavanagh, G.F., D.J. Moberg, and **M. Velasquez.** 1981. 'The Ethics of Organizational Politics', *Academy of Management Review,* 6: 363–374.

Chakraborty, S.K. 1985. *Human Response in Organizations: Towards the Indian Ethos.* Calcutta: Vivekananda Nidhi.

_____ 1987. *Managerial Effectiveness and Quality of Work Life: Indian insights.* New Delhi: Tata McGraw Hill.

_____ 1991. *Management of Values.* New Delhi: Oxford University Press.

Chatterjee, S.K. 1979. *Management of Public Entrepreneurs.* New Delhi: Surjeet Publication.

Chen, Al Y.S., R.B. Sawyers, and **P.F. Williams.** 1997. 'Reinforcing Ethical Decision Making Through Corporate Culture', *Journal of Business Ethics,* 16: 855–865.

Chinmayananda, S. 1992. *The Holy Geeta.* Mumbai: Central Chinmaya Mission Trust.

Chodorow, N. 1978. *Reproduction of Mothering.* Stanford, CA: Stanford University Press.

Chonko, L.B. and **S.D. Hunt.** 1985. 'Ethics and Marketing Management: An Empirical Examination', *Journal of Business Research,* 13: 339–359.

Christie, R. and **F.L. Geis.** 1970. *Studies in Machiavellianism.* New York: Academic Press.

Coch, L. and **J.R.P., Jr. French.** 1948. 'Overcoming Resistance to Change', *Human Relations,* 1: 512–532.

Colby, A., L. Kohlberg, J. Gibbs, and **M. Liberman.** 1983, 'A Longitudinal Study of Moral Judgement', *Monographs of the Society for Research in Child Development,* 48: 1–124.

Colhoon, R.P. 1969. 'Niccolo Machiavelli and the Twentieth Century Administrator', *Academy of Management Journal,* 2: 205–212.

Cooke, A. 1986. 'Is "Business Ethics" an Oxymoron?' *Business and Society Review,* 58: 68–69.

Costa, J.D. 1998. *The Ethical Imperative: Why Moral Leadership is Good Business,* Reading, Mass: Perseus Books.

Cravens, R.W. and **P. Worchel.** 1977. 'The Differential Effects of Rewarding and Coercive Leaders of Group Members Differing in Locus of Control'. *Journal of Personality,* 45: 150–168.

Cuilla, J.B. 1985. 'Do MBA Students have Ethical Phobia?', *Business and Society Review,* 53: 52–54.

Cullen, J.B., B. Victor, and **C. Stephens.** 1989. 'An Ethical Weather Report: Assessing the Organizational Ethical Climate', *Organizational Dynamics,* 50–62.

Dailey, R.C. 1978. 'Relationship Between Locus of Control, Perceived Group Cohesiveness, and Satisfaction with Co-Workers, *Psychological Reports,* 42: 311–316.

Dasgupta, S.A. 1957. '*A History of Indian Philosophy*', Cambridge University Press.

Davidson, K.M. and **K.G. Bailey.** 1978. 'Effects of "Status Sets" on Rotter's Locus Of Control Scale', *Journal of Consulting and Clinical Psychology,* 46: 186.

Davis. J.R. and **R.E. Welton.** 1991. 'Professional Ethics: Business Students' Perception', *Journal of Business Ethics,* 10: 451–463.

Dawson, L.M. 1997. 'Ethical Differences between Men and Women in the Sales Profession', *Journal of Business Ethics,* 16: 1143–1152.

Derry, R. 1989. 'An Empirical Study of Moral Reasoning Among Managers', *Journal of Business Ethics*, 8: 855–862.

Deshpande, S.P. 1996. 'Ethical Climate and the Link between Success and Ethical Behaviour: an Empirical Investigation of a Non-Profit Organization', *Journal of Business Ethics*, 15: 315–320.

DeVellis, R.F. 1991. *Scale Development: Theory and Applications*. New Bury Park, CA: Sage Publication Inc.

Dobbins, G. and **S. Platz.** 1986. 'Sex Differences in Leadership: How Real Are They?', *Academy of Management Review*, 11: 118–127.

Donaldson, J. 1992. *Business Ethics: A European Casebook*. London: Academic Press Ltd.

Donaldson, T. 1994. 'Ethics in Business: A New Look', in T. A. Mathias (ed.) *Corporate Ethics*. New Delhi: Allied Publishers Limited.

Drory, A. and **U.M. Gluskinos.** 1980. 'Machiavellianism and Leadership', *Journal of Applied Psychology*, 65: 81–86.

DuCette, J. and **C. Wolk.** 1973. 'Cognitive and Motivational Correlates of Generalized Expectancies of Control', *Journal of Personality and Social Psychology*, 26: 420–426.

Duke, M.P., J. Shaheen, and **S. Nowicki.** 1974. 'The Determination of Locus of Control in a Geriatric Population and a Subsequent Test of the Social Learning Model for Interpersonal Distances', *Journal of Psychology*, 86: 277–285.

Dunham, R.B. 1984. *Organization Behaviour—People and Process Management*. Illinois: Richard D. Irwin, Inc.

Eisenhardt, K. 1989. 'Agency Theory: An Assessment and Review', *Academy of Management Review*, 14: 57–74.

Enderle, G. 1987. 'Some Perspectives of Managerial Ethical Leadership', *Journal of Business Ethics*, 6–657.

England, G.W. 1978. 'Managers and their Value Systems: A Five Country Comparative Study', *Columbia Journal of World Business*, 13(2): 35–44.

Enz, C.A. 1988. 'The Role of Value Congruity in Intraorganizational Power', *Administrative Science Quarterly*, 33: 284–304.

Falkenberg, L. and **I. Herremans.** 1995. 'Ethical Behaviors in Organizations: Directed by the Formal or Informal System?', *Journal of Business Ethics*, 14: 133–143.

Fama, E. 1980. 'Agency Problems and the Theory of the Firm', *Journal of Political Economy*, 14: 288–307.

Ferrell, O.C. and **L.G. Gresham.** 1985. 'A Contingency Framework for Understanding Ethical Decision Making in Marketing', *Journal of Marketing*, 49: 87–96.

Ferrell, O.C. and **S.J. Skinner.** 1988. 'Ethical Behaviour and Bureaucratic Structure in Marketing Research Organizations', *Journal of Marketing Research*, 25: 103–109.

Ferrell, O.C., L.G. Gresham, and **J. Fraedrich.** 1989. 'A Synthesis of Ethical Decision Models for Marketing', *Journal of Macro Marketing*, 9(fall): 55–64.

Fiedler, F.E. 1967. *A Theory of Leadership Effectiveness*. New York: McGraw-Hill.

Fisse, B. and **J. Braithwite.** 1983. *The Impact of Publicity on Corporate Offenders*. Albany, NY: State University of New York Press.

Fleishman, E.A. 1953. 'The Description of Supervisory Behavior', *Personnel Psychology*, 37: 1–6.

Fleishman, E.A. 1957. 'A leader behavior description for industry', in R.M. Stogdill and A.E. Coons (eds.), *Leader behavior: Its Description and Measurement*. Columbus, OH: Bureau of Business Research, Ohio State University.

Ford, R.C. and **W.D. Richardson.** 1994. 'Ethical Decision-Making: A Review of the Empirical Literature', *Journal of Business Ethics*, 13: 205–221.

Forsyth, D.R. and **R.E. Berger.** 1982. 'The Effects of Ethical Ideology on Moral Behaviour', *Journal of Social Psychology,* 117: 53–56.

Frawley, David. 2000. *The Astrology of the Seers: A Guide to the Vedic (Hindu) Astrology.* Wisconsin: Lotus Press.

Freeman, S.J.M. and **J.W. Giebink.** 1979. 'Moral Judgement as a function of Age, Sex and Stimulus', *Journal of Psychology,* 102: 43–47.

French, J.R.P. 1950. 'Field Experiments: Changing Group Productivity', in J. G. Miller (ed.), *Experiments in Social Process.* New York: McGraw-Hill.

Freud, S. 1925. 'Some Psychical Consequences of the Anatomical Distinction Between the Sexes', in J. Srachey (ed.), *The standard edition of the complete psychological works of Sigmunal Freud,* Vol. 19. London: The Hogarth Press.

Fritzsche, D.J. and **H. Becker.** 1984. 'Linking Management Behaviour to Ethical Philosophy an Empirical Investigation', *Academy of Management Review,* 27(1): 166–175.

Fritzsche, D.J. 1988. 'An Examination of Marketing Ethics: Role of the Decision-Maker, Consequences of the Decision, Management Position, and Sex of the Respondent', *Journal of Macro Making,* 8: 29–39.

Galbraith, S. and **H.B. Stephenson.** 1993. 'Decision Rules Used by Male and Female Business Students in Making Ethical Value Judgement: Another Look', *Journal of Business Ethics,* 12: 227–233.

Gale Encyclopaedia of Psychology: 2001, 2nd ed. Gale Group.

Galli, I., Nigro and **G. Krampen.** 1986. 'Multidimensional locus of control and Machiavellianism in Italian and West German students: Similarities and differences', *International Review of Applied Psychology,* 35: 435–461.

Gardner, J.W. 1990. *On Leadership.* New York: The Free Press.

Gellerman, S.W. 1986. 'Why "Good" Managers Make Bad Ethical Choices', *Harvard Business Review,* 64: 85–90.

Gemmill, G.R. and **W.J. Heisler.** 1972. 'Machiavellianism as a Factor in Managerial Job Strain, Job Satisfaction, and Upward Mobility', *Academy of Management Journal,* 1(15): 51–62.

Gergen, K.J. 1969. *The Psychology of Behaviour Exchange* Reading. MA:Addison-Wesley.

Gilligan, C. 1977. 'In a Different Voice: Women's Conceptions of Self-Morality', *Harvard Educational Review,* 47: 481–517.

Gilligan, C. 1982. *In a Different Voice: Psychological Theory and Women's Development,* Cambridge: Harvard University Press.

Gilligan, C. 1987. 'Moral Orientation and Moral Development', in E.F. Kittay and D. T. Mayers (eds.), *Women and Moral Theory.* Totowa. New Jersey: Row man and Littlefield.

Gini, Al. 1996. 'Moral Leadership and Business Ethics', Loyola University Chicago in Ethics & Leadership Working Papers Academy of Leadership Press.

Girodo, M. 1998. 'Machiavellian, Bureaucratic, and Transformational Leadership Styles in Police Managers: Preliminary Findings of Interpersonal Ethics', *Perceptual and Motor Skills,* 86: 419–427.

Glover, S.H., M.A. Bumpus, J.E. Logan, and **J.R. Ciesla.** 1997. 'Re-examining the Influence of Individual Values on Ethical Decision Making', *Journal of Business Ethics,* 16: 1319–1329.

Goffman, E. 1959. *The Presentation of Self in Everyday Life.* New York: Double Day.

Goodstadt, B.E. and L.A. Hjelle. 1973. 'Power to the powerless: Locus of Control and the Use of Power', *Journal of Personality of Social Psychology,* 27: 190–196.

Grant, J. 1988. 'Women as Managers: What They Can Offer to Organizations', *Organizational Dynamics,* winter, 56–63.

Gullillen, M. and T.F. Gonzatez. 2001. The Ethical Dimension of Managerial Leadership Two Illustrative Case Studies in TQM.' *Journal of Business Ethics,* 33(2): 101–114, September.

Gupta, D. 2001: 'A Little Ethics can be Dangerous', *Business India,* 5–18 February, P. 92.

Gupta, L.J. and M. Sulaiman. 1996. 'Ethical Orientation of Managers in Malaysia', *Journal of Business Ethics,* 15: 735–748.

Halpin, A.W. and B.J. Winer. 1957. 'A factorial study of the leader behavior descriptions', in R.M. Stogdill and A.E. Coons (eds.), *Leader behavior: Its description and measurement.* Columbus, OH: Bureau of Business Research, Ohio State University, (pp. 39–52).

Hammer, T.H. and Y. Vardi. 1981. 'Locus of Control and Career Self-management among no Supervisory Employees in Industrial Settings', *Journal of Vocational Behaviour,* 18: 13–29.

Harris, J.R. 1989. 'Ethical values and Decision Processes of Male and Female Business Students', *Journal of Education for Business,* 8: 234–238.

Harris, J.R. 1990. 'Ethical Values of Individuals at Different Levels in the Organizational Hierarchy of a Single Firm', *Journal of Business Ethics,* 9: 741–750.

Harris, J.R. and C.D. Sutton. 1995. 'Unraveling the Ethical Decision-Making Process: Clues from an Empirical Study Comparing *Fortune* 1000 Executives and MBA Students' *Journal of Business Ethics,* 14: 805–817.

Harvey, J.H., R.D.Barnes, D.L. Sperry, and B. Harris. 1975. 'Perceived Choice as a Function of Internal-External Locus of Control', *Journal of Personality,* 42: 437–452.

Hegarty, W. H. and H.P. Sims. 1978. 'Some Determinants of Unethical Decision Behavior: An Experiment', *Journal of Applied Psychology,* 63: 451–457.

Hegarty, W.H. and H. P. Sims. 1979. 'Organizational Philosophy, Policies, and Objectives Related to Unethical Decision Behaviour: A Laboratory Experiment', *Journal of Applied Psychology,* 64(3): 331–338.

Heisler, W.J. and G. Gemmell. 1977. 'Machiavellianism, Job Satisfaction, Job Strain and Upward Mobility: Some Cross-Organizational Evidence', *Psychological reports,* 2(41): 592–594.

Hemphill, J.K. 1949. 'The Leader and his Group', *Journal of Educational Research,* 28: 225–229.

——————— 1950. *Leader Behavior Description,* Columbus, OH: Bureau of Educational Research, Ohio State University.

Hemphill, J.K. and A.E. Coons. 1957. 'Development of the leader behavior description questionnaire', in R.M. Stogdill and A.E. Coons (eds.), *Leader Behavior: Its Description and Measurement.* Columbus, OH: Bureau of Business Research, Ohio State University, (pp. 6–38).

Henderson, V.E. 1982. 'The Ethical Side of Enterprise', *Sloan Management Review,* 23: 37–47.

Hinman, L.M. 1977. 'The Ethics of Diversity: Gender, Ethnicity, and Individuality', in Alfred Prettyman, *National Civics in a Mosaid Democracy, Revised.* McGraw-Hill.

Hitt, W.D. 1990. *Ethics and Leadership: Putting Theory into Practice,* Columbus, OH: Battelle Press.

Hogan, R. 1973. 'Moral Conduct and Moral Character: A Psychological Perspective', *Psychological Bulletin,* 79(4).

Homans, G.C. 1958. 'Social Behaviour as Exchange', *American Journal of Social Psychology,* 63: 597–606.

Homans, G. 1950. *The Human Group.* New York: Harcourt Brace Jovanovich.

Honeycutt, E.D., J.A. Siguaw and **T.G. Hunt.** 1995. 'Business Ethics and Job-Related Constructs: A Cross-Cultural Comparison of Automotive Salespeople', *Journal of Business Ethics,* 14: 235–248.

Hood, J. 2003. 'The Relationship of Leadership Style and CEO Values to Ethical Practices in Organizations, *Journal of Business Ethics,* 43(4): 263–273.

Horn, J.L. 1967. 'Intelligence: Why it Grows, Why it Declines', *Transaction,* 4: 3–31.

Horn, J.L. 1982. 'The Ageing of Human Abilities', In B. B. Wolman (ed.), *Handbook of Developmental Psychology: Research and Theory.* Englewood Cliffs, NJ: Prentice-Hall.

Horn, J.L. and **R.B. Cattell.** 1966. 'Refinement and Test of the Theory of Fluid and Crystallized Intelligence', *Journal of Education Psychology,* 57: 253–270.

Hosmer, L.T. 1987. *Ethics in Management.* New Delhi: Richard Irwin-Universal Book Stall.

Hunt, J.G., R.M. Osborn, and **L.L. Larson.** 1975. 'Upper Level Technical Orientation of First Level Leadership within a no Contingency and Contingency Framework', *Academy of Management Journal,* 18: 475–488.

Hunt, S.D. and **S. Vitell.** 1986. 'A General Theory of Marketing Ethics', *Journal of Macro Marketing,* 8: 5–16.

Hunt, S.D. and **S. Vitell.** 1992. 'A General Theory of Marketing Ethics: A Retrospective and Revision', in J. Quelch and C. Smith (eds.), *Ethics in Marketing.* Chicago: Richard D. Irwin.

Hyman, M.R., R. Skipper, and **R. Tansey.** 1990. 'Ethical Codes are not Enough', *Business Horizons,* March–April 16.

Ilgen, D.R. and **D.S. Fujii,** 1976. 'An Investigation of the Validity of Leader Behaviour Description Obtained from Subordinates', *Journal of Applied Psychology,* 61: 642–651.

Izraeli, D. 1988. 'Ethical Beliefs and Behaviour of Managers: A Cross-Cultural Perspective', *Journal of Business Ethics,* 7: 263–271.

Jackall, R. 1988. *Moral Mazes,* New York: Oxford University Press.

Jackson, T. and **M.C. Artola.** 1997. 'Ethical Beliefs and Management Behaviour: A Cross-Cultural Comparison', *Journal of Business Ethics,* 16: 1163–1173.

Jensen, M. and **W. Meckling.** 1976. 'Theory of the Firm: Managerial Behaviour, Agency Costs, and Ownership Structure', *Journal of Financial Economics,* 3: 305–360.

Jones G.E. and **M.J. Kavanagh.** 1996. 'An experimental examination of the effects of individual and situational factors on unethical behavioural intentions in the workplace', *Journal of Business Ethics,* 15: 511–523.

Jones, E.E. 1985. 'Major Development in Social Psychology During the Past Five Decades', in G. Lindezey and E. Aronson (eds.), *The Hand Book of Social Psychology.* New York: Random House.

Jones, T.M. 1991. 'Ethical Decision-Making by Individuals in Organizations: An Issue-Contingent Model', *Academy of Management Review,* 16: 366–395.

Jones, T.M. and **F.H. Gautschi.** 1988. 'Will the Ethics of Business Change? A Survey of Future Executives', *Journal of Business Ethics,* 7: 231–248.

Jose, A. and **M.S. Thibodeaux.** 1999. 'Institutionalization of Ethics: The Perspective of Managers,' *Journal of Business Ethics,* 22(2): 133–43.

Julian, J.W., and **S.B. Katz.** 1968. 'Internal versus External Control and the Value of Reinforcement', *Journal of Personality and Social Psychology,* 8: 89–94.

Kabanoff, B. and **G.L. O'Brien.** 1980. Work and Leisure: A Task Attributes Analysis', *Journal of Applied Psychology,* 65: 596–609.

Kahle, L.R. 1980. 'Stimulus Condition Self-selection by Males in the Interaction of Locus of Control and Skill-chance Situations', *Journal of Personality and Social Psychology,* 38: 50–56.

Katz, D. and **R.L. Kahn.** 1952. 'Some Recent Findings in Human Relation Research', in E. Swanson, T. Newcomb, and E. Hartley (eds.), *Readings in Social Psychology.* New York: Holt, Rinehart, Winston, (pp. 650–665).

Katz, D. and **R.L Kahn.** 1978. *The Social Psychology of Organizations,* New York: Wiley.

Katz, D., N., Maccoby, and **N. Morse.** 1950. *Productivity, Supervision and Morale in an Office Situation,* Ann Arbor, MI: Institute for Social Research, University of Michigan.

Kaur P. 1992. *Success Options and Organizational Dynamics.* New Delhi: Segment Books.

Kaur, K.P. 1987. 'Bureaucratization in the Public and Private Sector: A Comparison of Large Scale Manufacturing in Punjab', in R.K. Sapru (ed.) *Management of Public Sector Enterprises in India Vol. II.* New Delhi: Ashish Publishing House.

Kidwell, J.M., R.E. Steven, and **A.L. Bethke.** 1987. 'Differences in the Ethical Perception of Male and Female Managers: Myth or Reality', *Journal of Business Ethics,* 6: 489–493.

Knoop, R. 1981. Age and Correlates of Locus of control', *The Journal of Psychology,* 108: 103–106.

Kochan, T.A., S.M. Schmidt, and **de T.A. Cotiis.** 1975. 'Superior-Subordinate Relations: Leadership and Headship', *Human Relations,* 28: 279–294.

Kohlberg, L. 1969. 'Stage and Sequence: The Cognitive–Development a Approach to Socialization', in D.A. Goslin (ed.), *Handbook of Socialization Theory and Research.* Chicago: Rand Mc Nally.

Kohlberg, L. 1981. *The Philosophy of Moral Development.* San Francisco: Harper and Row.

Kosambi, D.D. 1965. *The Culture and Civilization of Ancient India in Historical Outline,* London: Routledge and Kegan Paul.

Kreitner, R. and W.E. Reif. 1980. Ethical Inclination of Tomorrow's Managers: A Cause for Alarm?', *Journal of Business Education,* 56: 25–29.

Krolick, G. 1979. 'Changes in Expectancy and Attribution following Success, Failure and Neutral Consequences' (Doctoral dissertation, Syracuse University, 1978). *Dissertation Abstract International,* 39: 5074B (University Microfilms No. 79–08546).

Kuhnert, K.W. and **P. Lewis.** 1987. 'Transactional and Transformational Leadership: A Constructive/Developmental Analysis', *Academy of Management Review,* 12: 648–657.

Kulkarni, A.V. 1983. Relationship between Internal Versus External Locus of Control and Job Satisfaction', *Journal of Psychological Researches,* 27: 57–60.

Laczniak, G.R. and **P.E. Murphy.** 1991. 'Fostering Ethical Decisions', *Journal of Business Ethics',* 10: 259–271.

Lao, R.C. 1976. 'Is Internal-External Control an Age-related Variable?', *Journal of Psychology,* 92: 3–7.

Larwood, L. and **M.M. Wood.** 1977. *Women in Management.* Lexington, MA: Lexington Books, D. C. Heath & Co.

Laszlo, Christopher, and **J. Nash.** 2001. 'Six Facets Of Ethical Leadership: An Executive's Guide To The New Ethics In Business', *Electronic Journal of Business Ethics and Organization Studies* 8(1):

Lee, K.H. 1981. 'Ethical Beliefs in Marketing Management: A cross-Cultural Study', *European Journal of Marketing,* 15: 58–67.

Lever, J. 1978. 'Sex Differences in the Complexity of Children's Play and Games', *American Sociological Review,* 43: 471–483.

Lewin, K., Lippitt, R., and **R.K. White.** 1939. 'Patterns of Aggressive Behavior in Experimentally Created Social Climates', *Journal of Social Psychology,* 10: 271–299.

Lied, T.R. and **R.D. Pritchard.** 1976. 'Relationship between Personality Variables and Components of the Expectancy-Valence Model', *Journal of Applied Psychology,* 61: 463–467.

Lifton, P.D. 1985. 'Individual Differences in Moral Development: The Relation of Sex, Gender, and Personality to Morality', *Journal of Personality,* 2: 306–334.

Likert, R. 1959. 'Motivational Approach to Management Development', *Harvard Business Review,* 37: 75–82.

———— 1961, *New Patterns of Management.* New York: McGraw-Hill.

———— 1967. *The Human Organization: Its Management and Value.* New York: McGraw-Hill.

Lincoln, Y.S. and **E.G. Guba.** 1985. *Naturalistic Inquiry.* London: Sage Publications.

Litwin, G.H. and **R.A., Stringer Jr.** 1968. *Motivation and Organizational Climate.* Boston: Division of research, Harvard Business School.

Loden, M. 1985. *Feminine Leadership.* New York: Times Books.

Lodge, G.C. 1990. *Perestrika for America: Restructuring business-Government Relations for World Competitiveness.* Boston, MA: Harvard Business School.

Lord, R.G. 1976. 'Group Performance as a Function of Leadership Behaviour and Task Structure: Towards an Explanatory Theory', *Organizational Behaviour and Human Performance,* 17: 76–96.

Lunati, T. 1996. 'Market and Morality', in Alan Kitson and Robert Campbell (eds.), *The Ethical Organization.* London: Macmillan.

Luthans, F. and **R. Kreitner.** 1985. *Organizational Behaviour Modifications and Beyond: An Operant and Social Learning Approach.* Glenview, IL: Scot Forsman.

Lyons, N.P. 1983. 'The Perspectives: On Self-Relationships and Morality', *Harvard Educational Review,* 53: 125–145.

Lysonski, S. and **W. Gaidis.** 1991. 'A Cross Cultural Comparison of the Ethics of Business Students', *Journal of Business Ethics,* 10: 141–150.

Maddi, S.R. 1976. Personality Theories: A Comparative Analysis, 3rd ed. Homewood, Illinois: The Dorsey Press.

Maheshwari, B.L. 1985. 'Managerial Effectiveness in Public Enterprises', in T.L. Sankar, R.K. Mishra and Ravi Shanker (eds.), *Leading Issues in Public Enterprise Management,* Bombay: Himalaya Publishing House.

Maheshwari, R. and **P. Maheshwari.** 1985. 'Public Enterprises: A Case for New Managerial Order', in R. K. Mishra and S. Ravishankar (eds.), Current Perspectives *in Public Enterprise Management',* New Delhi: Ajanta Publications.

Majumdar, R.K., A.P. MacDonald, and **K.B. Greever.** 1977. 'A Study of Rehabilitational Counselor: Locus of Control and Attitudes toward the Poor', *Journal of Counseling Psychology,* 24: 137–141.

Malikiosi, M.K. and **R.M. Ryckman.** 1977. 'Difference in Perceived Locus of Control among Men and Women, Adults and University Students in America and Greece', *Journal of Social Psychology,* 103: 177–183.

Mann, F.C., and **J. Dent.** 1954. 'The Supervisor: Member of two Organizational Families', *Harward Business Review,* 32: 103–112.

Mann, F.C., and **L.R. Hoffman.** 1960. *'Automation and the Worker: A Study of Social change in Power Plants',* New York: Holt, Rinehart, Winston.

March, J.G. 1955. 'An Introduction to the Theory and Measurement of Influence', *American Political Science Review,* 49: 431–451.

March, J.G. and **H.A. Simon.** 1958. *Organizations,* New York: Wiley.

McBer and Company. 1980. Managerial Style Questionnaire.

McCall, M.W. Jr. 1977. 'Leaders and Leadership: Of Substance and Shadow', in E.E. Lawler and L. W. Porter (eds.), *Perspectives on Behaviour in Organizations.* New York: McGraw-Hill.

McCoy, S.C. 1985. *Management of Values: The Ethical Difference in Corporate Policy and Performance.* New York: Harper and Row Publication.

McCuddy, M.K. and **B.L. Peery.** 1996. 'Selected Individual Differences and Collegians' Ethical Beliefs', *Journal of Business Ethics,* 15: 261–272.

McCuddy, M.K., K.E. Reickardt, and **D.L. Schroeder.** 1983. 'Ethical Pressures: Fact or Fiction?' *Management Accounting,* April, 57–61.

McDonald, G. and **P.C. Pak.** 1996. 'It's All-Fair in Love and Business: Cognitive Philosophies in Ethical Decision-Making', *Journal of Business Ethics,* 15: 973–996.

McKenna, R.J. 1996. 'Explaining Amoral Decision-making: An External View of a Human Disaster', *Journal of Business Ethics,* 15: 681–694.

McNichols, C.W. and **T.W. Zimmerer.** 1985. 'Situational Ethics: An Empirical Study of Differenciators of Student Attitudes', *Journal of Business Ethics,* 4: 175–180.

Mead, G.H. 1934. *Mind, Self, and Society.* Chicago, II: University of Chicago Press.

Miseing, P. and **J.F. Preble.** 1985. 'A Comparison of Five Business Philosophies', *Journal of Business Ethics,* 4: 175–180.

Mill, C.R. 1953. 'Personality Patterns of Sociometrically Selected and Sociometrically Rejected Male College Students', *Sociometery,* 16: 151–167.

Mill, John Stuart. 1991. 'Utilitarianism' in J.M. Robson (ed.) *Collected Works of John Stuart Mill.* London: Routledge and Toronto, Ont.: University of Toronto Press.

Miller, D., K.D. Vries, F. Manfred and **J.M. Toulouse.** 1982. 'Top Executive Locus of Control and its Relationship to Strategy Making, Structure and Environment', *Academy of Management Journal,* 25: 237–253.

Minkes A.L., M.W. Small and **S.R. Chatterjee.** 1999. 'Leadership and Business Ethics: Does It Matter? Implications for Management', *Journal of Business Ethics,* 20(4): 327–335.

Moore, G.E. 1903. *Principia Ethica.* Cambridge: Cambridge University Press.

Moore, J. 1993. 'What is Really Unethical about Inside trading', in T. I. White (ed.) *Business Ethics,* New York: Macmillan.

Moore, L.H. 1932. 'Leadership Traits of College Women', *Sociol. Soc. Res.* 17: 44–54.

Morgan, G. 1986. *Images of Organizations.* Newbury Park, CA: Sage publication Inc.

Morales, Frank. 1998. http://www.dharnacentral.com/aboutfm.htm

Morrison, A.M., R.P. White and **E. Van Velsor.** 1987. *Breaking the Glass Ceiling.* Reading, MA: Addison-Wesley.

Munson, E.L. 1921. *The Management of Men,* New York: Holt, Rinehart, Winston.

Murphy, P.E. 1989. 'Creating Ethical Corporate Structures', Sloar Management Review, 30(2): 81–87.

Murphy, P. and G.R. Laczniak. 1981. 'Marketing Ethics: A Review with Implications for Managers, Educators and Researchers', in B.M. Enis and K.J. Roering (eds.), *Review of Marketing Association.* Chicago:

Newell, A., and H.A. Simon. 1972. *Human Problem Solvin.* Englewood Cliffs, NJ: Prentice-Hall.

Nielsen, R.P. 1988. 'Limitations of Ethical Reasoning as an Action (Praxis) Strategy', *Journal of Business Ethics,* 7: 725–33.

Nowicki, S. Jr. and M.P. Duke. 1974. 'A Locus of Control Scale for College as well as non-college adults', *Journal of Personality Assessment,* 38: 136–137(a).

Nowicki, S.J. and M.P. Duke. 1983. 'The Nowicki-Stricki and Lifespan Locus of Scales: Construct Validation', in H.M. Leafcourt (ed.), *Research with Locus of Control.* New York, London: Academic Dress.

Nunnally, J.C. 1978. *Psychmetric Theory.* New York: McGraw-Hill.

Ouchi, W.G. 1981. *Theory 2.* Reading, MA: Addison-Wesley Publishing Company.

Pareek, U. 1989. 'Motivation Analysis of Organizations-Climate (MAO-C)', in J. W. Pfeiffer (ed.), *The 1989 Annual: Developing Human Resources.* San Diego, CA: Pfeiffer & Company.

Parry K.W. and S.B. Proctor-Thomson. 2002. 'Perceived Integrity of Transformational Leaders in Organisational Settings', *Journal of Business Ethics,* 35(2): 75–96.

Parthasarthy, A. 1984. *Vedanta Treatise* (3rd ed.). Bombay: Vedanta Life Institute.

Petrick, A.P. and J.F. Quinn. 2001. 'The Challenge of Leadership Accountability for Integrity Capacity as a Strategic Asset', *Journal of Business Ethics,* 34(3–4): 175–189, December.

Pettersen, N. 1985. Specific versus Generalized Locus of Control Scales Related to Job Satisfaction', *Psychological Report,* 56: 60–62.

Pfeffer, J. 1997. 'The Ambiguity of Leadership', *Academy of Management Review,* 2: 104–112.

Pfeffer, J. and G.R. Salancik. 1975. Determinants of supervisory behavior: A role set analysis, Human Relations, 28: 139–153.

Piaget, J. 1932. *The Moral Judgement of the Child.* New York, NY: The Free Press.

Pigors, P. 1935. *Leadership or Domination.* Boston, MA: Houghton, Mifflin.

Posner, B.Z and W.H. Schmidt. 1984. 'Values and the American Manager: An Update', *California Management Review,* 26: 202–216.

———— 1992. 'Values and the American Manager: An Update Updated', *California Management Review,* 34: 86.

Prakash, J. 1987. 'Public Enterprise Efficiency: Some basic Issues', in R.K. Sapru and T.N. Chaturvedi (eds.), *Management of Public Sector Enterprise in India.* New Delhi: Ahish Publishing House.

Prasad, J. and C.P. Rao. 1982. 'Foreign Payoffs and International Business Ethics: Revisited', *Southern Marketing Association Proceedings,* 260–264.

Premeaux, S.R. and R.W. Mondy. 1993. 'Linking Management Behavior to Ethical Philosophy', *Journal of Business Ethics,* 1: 349–357.

Pryer, M.V. and Distefano, M.K., Jr. 1971. 'Perceptions of Leadership Behaviour, Job Satisfaction and Internal-External Control Across Three Nursing Levels. *Nursing Research,* 20: 534–537.

Radhakrishnan, S. 1948. *The Bhagavad-Gita.* Great Britain: George Allen & Unwin Ltd.

Rayburn, J.M. and **L.G. Rayburn.** 1996. 'Relationship between Machiavellianisms and Type A Personality and Ethical–orientation', *Journal of Business Ethics*, 15: 1209–1219.

Reichers, A.E., and **B. Schneider.** 1990. *Climate culture: An Evolution of Constructs. Climate and Culture.* San Fransisco: Jossey-Bars.

Reidenbach, R.E. and **D.P. Robin.** 1991. 'A Conceptual Model of Corporate Moral Development', *Journal of Business Ethics,* 10: 273–284.

Rest, J. 1986. *Moral Development: Advances in Research and Theory.* New York: Praeger.

Rice, W.R., D. Instone and **J. Adams.** 1984. 'Leader Sex, Leader Success, and Leadership Process: Two Field Studies', *Journal of Applied Psychology,* 6: 12–31.

Ricklets, R. 1983. 'Executives and General Public Say Ethical Behaviour is Declining IN U.S.,' *The Wall Street Journal,* October, 31–33.

Robinson, J.P. and **R. Shaver.** 1973. *Measurement of Social Psychological Attitudes.* Ann Arbor, MI: Institute for Social Research.

Rokeach, M. 1973. *The Nature of Human Values.* New York: Free Press.

Rosener, J.B. 1990. 'Ways Women Lead', *Harvard Business Review,* November-December, 119–125.

Rotter, J.B. 1966. 'Generalized Expectancies for Internal versus External Control of Reinforcement', *Psychological Monograph,* 80: 1–28.

Ruegger, D. and **E. King.** 1992. 'A Study of the Effect of Age and Gender upon Student Business Ethics', *Journal of Business Ethics,* 11: 179–186.

Russel, G.W. 1974. 'Machiavellianism, Locus of Control, Aggression, Performance and Precautionary Behaviour in Ice Honey', *Human Relations,* 27: 825–837.

Salthouse, T. A. 1988. 'Initiating the Formalization of Theories of Cognitive Ageing'. *Psychology and Ageing,* 3: 3–16.

Sapru R.K. and **K. Matta.** 1987. 'Public Enterprize Management in India: An Overview', in R.K. Sapru and T. N. Chaturvedi (eds.), *Management of Public Sector Enterprize in India.* New Delhi: Ahish Publishing House.

Sastry, A.M. 1981. *The Bhagwad Gita: With the Commentary of Sri Sankaracharya.* Madras: Samta Books.

Sathe, V. 1983. 'Implications of Corporate Culture: A Manager's Guide to Action', *Organizational Dynamics,* 9: 333–354.

Schein, E.H. 1985. *Organizational Culture and Leadership.* San Francisco: Jossey-Bass.

Schein, V.E. 1975. 'Relationships between Sex Role Stereotypes and Requisite Management Characteristics among Female Managers'. *Journal of Applied Psychology,* 6: 340–344.

Schminke, M. and **D. Wells,** 1999. 'Group Processes and Performance and their Effects on Individuals' Ethical Frameworks', *Journal of Business Ethics,* 35(2): 75–96, January.

Schminke, M. 1997. 'Gender Differences in Ethical Framework and Evaluation of Others' Choices in Ethical Dilemmas', *Journal of Business Ethics,* 16: 55–65.

Schminke, M., M.L. Ambrose and **T.W. Noel.** 1997. 'The Effect of Ethical Frame works on perceptions of Organizational Justice', *Academy of Management Journal,* 40(5): 1190–1207.

Schneider, B. 1983. 'Interactional Psychology and Organizational Baehaviour', in B.M. Staw and L.L.Cummings (eds.), *Research in Organizational Behaviour* (Vol. 5). Greenwich, CT: JAI Press.

Schultz, D.P. 1982. *Psychology and Industry Today.* New York: Macmillan.

Schwab, D.B. 1980. 'Content Validity in Organizational Behaviour in B.M. Staw and L.L.Cummings (eds.), *Research in Organizational Behaviour,* (Vol. 2). Greenwich, CT: JAI Press.

Sekhar, R.C. 1998. *Ethical Choices in Business,* New Delhi: Response Books.

Selznik, P. 1957. *Leadership in Administration: A Sociological Interpretation.* Row, Peterson, Evanston, IL.

Serwinek, P.J. 1992. 'Demographic & Related Differences in Ethical Views Among Small Businesses', *Journal of Business Ethics,* 11: 555–566.

Shamasastri , R. 1951. *Arthashastra* .Edited by T. Ganapati Sastri, Mysore.

Sharma, I.C. 1965. *Ethical Philosophies of India.* Lincoln, Nebraska: Johnsen Publishing Co.

Sharma, P. and **K.T. Bhal.** 2001. Ethical Decision-Making by Indian Managers: Identification of the Constructs, their Measurement and Validation' *Management and Labour Studies,* 26: 145–163.

———— 2001. 'Ethical Decision Making by Managers in Public and Private Sector Organizations: A Qualitative Analysis'. *Psychological Studies,* 46(3): 222–232.

———— 2003. 'Impact of personality factors on ethical frameworks and ethical decision making' *Indian Journal of Industrial Relations,* 38(3): 297–317.

———— (2004). Ethical Frameworks and Ethical Decision Making: Role of Age Group and Gender. *Gitam Journal of Management,* 2(1): 44–59.

Shartle, C.L. 1956. *Executive Performance and Leadership.* Englewood Cliffs, NJ: Prentice-Hall.

Sheehy, G. 1990. *Character. America's Search for Leadership.* New York: Bantam Books.

Shukla, A. and **A.D. Costa.** 1994. 'Are Women More Ethical Then Men?', *Journal of Business Ethics,* 13: 859–871.

Siegel, J.P. 1973. 'Machiavellianism, MBA's and Managers: Leadership Correlates and socialization Effects, *Academy of Management Journal,* 3(16): 404–412.

Simons, J.A., D.B. Irwin and **B.A. Drimin.** 1987. *Instructor's.* Manual to Accompany Psychology: The Search for Understanding. St. Paul: West Publishing.

Sims R. and **R. Johannes Brinkman.** 2002. 'Leaders as Moral Role Models: The Case of John Gutfreund at Salomon Brothers', *Journal of Business Ethics,* 35(4): 327–339.

Sims, R.L. and **T.L. Keon.** 1997. 'Ethical Work Climate as a Factor in the Development of Person-Organization Fit', *Journal of Business Ethics,* 16: 1095–1105.

Sims, R.R. 1992. 'The Challenge of Ethical Behavior in Organizations', *Journal of Business Ethics,* 11: 505–513.

Sinclair, A. 1993. 'Approaches to Organizational Culture and Ethics', *Journal of Business Ethics,* 12: 63–73.

Singh, A.K. 1990. 'Organizational culture and leadership fit', *Decision,* 17: 103–108.

Singh, M.R.G. 1978. 'The Relationship of Job Satisfaction with Locus of Control, Organizational Setting and Education', (Doctoral dissertation, University of Michigan, 1978). *Dissertation Abstracts International,* 38: 684A (University Microfilm No. 78–13735).

Singhapakdi, A. and **S.J. Vitell.** 1990. 'Marketing ethics: Factors Influencing Perceptions of Ethical Problems and Alternatives', *Journal of Macro Marketing,* 12: 4–18.

Singhapakdi, A. 1990, 'Perceptual Framework of Marketing Ethics Decision Making: An Exploratory Comparison Between Students and Practitioners', in R. Viswanathan (ed.), *Marketing Magic.* Chicago: American Marketing Association.

Sinha, J.B.P. 1973. *Some Problems of Public Sector Organizations.* New Delhi: National Publishing House.

———— 1980. *The Nurturent Task Leader: A Model of Effective Executive.* New Delhi: Concept.

———— 1995. *The Cultural Context of Leadership and Power.* New Delhi: Sage Publications India Pvt Ltd.

Smith Adam. 1952. *An Enquiry into the Nature and Causes of Wealth of Nations.* Chicago: Benton.

———— 1976. *The Wealth of Nations.* With introduction, Bibliography, and Chronology by David Champbell Publishers Ltd. (1991). Oxford: Everyman's Library.

Spector, P.E. 1982. 'Behaviour in Organizations as a Function of Employee's Locus of Control', *Psychological Bulletin*, 91: 482–497.

Stanga, K.G. and **R.A. Turpen.** 1991. 'Ethical Judgements on Selected Accounting Issues: An Empirical Study', *Journal of Business Ethics*, 10: 739–747.

Stead, W.E., D.L. Worrell and **J.G. Stead.** 1990. 'An Integrative Model for Understanding and Managing Ethical Behavior in Business Organization', *Journal of Business Ethics*, 9: 233–242.

Steiner, G.A. and **J.E. Steiner.** 1988. *Business Government and Society: A Management Perspective* (4th ed.). Random House.

Stoller R.J. 1964. 'A Contribution to the Study of Gender Identity', *International Journal of Psycho-Analysis*, 45: 220–226.

Swami Dayananda. 1999. *The Teachings of the Bhagavad Gita.* New Delhi: Vision Books Publishers.

Swami Vivekananda. 1976. Calcutta: Rajyoga Advaita Asharam.

Taka Iwao. 1996. *Business Ethics in Countries and Related Regions.* Tokyo:

Takala, T. and **O. Uusitalo.** 1995, 'Retailers' Professional and Professio - Ethical Dilemmas: The Case of Finnish Retailing Business', *Journal of Business Ethics*, 14: 893–907.

Tandon, K. 1990. 'Quality of Interaction in Leader-Member Dyads: Measurement, Antecedents, and Consequences' (Doctoral thesis submitted to Indian Institute of Technology, Kanpur, India).

Tannenbaum, R., I.R. Weschler and **F. Massarik.** 1961. *Leadership and Organization.* New York: McGraw-Hill.

Taylor, R.W. 1975. *Principals of Business Ethics: An Introduction.* California: Dickenson, Encino.

Thapar, Romila. 1966. *A History of India.* Vol I. UK: Penguin.

Thibaut, J.W. and **H.H. Kelley.** 1959. *The Social Psychology of the Group.* New York: Wiley.

Thomas P. J. and **R.H. Waterman, Jr.** 1982. *In Search of Excellence.* New York: Harper and Row.

Trevino L.K. 1986. 'Ethical Decision-Making in Organizations: A Person—Situation Interactionist Model', *Academy of Management Review*, 11: 601– 617.

Trevino, L.K. 1990. 'A Cultural Perspective on Changing and Developing Organizational Ethics', *Research in Organizational Change and Development*, 4: 195–230.

Trevino, L.K. and **S. Youngblood.** 1990. 'Bad Apples in Bad Berrels: A Cultural Analysis of Ethical Decision-making Behaviour in Organizations', *Journal of Applied Psychology*, 75(4): 378–385.

Trevino, L.K., M. Brown and Pincus-Hartman. 2003. 'Moral Person and Moral Manager: How Executives Develop a Reputation for Ethical leadership', *California Management Review*, 42(4): 128–142.

Tsalikis, J. and M. Ortiz- Buonafina. 1990. 'Ethical Beliefs' Differences of Male and Females, *Journal of Business Ethics*, 9: 509–517.

Tsalikis, J. and O. Nwachukwu. 1988. 'Cross-Cultural Business Ethics: Ethical Beliefs Differences between Black and White', *Journal of Business Ethics*, 7: 745–754.

Van Maanen, J. 1976. 'Breaking in: Socialization to work', in R. Dubiu (ed.), *Handbook of work organization and society*. Chicago: Rand Mc Nally.

Vecchio, R.P. 1981. 'Workers' Belief in Internal versus External Determinants of Success', *Journal of Social Psychology*, 114: 199–207.

Velasquez, M.G. 1992. *Business Ethic*. New York: Prentice-Hall Inc.

_____ 1998. *Business Ethics: Concepts & Cases. IV Edition*. New Jersey: Prentice-Hall.

Victor, B. and J. Cullen. 1987. 'A Theory and Measure of Ethical Climate in Organisation,' *Research in Corporate Social Performance and Policy*, 9: 51–71.

Victor, B. and J. Cullen. 1988. 'The Organizational Basis of Ethical Work Climate', *Administrative Science Quarterly*, 33: 101–125.

Vitell, S. and T. Festvand. 1987. 'Business Ethics: Conflicts Practices and Beliefs of Industrial Executives', *Journal of Business Ethics*, 6: 111–122.

Vleeming, R.G. 1979. 'Machiavellianism: A Preliminary Review' *Psychological Reporter*, February, 295–310.

Vroom, V.H. 1964. *Work and Motivation*. New York: Wiley.

Walker, L.J. 1984. 'Sex Differences in the Development of Moral Reasoning: A Critical Review', *Child Development*, 55: 677–691.

Walls, R.T. and J.J. Miller. 1970. 'Delay of Gratification in Welfare and Rehabilitation Clients', *Journal of Counselling Psychology*, 4: 383–384.

Webb, U. 1915. 'Character and Intelligence', *British Journal of Psycholo. Monogr.* No. 20.

Whetstone, J.T. 2001. 'How Virtues Fits Within Business Ethics', *Journal of Business Ethics*, 35(2): 75–96, January.

Wimbush, J. and J. Shepard. 1994. 'Towards an Understanding of Ethical Climate: Its Relationship to Ethical Behavior and Supervisory influence', *Journal of Business Ethics*, 13: 637–647.

Wimbush, J., J. Shepard and S. Markham. 1997. 'An Empirical Examination of the Relationship between Ethical Climate and Ethical Behavior from Multiple Levels of Analysis', *Journal of Business Ethics*, 16: 1705–1716.

Whipple, T.W. and D.F. Swords. 1992. 'Business Ethics Judgements: A Cross-cultural Comparison', *Journal of Business Ethics*, 11: 671–678.

Yukl, G.A. 1981. *Leadership in Organizations*, Englewood Cliffs, NJ: Prentice Hall.

Zedeck, S. 1971. 'Problem with the Use of "Moderator" Variable', *Psychological Bulletin*, 76: 295–310.

INDEX

ABOUT THE AUTHORS

Poonam Sharma, a Ph.D from the Indian Institute of Technology (IIT), Delhi, is currently a scientist at the Indian Agricultural Research Institute, Delhi. Actively involved in research on managerial ethics, especially of Indian managers, she has published several articles on various aspects of the subject. She has taught and trained managers from different organizations and has done sponsored research for organizations like the ICAR and the World Bank.

Kanika T. Bhal, a Ph.D from IIT, Kanpur, is currently Associate Professor and Area Chair of the Organisation Management Group, Department of Management Studies, IIT, Delhi. She has also been a Visiting Fellow at the Sloan School of Management, MIT, Cambridge, USA. Dr Bhal has trained managers in different sectors and published over 50 articles and three books, including *Managing Dyadic Interactions in Organizational Leadership*. She has also been a consultant to various public and private sector organizations and has been involved in international assignments with Fordham University and Wharton School of Management, USA, University of Birmingham, UK and University of Lethbridge, Canada. Her current areas of research include managerial ethics, leadership and culture.